SLAVE STEALER

SLAVE STEALER

Vol. II Reyna Royale Chronicles

by

Jim Duggins

Smoke Tree Press
Rancho Mirage, CA
www.smoketreepress.com

SLAVE STEALER is a work of fiction. The sole purpose of the writer has been to create an adventure taken by an incredible 19th century African-American woman. Any resemblance to any specific person, place, or event is purely coincidental.

Copyright 2010 Jim Duggins

No part of this publication may be reproduced in any form except for the use of brief quotes as a review without the written permission of the author.

ISBN 978-0-9825337-2-7

Printed in the United States of America

Smoke Tree Press
Rancho Mirage, CA

Dedication: I am grateful for the many people who have helped me learn more about writing, about life, and about myself. I am humbled by their generous gift of themselves. In addition to a long list of teachers who have given more to me than I could fairly expect, specific public institutions, the University of Illinois, San Francisco State University, and the University of California, Berkeley – abetted by the G.I.Bill – provided resources without which I could never have fared so well. Most recently, my weekly Critique Group of the Palm Springs Writers Guild has been an invaluable source of inspiration and guidance.

FOR

Catharine Lucas who taught me more than I knew
Katherine V. Forrest who tested what I learned

Contents

Part One
What You Don't Know, You Can't Tell

Part Two
The Station Master

Part Three
The Fugitive

Part Four
The Rebel

Part One

What You Don't Know, You Can't Tell

Chapter 1

Lula was wearing her gold tooth. That alone was an omen. It wasn't exactly *her* tooth, at least not in the sense that she grew it or had it made, but nevertheless she owned it. It had originally belonged to Granny Grimes and Lula had frequently said it was the most beautiful thing she'd ever seen and so it seemed fitting for Granny to leave it to Lula when she passed. Lula wore the tooth only on special occasions.

Although she'd had no missing teeth, it was a simple matter to pull one out so she could replace it with her inheritance. That Granny's was slightly smaller and that it must be held in place with her tongue to show it off to best advantage seemed a minor inconvenience, rather like suffering for the sake of art.

But, the fact that Lula was wearing her tooth on the day that Edward Shield arrived could not be considered insignificant. At the first sight of him, she bawled out, "Mrs. Royale! Mrs. Royale! Company's coming!"

Reyna Royale, San Francisco's reigning Queen of Voodoo, planned to receive the man in her seance room where her sacred objects would unsettle a non-believer. To confirm her superiority further, she had also mastered the ability to fake a trance when she wanted time to think before an answer. No one staged a more credible trance than Reyna, also known as Mamaloi, interpreter of voodoo sign.

She had arranged herself artfully on a golden yellow silk divan when he entered. Her mourning garb, layers of gray and black watered silk, shone gloriously against the yellow, and the combination of the two colors rendered her creamy skin even fairer. She used no cosmetics other than a touch of olive oil across her eyebrows and lids to brighten and emphasize her large, feline eyes.

Not a day passed that Reyna did not offer thanks to Vodu for the inheritance of her flawless white skin, the product of her mother's café au lait lightened further by a master's dalliance. The trickery of passing as white, however, never softened her heart: in that chamber, her identity remained solidly, fiercely African. Her luscious beauty and white skin were simply tools that slavery had forced her to learn to use.

At the head of the divan lay a wicker basket, home of Mojo Hand, her ritual snake, a copperhead she was especially fond of. At the other end, a wooden cage held Caesar, a large black game cock who frequently jumped up as though in combat then settled down to crow loudly as though he'd won a furious battle. On the wall behind her, a collection of beaded and feathered conjure bags hung from brass hooks.

Leaving his servant on the porch, the visitor followed Lula into the seance room and crossed over to touch Reyna's fingers in respectful greeting. Although his look swept the room, he did not express the surprise she'd hoped for. He hardly glanced at Mojo Hand who'd raised his head to see who had come near his basket. Disappointed by her failure to startle him, Reyna was further disconcerted by his cool appraisal.

"Madam," he said. "It is my pleasure to meet you."

He was older than she'd guessed; probably close to sixty, but a handsome, vigorous-looking man all the same. His square cut jaw was determined, not arrogant or haughty. Sandy hair, shot through with silver, led to stylish mutton chop sideburns against his ruddy complexion. He wore a tan suit with big brown buttons — and a glove on his right hand and carried the other. The gloves matched the buttons of his suit. Whether this was a personal fetish or some effete convention of etiquette she couldn't guess.

Reyna had accepted his desire to meet with her only to satisfy her curiosity about this extraordinary white man who had come to one of her voodoo ceremonies. Now, close at hand, she wondered if she'd made a mistake. His eyes, a dark, warm brown framed by long, curling lashes, stared openly at her in a way that white people rarely did. His expression in that instant exchange seemed actually to leap across the room and caress her. She felt her cheeks redden for harboring such thoughts about a white man. *Velvet Eyes. I shall call you Velvet Eyes.*

He said, "I was referred to you by Reverend Thomas Randolph, a man you know."

Despite her effort to remain calm, her heart jumped in her chest.

"Yes," she said, leaning forward a tiny bit, fighting to keep her composure. "Yes, I am acquainted with the man."

He coughed behind the gloved hand. "Over the years we have done business together."

His scrutiny grew more intense, as though not believing this lovely young woman, sitting in this weird parlor, could have been the one recommended by Thomas Randolph. Furthermore, on the frontier, it was unusual to find a self-sufficient and beautiful young woman who was not a prostitute.

"And, he wanted especially for me to tell you how grateful he is for your help — "

All at once, Caesar, her game cock, leaped up in the air, flapped his wings, and threw his legs about as though his feet were equipped with the razor-sharp spurs of cockfights. Then, as quickly as he'd begun, he dropped back to the floor of his cage where he strutted back and forth, crowing madly.

Apparently unperturbed, Shield bent forward, searching her face. "I wonder," he said. "Can I trust you?"

The direction of their conversation set off danger signals in her head. Working as she did with large numbers of people, rich and poor of every color, a voodooienne needed to be continually alert to trouble and all her warning senses rang as loud as fire bells. But, it was also true that Reyna had not become rich and powerful because she was faint of heart.

After a moment, she said, "You can trust me."

He paused, as if pained and in deep thought, then blurted out, "I must say this plainly if we are to talk at all. I'm taking a chance in trusting you, but you must know that I also know that you're not entirely innocent in the matter I want to discuss."

Reyna looked away from him, a hardness set in the line of her mouth. She couldn't allow emotion to betray her.

"Your reputation for the work you've done with Reverend Randolph has reached the ears of important people in the east." He paused as though embarrassed by his outburst, then went on, "Many persons are in prison at this moment for less than you've done, helping runaway slaves."

His brief speech ricocheted around in Reyna's head and the old, familiar panic returned. As clear as day she saw her mama beaten on the cross of the workmaker at Riverview Plantation; she felt again the suffering of the beatings she had received at the hand of Mistress Suzanne; and the pain and degradation Master Hamber inflicted upon her when he raped her and sold her away.

Still, she found the steel to force a calm if tentative voice to form a reply. "So? What do you want here? What do you want of me? To put me in prison?"

At that last, Mr. Shield looked stricken and fell to one knee, his great brown eyes pleading. "Oh, no dear lady. Far from it. I commend what you've done. I'm here because of your success. I merely came here to bring you greetings from my friend. And, to ask for your help if I may."

"You speak of trust," she said. "Who are you?"

"I am Edward Shield. I have a home in Boston and a farm in Virginia, but I can't tell you where I've been staying in California."

"Then, what is trust if you can't even tell me where you live?"

"I can't tell you for the same reason I'd never tell someone else about you. We're better off not knowing some things. What I don't know, no one can make me tell. If you become one of us, only you and I will know that."

"One of us?" she asked. "One of who?"

Perspiration beaded his forehead and his jaw clenched. At last, he said in a guttural voice so low she could scarcely hear, "I want you to join in our operation in the Underground Railroad. What you've done here is amazing. You have an intuitive quality of leadership that many men never develop. You've . . . so many gifts to offer us. The large number of people who attend your ceremonies. I've thought about it for several months and your situation is perfect. I am a conductor, one who assists passengers on the line. I've been staying at a station up north. That's why I can't tell you where I've been living. Now, do you understand why I have great difficulty confessing to you? I made the mistake of trusting someone once before."

Reyna's brow wrinkled with her confusion. "Pardon me, sir. I know of no railroad to California. What is this railroad you speak of?"

"Forgive me," he said. "I didn't stop to think. Let me explain."

When he'd finished, Reyna sat a long moment considering the wonder of what she'd heard. Her eyes moisted over at the kindness shown by the abolitionists toward hapless fellow creatures. Then, color drained from her face, she said, "You're right. We can be arrested even for having this conversation. A voodoo woman has many enemies and a white man who talks of helping slaves also has a price on his head. But, how do I know who you are, Mr. Shield? How do I know that you are who you say you are?"

Shield hung his head as though deeply ashamed. "I think this will tell you what you want to know."

Carefully removing his elegant brown suede glove, he held out the palm of his hand. A great white scar, etched by a branding iron on that tender skin, formed the initials 'SS,' the brand used to punish those who helped runaway slaves. By that crude tattoo, Edward Shield would be forever known as a Slave Stealer.

Had she believed in lucky coincidence, Reyna would have thought it pure chance, but the voodoo queen put no faith in accidents, lucky or not. Voodoo religion considered all matters, material and spiritual, to be so intertwined that there were no accidents. What she found this day was too perfect not to have been put there for her by the great father, Vodu.

The two weeks had left her little time for anything but seemingly endless preparations for her journey. As she went through the steps of delegating to her most intelligent and responsible followers the management of her affairs while she was away, she came to realize the extent of her business enterprises. No wonder her days were so full that her life had sped past like a runaway race horse.

Although competent in their duties, her workers knew only to follow her orders. Now, she must teach them to operate without her direction. She must appoint and train lead cooks and managers for the three guest houses. No less awesome was the task of seeing to the staffs in her parlor houses. In addition she owned a public stable and two rental homes. And then there were her laundries where black people competed for jobs where the majority of the proprietors were Chinese. Reyna won the competition easily because of her firm business hand and the respect her voodoo leadership had among the workers.

At last she had packed a steamer trunk — in fact, packed and repacked it several times to be certain — with the clothes she thought she'd need back East in a variety of climates. It was in the City of Paris, the dry goods store named after the French ship that had been San Francisco's foremost supplier, that she stumbled upon the miracle.

In the Notions' Department, she found a Ladies' Secretaire, a small box covered in pale-blue padded leather. Measuring two feet long and eighteen inches wide, it was ten inches deep. Opening the tiny brass lock and lifting the lid, she saw that the inside was lined with a series of small pockets to hold stationery, envelopes, paper, and perhaps calling cards. A fitted mahogany writing top separated the lid from the lower compartment of the portable desk. In that area, a lady might keep inkwells, pen nibs, sand for blotting wet ink, and wax seals. Reyna could scarcely keep herself from shrieking out loud with delight. The beautiful and cleverly designed little lap desk would be excellent for her use as a portable altar, a cabinet of the so-called "mysteries" of her faith. A perfect companion for her travels.

The two compartments seemed to have been deliberately designed by the spirit loas to hold the herbs and seeds she used in ritual: the upper lid could contain a supply of peppermint for purification, sage for wisdom, thyme for healing. In the lower half she'd hide her more sacred remedies: Adam and Eve root for love, juniper for sexual advance, and valerian root to summon devils to defeat enemies. She snatched up her new prize, hurried home, and began immediately to pack the herbs and magic potions she used in Voodoo.

Each of Reyna's Presentation Sisters, her acolytes in the faith, worked as maids in rich, white households. They scrubbed and dusted, emptied and washed the chamber pots, made the beds and ironed the laundry ten hours a day, six days a week, not much different from their sisters in slavery. For those who'd come up from laboring as field hands, Reyna herself trained them to domestic work and found them employment just as Marie Laveau had once done for her in New Orleans. When Reyna left "to visit family back East," she left a gaping hole in the life of many of her followers.

This evening, when Lula returned to her home, a makeshift dormitory for the Presentation Sisters in the hay loft of a barn in nearby Rancho San Miguel, she knew why she felt gloriously happy most days. Against skin as dark and shiny as a blackberry, her gold tooth shone in her smile like the new sun; and she spent her days humming the church hymns she knew from First Methodist Church of Christ, A.M.E.

The word *freedom* played on her lips and almost nothing dragged her down now that she was free. No matter how exhausted or sore her muscles from ten hours in Miz' Richmond's kitchen, the minute Lula opened the barn door and climbed the ladder leading up to their room, a breath of air as sweet as new mown hay filled her lungs and she knew. After a long day in the white man's world, cleaning his house, minding his kids, emptying his slops, it came over her like a spell in the light of a new moon. Here, in the barn with her black sisters, all of them smelling of sweet grasses on the floor, Lula could take off her shoes, wiggle her bare feet in the straw and just feel free and black all over.

Sister Ruth and Sister Martha were there when her head cleared the ladder to the loft. Sister Ruth, a skinny, dark brown creature with pickaninny braids worked like the knobs of a prickly pear sticking out all over her head, looked over as Lula stepped off the ladder. Sister Martha didn't open her eyes, feigning a nap on her pallet in the straw.

"Hey. How ya doin' Lula?" Ruth asked.

"I fine, thank you, Sister. How 'bout yo'self?"

"We be fine . . . no, we ain't be fine. Both me and Martha got the blues over Mamaloi goin' away."

Martha lifted her head, looked over at Lula, "It just don't seem right, her leavin' us like this. Shoot!"

"Mamaloi got family back East. You know, you gotta go when it's family," Lula said.

"What family she got back there? You ever heard her mention some family back East?"

Their conversation was interrupted by the slam of the barn door below, then steps Lula recognized as those of Sophia crossing the barn, then mounting the ladder. In another moment, her round, brown face appeared. "What's goin' on?" she asked. "You three look like sick puppies."

"We just talkin' about where Mamaloi go? . . . an' how bad we feel."

"To be honest and fo' true," Lula said, "it's just that life is so excitin' with her aroun' and so boring when she not. Now, she gone and she don' say when she come back."

Nodding her head, Sophia, put in, "Makes me mad, too. Her goin' off with a white man like that."

Martha sat up in bed, "It's not the white man that I find 'spicious, it's that friend of his, that Indian fellow, Hawk. What she want with a no account Indian? White man ain't funny for her, her being white an' all herself."

At that the Sisters Lula, Ruth, and Sophia chorused, "Girl! What you talkin' about? Her bein' white an' all?"

"You some kind of dumb or what?"

"Whoever put that in your head?"

Sophia added a shrill, mocking laugh "I can't believe you said that."

"Well," Martha said defensively. "She gotta be white. All her friends be white. And she be rich. Ain't no white man gonna let a nigger be rich."

"Get some logic in your brain, child." Sophia said. "Where you think Mamaloi got the power, the power of Vodu. Where you think she got that?"

"Well . . . :"

"You ever seen a white woman got that? Any ol' raggedy-assed white woman who say she gots the power ain't nothing but a common witch, an' a crazy one at that."

"Well . . .what about her color?"

"Lots of high yellow girls where she come from, down New Orleans way, they all white as milk. But mind this, the law say that if you got one drop of black blood, you be colored."

Well . . .I don't know."

"I do an' I know because I just *feel* that she be colored. Don't you know it's more than looks and fancy manners? Don't you *feel* that way? Don't you *feel* that there's something differnt about her, differnt in the way she moves in her skin? It just *feel* like she's one of *us*." Sophia paused a moment, cocked her head back as though reflecting on the movements of her Voodoo Queen, then went on, "If'n I was her, I'd pass as white, too, 'specially if I had something to hide back where I come from. Like they was someone lookin' for me . . . like they was a certain master whose property done run away."

Martha bit her lower lip, pouting, said, "Well, I just don't know."

"Well, you just trust old Sophie. Believe on it." She thought a moment, then added, "'Sides all that, girl. Ain't a white girl alive can dance like Mamaloi."

Chapter 2

The odor of fish and the squawk of seagulls pierced the gray winter morning as the *SS Egypt* made its way into Boston's India Wharf. Atop a debris box on the pier, two large gulls, wings arched in the "V" of combat, faced one another in a tug of war over a rope of entrails from an animal of undetermined species. Thirty yards away, a long line of drays had stopped, delayed by a wagon whose mangy brown nag refused to move. Curses in Italian, Greek, German, French, and thick-tongued Gaelic scorched the air like a crowd scene in a Verdi opera. As a third generation Bostonian, Shield, who had lived in this city most of his sixty years, gave scant attention to the pandemonium below.

The purser's manifest for Suite 2B indicated it belonged to Mr. Edward Shield who was returning home after a business trip of three months' duration. Shield was accompanied by his ward, Miss Reyna Shield, a young woman who it was said, had been raised by nuns at the Ursuline Convent in New Orleans. With them was his manservant, King Hawk, a Natick Indian.

Gripping the railing with his strong right hand, he put a protective arm around his "ward." His large brown eyes misted over and a sigh escaped him. All that mattered was the young woman he sheltered in the crook of his left arm. He could not remember a time when he'd been happier.

Bending toward her ear, he muttered, "You have given me the family I've wanted for a long time. My wife and child died in childbirth in '43, and then my parents passed on . . . in the influenza epidemic of '45 . . . I was nearly twice your age . . . I've yearned for a family all those years and here you are, a full grown . . . er, ahem . . . niece."

Shield considered Reyna no more than a girl. Her intelligence and organizational ability, the qualities that had brought him to recruit her for the underground, were as nothing alongside his delight in her childlike wonder as she explored a world she'd never imagined.

By nature a quiet man and somewhat formal, he had been singularly driven all his life by his compassion for others. He did not examine the source of his compulsive need for philanthropy, he simply knew that his greatest rewards came from helping less fortunate people. In that, he found their meeting prophetic because they had each appeared at the exact moment they were ready for one another: she to be cared for and he to do the caring.

It was a measure of his abiding sense of morality that Shield never once considered the beautiful young woman as anything other than apprentice and partner in his underground railroad work. As Reyna was twenty-eight and he was thirty years her senior, he'd have been outraged by the suggestion that their relationship could be other than business and the affection due a child. He was sometimes embarrassed when he caught a raised eyebrow on the face of a man he was introducing to this "niece," but he dismissed the attitude as that of a cad. When he thought of Reyna, he thought of her as a young relative in his care; hence the notion of intimacy was as repugnant as incest.

While Shield had simply wanted to use her many businesses in San Francisco as stations for the railroad, he began to see that it had been foolish of him to think that the powerful Voodoo Queen could be a mere cog in someone else's wheel. Once she agreed to become a part of the railroad, she'd insisted upon traveling the line to know more about its operation. Reluctantly, he had consented to show her that part and those stations of the underground railroad where he was a conductor. In private moments, he secretly admitted to himself, too, that he feared the mysterious power of the voodoo ritual. Was it superstition, or was it real? Could such things touch white people? Him?

Leaning against his arm, Miss Reyna Shield seemed as different from Mrs. Reyna Royale as it was possible to imagine, a transformation that had come about in eight short weeks. Gone was the rice powder and paint, the sultry throb of the cult, the steel-hard edge of Mamaloi. Gone was the powerful businesswoman in widow's weeds at the heart of the new frontier. Now, her complexion was that of a lovely peach, rose and dark cream, and her pouting, full lips were like the inner flesh of ripe plums. Her life before this new undertaking had taught her to survive as a slave, then as a voodooienne, then as a beautiful woman in a rough mining camp — all of this by means of artifice, pretense, and an ability to burrow and hide deep within her own mind to a place no master or foe could reach.

This journey had been relatively uneventful for Shield, but not a single day passed without astonishing experiences for her. From San Francisco they had traveled by riverboat to Sacramento where they boarded a Wells Fargo coach for the trip over the Sierras and as far as the Mormon settlement in Utah. From there, they went by horseback to Cape Girardeau, Missouri, to connect with paddle wheel vessels for the trip up the Mississippi River to the Great Lakes where they met the *SS Egypt*.

For all Reyna's power in the secret religion and her business acumen, every day of the journey left her speechless. She'd lived among miners for five years, but had never seen the mountains honeycombed with the rabbit holes they dug in search of their fortunes. Now she could appreciate their courage and stamina. The vastness of the territories of Nevada and Utah with their limitless herds of buffalo spread out to the horizon took her breath away. She was strangely moved by the silent files of ferocious-looking Indian warriors who passed at a distance.

Their stop at the first railroad station, Cincinnati, had been to outfit her as an urbane young lady. In a way she hadn't expected, Reyna's new wardrobe broadcast her new life. Her stylish gowns required eight petticoats filled with six pounds of horsehair to maintain their hourglass shape. When she protested the weight and heat of them, the dressmaker assured her that twice as many were necessary for fashionable ladies in Paris and New York. Reyna had been further astounded the first time she tried on a hat. The enormous silk and lace creations sat uneasily on the head of one accustomed to a simple bonnet and widow's veil.

While her clothes were being made, they'd stayed in a station run by a certain Mr. Williams. There in Cincinnati, Queen City of the West, where 40,000 people gathered on rolling hills nestled between three rivers, her true education had begun. This first "depot" was but one of dozens spaced some thirty miles apart on the way north. There, too, she had met her first white man whose sole motivation for helping slaves escape was mercenary. Completely without deceit in the matter, Williams accepted the dangers of the underground only so long as Shield made regular payments. In some wryly distorted way, his indifferent manner worked to the advantage of the railroad because he was always cautious, never influenced by emotions that led to taking dangerous chances.

Further, Williams' suspicions, his overt questions and cocked eyebrow, led Reyna and Shield to bolster the invention of her as his ward. Her father, Mr. Shield's younger brother, they said, had been aboard a sailing ship that sank off the coast of Florida. Now an orphan, Reyna was Shield's niece and legally his ward. The story was so convincing that if Williams had any doubts, they focused upon his curiosity about her peculiar eyes. The fact that one could be born with golden eyes fascinated him beyond telling.

Reyna fell in love with the station on Drummond Island. The fishermen accepted the windblown island as their home because of its natural harbor and its proximity to the living they wrested from the water. The savage look of the sailors and the tales they told, the heavy odor of fish oil clouding the air, the hanging nets drying on the docks at Whitby Bay, and the cleaning, skinning, and butchery of a dozen species fresh caught for the tables of all the northern states, all of it excited a chord deep in Reyna's breast. There, too, Reyna noted that the island wrenched heartsick sighs from the servant, Hawk, the ex-whaling man.

The station at Drummond was operated by an old woman known to them only as Grandma. Worsening arthritis and a succession of heart attacks had slowed her down and doubled her over a little, but her spirit soared as strong as ever in her weakened body. Grandma owned the general store, a big, peak-roofed, weather-beaten barn of a building that guarded the entrance to the town. There, carefully concealed brass pulls lifted a set of trap doors into the cellar where Grandma stored her collection of homemade wines and the human cargo of the station. Grandma lived across the road in a two story stone house that was painted with the gray-green lichen of wet wind and rain.

When it was time to leave, Reyna took the old woman's two hands in hers and spent several minutes staring into her eyes. At last, the lump in her throat had eased enough for her to mumble, "Thank you, Grandma. I won't forget your kindness and we'll meet again by and by." Then, she impulsively hugged the frail old body so hard she could feel the ancient heart beat stiff against her ribs.

Entering Boston Harbor, Reyna wore a fashionable gown of rose-colored wool. Leg of mutton sleeves began at her lace collar and fell to her wrists where they met dainty, crocheted mittens. An ankle length maroon cape protected her from sharp winds. Her face was hardly visible beneath an enormous hat piled high with flowers and lace. The point of her wispy parasol touched the tiny toe of her high-heeled rose slippers.

A sudden gust of wind raked the deck of the *SS Egypt* and sent Reyna's hand to her hat. Even now, her mind reeled at her own audacity — to leave San Francisco and the security she'd built there — to join a lawless group of abolitionists assisting runaway slaves. True, Shield offered her protection, but she had a past, a slavery past, to conceal. If caught, he would go to prison; she would return to slavery, a slavery that included the brand "R" on her cheek for "runaway," and the harsh treatment of any master who dared to buy such chattel.

There was something else, something incomprehensible and frightening about what she was about to do. She'd toiled for five years to establish her successful and comfortable refuge in San Francisco. What on earth had possessed her to gamble everything? Although the admission that she had no choice terrified her, it was true. The beatings, the rape, the indecencies she herself had suffered and those she'd witnessed upon her people had hardened something deep inside her, a force so strong it could never be denied. Now, protected by the skin, the clothes, and the manners of a white woman, that thing inside lay coiled like her talisman serpent, ever ready to strike a blow for her people still in chains. She was prepared to risk it all in that cause.

She gasped at the sight of India Wharf when their ship banged to rest against the fenders of the dock. Not in her headiest fantasy had Reyna imagined such things could exist; neither buildings of such size nor such throngs of people.

On the dock below, sailors scurried about hauling and securing the ship's lines and lowering the gangplank for passengers' debarkation. India Wharf, at the foot of Broad Street, an enormous pier of three and four story granite buildings stretched out as far as she could see. The buildings, the transverse streets, the dozens of ships at dock, boiled like a cauldron with stevedores, warehousemen, and bustling merchants directing the storage and consignment of cargo. Bully boys carrying bags, boxes and chests on their backs, hurried here and there as if the loads were feathers. Riders on horseback, carriages, wagons and drays, a restless sea of humanity roiled between the ships and buildings. At the far end of the wharf, still more activity surrounded the customs house, a massive, granite Doric temple.

The boatswain piped the signal for passengers to disembark and the animated travelers pointed out luggage, then scrambled after baggage carriers. Reyna followed Hawk with their bags down the steep, bouncy gangplank.

A row of sleek Victoria's, open-topped, four-wheel carriages for hire, waited at one side of the gangplank. Drivers in black silk top hats and coats matching the plum-colored cushions of their coaches nonchalantly eyed prospective customers. Hawk unceremoniously tossed their bags onto the floor of a cab and held the door for them before climbing up to the buckboard.

"Louisberg. Number Ten Louisburg Square," Shield ordered regally.

Hiking up to the high seat behind the horse, the driver drew a thin, black buggy whip from a fitted leather holster on the dashboard and flicked the flanks of the chestnut mare.

As they wheeled across town, up Broad Street, down Kings to Walnut, then to Beacon Street past the Commons, then to Mount Vernon Street, she'd have liked to question Shield, but perversely pretending to be blasé, she denied herself the pleasure of his interpretation of what she saw. It seemed that all of Boston's 90,000 citizens were out on the streets, walking, riding. The city seethed with the energy of its citizens. Outside the United States Hotel, they inched their way through a sea of carriages so dense they moved only at a snail's pace. Shield merely grunted at her excitement with the melee.

Despite the side-by-side crowding of three story brick houses, so different from the open space of Drummond, Reyna gasped at the loveliness of Louisburg Square as soon as they turned off. Of bright, red brick, undarkened by the smoke of the factories beginning to invade the city, the houses were prettily trimmed with federal style porches and white-painted window sashes. A small wrought-iron fence enclosed a grassy park in the middle of the street and a fanciful iron horse trough on a pedestal was duplicated in miniature for neighborhood dogs. Just to the left of the door of the third house on the street, polished brass numerals proclaimed, "Number Ten."

When the maid answered, Reyna nearly leaped from her skin. The servant wore a black bombazine domestic's costume with a snowy lace apron and pelerine. A wisp of lacy ruffle perched precariously in her woolly hair. Blacker than black, her skin was midnight blue. Thick-lipped, squash-nosed, and bulging-eyed; and an African's mounded, high-hipped rump protruded further behind than her bosom in front. Reyna gaped as at a ghost.

After three months traveling as a white woman among white people, almost unrelieved by contact with blacks, Reyna found herself going weak in the knees. She wanted to rush forward and hug her, woman to woman, black to black for the solid feeling of community such action engendered.

She stifled the urge. Instead, following a butler with her luggage into the house, she avoided the maid's eyes.

Chapter 3

Reyna awoke the next morning feeling as low as a coffle of slaves. Her head hurt, her muscles cramped, and her mind seemed unable to focus. Her heart felt ripped out of her chest, as it had following the death of her murdered friend in New Orleans. To make matters worse, she knew that the problem behind her misery came from the life she led.

In assuming the guise of a white widow, she had cut herself off from more than work-related contacts with black people. Walking a tightrope between the two worlds, black and white, she belonged to neither. Although she was comforted by her voodoo rituals, her relationships with blacks could never be public. She could never be white, nor could she return to the arms of her black community. Coming to Shield's house as a white woman had opened a wound she had no way to heal.

She told herself she passed as white in order to help her race, but that was only lately and it was only partially true. The plain fact was that passing as white had enabled her to escape from slavery. The nub of the matter lay in a place deep inside herself where she dared not go. She could trust no one, black or white. Mama. Mistress Suzanne. Master Hamber. The Sisters of the Ursulines. Marie Laveau. Robert MacGill. Black and white, they had all betrayed her. And when she sold her black heritage for a white face, she accepted a debt of guilt she could never expiate.

Eyes scratchy with sleeplessness, she came down to breakfast early and sat primly in the morning room waiting for him. Underneath her steadied poise, her mind boiled with misgivings. How could she have been so stupid as to make this trip without careful investigation? What did she *really* know of Mr. Edward Shield? Was his seeming affection a masquerade for some ulterior motive? What had she seen in the black face of the maid, Florette, yesterday? Would she be friend or foe? Now, here she was in a world of strangers without a single friend or ally.

Although it was cold outside and snow lay in drifts against the shrubs of the side yard, a clear winter sun warmed the steeple-ceilinged conservatory glass and speckled her pale blue gown with rainbow reflections. Just within her vision, a brilliantly-colored bluebird hopped across the icy slick on the fountain and bullied a pair of sparrows away from a juniper bush he claimed as his. To complete the chain, a sleek, gray tomcat hunkered down in the pounce position to eye the bluebird. The unfolding drama of cat and bird distracted Reyna for a moment from her own dilemma.

Shield rushed in, crossed over to her, kissed the top of her head, and greeted her heartily. "Good morning, child. I trust you slept soundly." Nothing about him indicated anything amiss.

Reyna, guarding against the slightest tremor in her voice, said, "Yes, Mr. Shield, I did. My room is quite comfortable, thank you."

Florette brought their tea and toast and treated Reyna to the same look she'd give a cockroach in the kitchen. Each time the maid's eyes flashed in her direction, Reyna felt demeaned. Still, reaching back to a lesson she had learned as a maid for a sadistic mistress, she put herself in that place in her mind where she could not be hurt. Moreover, she also knew she had the power to take revenge when the time was right. Mistress Florette would be wise to watch her step.

At last, after she'd sipped at her tea and tasted the toast, she stood. "I'm sorry, but I'm feeling peaked and feel that I must rest."

Shield leaned toward her, concern written on his face. "Are you unwell? Should I summon a physician?"

"No, thank you. It's nothing serious. Perhaps only a letdown after the voyage."

"Are you certain?"

Once more, his courtly airs of concern had begun to put her at ease. If it indeed were pretext, he was a master of the art. *But, no,* she said to herself. *I dare not drop my guard. Not ever.* She said aloud, "Yes, I'm certain. Please don't worry about me."

As she reached the door, he called out, "Oh, I'd nearly forgotten, Reyna. We're invited for dinner at the home of a potential business associate. They live in an impressive new development called Pemberton Square. Captain James Gardner is a retired sea captain, now a lawyer, but are you sure that you're well enough to go? I could easily set another time."

"That's not necessary. I'm sure I'll be well enough to go."

"Ah, well, then, you go along and rest. I'll meet you in the drawing room at six o'clock."

That night Shield had hired a hansom cab outfitted with sleigh runners and a driver high in the box at the rear. Freezing temperatures made the hard packed snow and ice of the roadway perfect for sleigh riding. After her emotional turmoil of the last twenty-four hours, Reyna gratefully seized the opportunity to be away from the house and in the company of others. *Perhaps,* she thought, *I've been too close to Shield and Hawk as my only companions of the past three months. I probably just need a change.*

The coachman followed the favored route for sleigh-riding lovers, out Beacon Street, over Mill Dam, and onto Bright Road. Strings of diamond ice clung to the frozen branches of trees and shrubs along the way. The hollow clop of horses' hooves, the brassy tinkle of sleigh bells and the creak of harnesses punctuated the hilarity of mischievous boys stealing rides on the rear runners of passing carriages. She kept her distance as best she could for there was only a single robe for them to share in the cab.

At Pemberton Square, a Negro maid answered the door. Reyna was not taken aback, but the maid blocked the door, apparently dumbfounded by the sight of them.

"Good evening," she said, distantly. She had seemed about to say something more but restrained herself. *A most inhospitable response from a clumsy girl*, Reyna thought. *If she were my employee she'd be gone in half an hour.*

An instant later, Captain James Gardner appeared behind the maid.

A long-faced man of fifty, Gardner's lifeless gray eyes never settled on hers. His longish gray hair straggled about his collar and his cheeks had an unhealthy, sick-bed pallor. There was about him, too, an evasive quality that made her uneasy. He kept his lips pursed above his pointy chin.

"Halloo," he said. "You must be Shield. Yes. And this must be your lovely niece. Halloo, Mistress Shield. Welcome to this house."

As quickly as he had appeared, Gardner whirled on his heel, took Reyna's hand to lead her to the burgundy-draped dining room where servants had laid out what looked like a ton of polished silver on an enormous table and sideboard. He directed Reyna and Shield to places set opposite one another while he took the master's chair facing that of his wife at the other end. Reyna shifted nervously, not sure how to behave. *What was wanted after so begrudging an introduction? Furthermore, the sullen silence among strangers was also ominous.* Beyond the arms of a massive silver candelabra Shield seemed no less uncomfortable. The candles twinkled in his soft, velvet eyes and reflected on his cheeks still ruddy with cold.

Phoebe Gardner was not at all the matron Reyna had expected to meet. Rather, she seemed to be in her early thirties and exuded the warmth her husband lacked. She had brilliant blue eyes that sparkled above a merry smile so constant it seemed to be sculpted. This night, in a wine-red velvet hostess gown, she rose at her end of the long table, held out her hand in greeting, said ceremoniously, "We are pleased to have you here, Mr. Shield. Mistress Shield, I've looked forward to meeting you." *How could she say that?* Reyna wondered. *This dinner party had been so lately planned: how could the woman know anything at all about me?*

"I am most pleased to be here," Shield murmured, seeming mesmerized by the mass of tapers in the candelabra. "Thank you for this."

Phoebe rescued the awkwardness by addressing Reyna. "I hear you're new to Boston, Mistress Shield. Where are you from?"

"New Orleans."

She leaned forward. "New Orleans! I've never been there, but I understand it's a very colorful city. Your family lived there?"

Reyna answered, reciting their practiced lie. "No, my parents were from Hartford. Mr. Shield is my uncle, my father's brother. When my parents passed on, their solicitor enrolled me in school at the Convent of the Ursuline Sisters in New Orleans."

Phoebe's face brightened, her dazzling smile broadened. "Oh! How interesting! The Ursuline Convent here in Boston was the first Catholic order in the United States."

All at once, without warning, Gardner interrupted her. "Phoebe, don't go into that for pity's sake."

At his rebuke, the eternal smile left his wife's face. "But it's true, James!"

He said, "It's also true that the Protestants burned the convent to the ground."

"Oh, that's terrible!" Reyna cried out. "Why did they do that?"

"Because the new Americans hated papists. And . . ." He paused as though hesitating to say the words. "And, because the nuns were teaching Indian children to read."

The room went silent. Reyna sat still with her head at her breast, eyes distant, imagining what it must have been like for the innocent women to be martyred like their founder, Saint Ursula. She remembered all too well, a similar story of the courageous Ursulines in New Orleans. Her recall of the Ursulines, a flickering thing at best, was still enough to remind her that the Ursulines had given her up to slave catchers.

"How very awful," she said distantly.

Gardner turned to Shield. "As I understand it," he said, suddenly changing the subject, "you've come about a matter of shipping."

A puzzled look wiped across Shield's face. "Shipping?" he repeated. "Shipping?"

"Yes, several shipments throughout the year." Gardner's thin, pursed lips lingered over the words. For some reason she could not figure out, the sea-captain attorney never once looked his guest in the eye.

Shield recovered from his confusion, brightened, and said, "Oh, yes, shipping. I guess you could call me a farmer. I have a house here, but I spend most of my time at the farm. Tobacco. Charles Town, Virginia. We've just begun to use Boston Harbor. Roads are too bad to travel up the coast." Shield spoke freely and his revelations clarified some of her doubts but still a smell of something false tainted his discussion.

At that a twisted smile broke out on the faces of both Gardners. Her mind racing rapidly for solutions, Reyna gasped, *Rum? Smuggling? Were they criminals?*

Their talk mystified Reyna. Starved for information about Shield, she hung on his every word, yet she sensed that their conversation masked something nefarious. The flow of questioning and answering seemed to be a charade — no one listened to the others. Nor did the three study each other as strangers do. She could not discern whether they were bored or mildly antagonistic.

At last the ordeal was finished. They stood simultaneously by unspoken agreement and exchanged good byes. In that brief moment, Reyna had the impression that the three who had appeared indifferent at the table nodded meaningfully, as if acknowledging a secret. Before she could think, Captain Gardner embraced her and said over her shoulder. "This is just fine. I'm glad you could come here, Mistress Shield. You'll always be welcome. Perhaps a special companion for Phoebe."

Under the fur robe in the cab, Shield sat stiff and straight. His shoulder touched hers only when the sleigh turned corners.

At last, breaking away from her deep thoughts, Reyna said, "They seem like good people."

He said, "Gardner's company has been recommended as completely trustworthy, but I wanted to size him up before I sent him business."

After a long pause, he stammered, "I'm not accustomed to talking about my feelings, Reyna. But I must talk to you now about feelings I have. I sense that you've been hurt some time in the past. I don't know where or when, but I know people can be quite cruel and I fear that someone has been so to you. It's none of my business, but I'd like to protect you from that."

"I have enjoyed your company, too, sir."

"You have made me happier in the past two months than I have been in many years."

"I also . . ."

"No, please. Allow me to finish. When my wife died . . . that was thirteen years ago . . . I thought I would never have a family. Then I met you, child."

"I'm not a child," she said sharply, stirring under the robe.

He found her hand and held it until her tension dissipated. "Please hear me out. I will soon be sixty. You may not think of yourself as a child, but you're closer to the age my daughter would have been had she lived than you are to me."

They rode the rest of the way to Number Ten Louisburg Square in a deep silence that she dared not break. A part of Reyna felt enraged to be considered a child after all she'd accomplished. Yet, another part yearned for the warm feeling of security and protection he claimed to offer. But, dinner with the Gardners convinced her that there was much to learn about Mr. Edward Shield before she could trust him.

Chapter 4

A reverie touched with sadness settled about Reyna as she packed for the trip to Charles Town, Virginia. They'd spent nearly a month in Boston, time sorely needed to evaluate what she'd seen and heard. The underground stations they'd visited had all been operated by whites, and blacks worked for pay, not as slaves. The world she'd so suddenly entered was upside down, and confusing. She lacked the words to describe her experience in this city sometimes called the Athens of the New World. Had she been able to gather all her experiences together, she thought, there wasn't a sack nearly big enough to hold them. She pretended to be sophisticated, knowing all the while it wasn't true.

She'd loved the adventure, the fashions, the stylish homes, music and theater, so many new things to do and see and learn after San Francisco — she'd admit that, if any one asked. But, unhappily, she'd learned little about the Underground Railroad and often sensed that Shield was hiding something from her. When she asked him blunt questions about the work and when she could begin, he'd look as though she'd opened a forbidden door, and only say, "All in good time, child. All in good time."

Reyna had learned to accept a platonic love unlike any she had ever known. She had never received such kindness and reached for it like a water-starved plant to spring rain. She thought of Maurice, her former lover. Their lust had outlasted their love, and had refused to free them when it should have been time to break away.

The night of the dinner with Captain and Phoebe Gardner had changed something in her. Her intuition, sharpened by her years of slavery and being a woman alone in the rowdy town of San Francisco, warned her that Shield was more complicated than he'd seemed. There was something, perhaps a dangerous something, he kept hidden from her. That thought chilled her heart.

The day they left for Virginia they climbed into a forest green brougham pulled by a team of geldings the same color as its mahogany trim. Fitted with velvet handholds and beige suede cushions, its leather curtains kept the cold March winds outside. High on the driver's box, Hawk, the silent, faithful manservant, clucked at the team and they were off.

The carriage traveled out of Boston to New York following the Boston and Worcester railway road past the Mill Pond development. Despite her fatigue, Reyna could not resist leaning forward every few minutes to part the side curtains to peer at the changing landscape. A hundred times before the first afternoon ended, she asked, "Oh, Mr. Shield, how much farther is Virginia?" For reasons not yet understood the place held a magical attraction for her.

They sped through Maryland, passed Taneyton and Fredrick, and crossed the Potomac at Harper's Ferry. It was not until they entered Virginia on the Northwestern Turnpike that Reyna realized what was drawing her there. Phantoms from the past took shape and made her tremble. Reyna dropped back on the seat and clamped her jaws tight against nausea. Jerfferson County, Virginia. Jefferson.

Startled, alarmed by the change in her, Shield bent forward and cupped her back with his gloved right hand. "What is it Reyna? What's wrong? What is it? Are you ill? We're almost there now. Can you hold out another forty minutes? We can send for a physician then. Or, should we stop in Bolivar?"

"Jefferson County," she whispered. "Jefferson County. Thomas Jefferson?"

"Yes, of course. The county's named after Thomas Jefferson. If I'm not mistaken, his grandson's still in the statehouse. Why?"

She caught her breath. "I'm not sure. It's an old memory — or maybe a nightmare. Something from my mother."

He drew her to him and squeezed hard. Although unable to guess the cause, Shield felt the quaking in her back. "Don't worry, child. I'm here. Let me make up for the bad things that have happened to you. Let me take care of you." He held her until the trembling ceased.

Suddenly she recalled her mother's words. Pulling away from him, eyes averted, staring blindly into her lap, she asked, "Mr. Shield, have you ever heard of a man named John or James Hampden Pleasants?"

Smith paled at the name. "Why do you ask? "

"I don't know, or at least I'm not sure. But, tell me. Do you know such a name?"

"Well, John Hampden Pleasants is a newspaper editor in Richmond. For the Richmond *Whig*. I don't know him, but he is called a political radical and an outspoken abolitionist. He's been imprisoned for his editorials. Men have been flogged in other states simply for having his articles in their possession. "

"But that's wonderful, Mr. Shield. What courage! How could they arrest him for speaking his mind? What's happened to freedom of speech?"

"Not in the south. Southerners fear abolitionist materials will stir up anti-slavery folks down there. Anyway, this Mr. Pleasants is a marked man if he stays in the south."

"Oh, how terrible," she moaned.

"How are you feeling now? Better?"

"Yes, Mr. Shield, I am. Whatever the feeling was, it's gone now."

But, twenty-five years had come crashing down about her. Her slave beginnings, any heritage she had, as hateful as it might be, began here in Virginia.

"Please call me Edward," he said as he snugged her closer in his arms, sensing the tension relax. "You will soon be legally my niece, my family. Call me Edward."

"If that would make you happy, sir." She smiled at him face to face over his embracing arm. "It feels good to me, also, to have a family. You know, Edward, I feel quite at home in Virginia. I just feel it in my bones. Virginia is as much my home as any place ever has been."

Shaking her head, she held back a tear for her father, a man she'd never known, the man who had raped her mother.

Chapter 5

At journey's end, Fairfield Farm appeared through the tulip trees lining a circular drive, a palace, two stories high and solid brick, girdled with gleaming white porches. Doric columns marched majestically across the front to support a regal second story balcony. Double doors, flanked with ten foot windows, opened onto the front gallery while French doors at the sides led directly to the gardens.

When their carriage turned onto the driveway, all the doors burst open to spill a host of maids and butlers and cooks onto the porches and lawns to greet them. Every last one of them, Reyna observed, was black.

They flocked around the carriage before it fully stopped, men, women and children, big eyed and with broad smiles, a veritable sea of black skin. "Heh, heh, howdy Mistuh Shield. Welcome to Fairfield, Miz Shield." *Thank God*, she noted, *not 'Mastuh. They said, 'mistuh' and 'miz,' a sign that they were free.*

They lined up, house servants and field hands, in a triple row along the porch to be introduced. Charlesetta and her kids, Jamie and Colline, Georgette and Georgine. J.P. and John James, obviously plantation functionaries by the proud look of them, bowed from the waist. After a half dozen, she lost count and heard only the rhythmic sounds of the syllables of the names, realized she'd have to memorize them. To her dismay, she found herself searching their features for family resemblances to herself, relations, perhaps cousins or aunts, a brother or sister even if only a half. She wondered, nervously, what they saw in her.

Her hand flew to her mouth at the sight of one man among them. A head taller than anyone there and lankier, his plain, farmerish style contrasted with his European features, his small white teeth and patrician, slightly bridged nose. Further, his nappy chestnut hair and butterscotch complexion offset sparkling aquamarine eyes. Startled by the sight of him here at the other end of the continent, Reyna fought to keep from crying out: *Maurice! Maurice! Maurice, here! Maurice, not lost to me in San Francisco!*

She alighted from the carriage as soon as a footman held the stair step, but was quickly engulfed in the crowd of domestics, where she could only look and nod and smile foolishly at the man who had seemed so like Maurice from a distance. Caught up in the enthusiastic, celebrating Negroes, Reyna became aware that their voices brought back the dialect of her childhood.

As the servants thinned out to return to their duties, the tall, thin man edged forward, self-consciously.

Shield cried out, "Well, Ned! Look who's here!"

The farmer thrust out his hand to take hers. "Welcome to Fairfield, Miz Shield. Mister Shield wrote to tell me about you." A tremor in his voice set her to trembling, too.

The crowd of domestics quieted then, seeming embarrassed with eavesdropping, but too curious for good manners.

"Thank you," she said, conscious of the rough hand holding hers. "But, please call me Reyna."

His aquamarine eyes, as blue-green as a reflecting pool, found and held hers. Up close, he was not at all like Maurice, but he had an inescapable magnetism and she couldn't stop staring, though she knew it was rude and foolish.

Seeing their awkwardness, Shield stepped between them.

"Ned," he said. "Come to supper tonight." He swept his arm about at the servants still lingering, the happy confusion of luggage and everyone talking at once. "Obviously, we can't make sense out here. We have some catching up to do."

Something in his imprecise enunciation sparked Reyna's suspicions. That feeling she'd come to recognize, exactly like the one she met at the Gardner's dinner party, was here in the exchange between Shield and the farmer. It sparked in the air at Fairfield as open and electric as it had in the Gardner's dining room.

"Thank you, sir. I'd like that," Ned said, boldly nodding toward Reyna. "All of us have a lot of talking to do."

After servants had dispatched the baggage to their rooms and were unpacking, shaking out wrinkles and hanging their garments, Shield and Reyna retired to the sweeping front porch to sit in lyre-backed Windsor chairs with goose down pillows and to drink glasses of cool lemonade. At last, Reyna allowed herself to fall into the deep relaxation of a gentle, breeze-cooled spring afternoon. It was that time of day when a retreating sun, the color of an Irish setter, washed the horizon in lavender streaks. After Boston and two days in the carriage, the abrupt calm of Fairfield hypnotized her with its beauty.

They were joined by Hawk, a knapsack over his shoulder, leading a magnificent coal black yearling. Reyna sensed that the Indian was ill at ease, unused to formal goodbyes. She flashed her most engaging smile to encourage him.

He spoke gruffly, his voice a growl deep in his throat. "I just wanted to stop by and say farewell and to thank you for our time together . . . and to thank for *this,* sir. I never thought to own such an animal." He yanked on the bridle of the young stallion, too overwhelmed by the gift to meet Shield's eyes.

Fairfield's master beamed a broad ear-to-ear grin, taking pleasure in Hawk's delight. "You're certainly welcome, King. And I know we'll see each other again soon."

Reyna left her chair and stepped down the three steps to the yard where he stood with his handsome horse. Then, she hugged him fiercely, reached into the cozy pocket in her sleeve and withdrew a small leather bag held together by a leather thong. Tying the thong about his neck, she traced the scar running down his face with her fingertips, closed her eyes, and mumbled a sacred chant.

"Tigui li papa," she intoned. "Tigui li papa." *Serpent father come be with us now.*

When she had finished, a tear rolled from his sightless eye.

A nagging foreboding led Reyna to take extra pains while dressing for dinner. Tonight, she vowed, she'd get to the bottom of Shield's skulking around, his disturbing inuendos and hints of intrigue. She had noted Ned's interest in her and done her best to signal him. Tonight, she hoped, would end Shield's treatment of her as a child.

After a maid had tugged her corset to a rib cracking seventeen inches, she pulled a new lemon-yellow silk gown over the horsehair bustle. She dressed her eyes and hair, then wound her long braids in a beehive at the back of her head, softening the look with a piece of snowy Belgian lace.

That night, she could see that someone with a sense of decor had arranged the dining room for this first supper of the three of them. *Who was there on a farm to create such clever accents in a room? Someone at Fairfield she had yet to meet? Was this another of Shield's surprises?* Side tables had been moved to make the formal room seem smaller and draperies had been drawn for intimacy. Candle stands at either end of the table lighted a cozy part of the room just for three. English china with a sailing ship design in cream and maroon was flanked with heavy, masculine silver which lay on linens so thick they could only be folded, not creased. Hattie, the cook, a cinnamon-colored woman with bright blue eyes, had prepared a menu that began with crayfish and finished with her special cream cheese pie.

When Reyna joined them in the dining room, she received the stares she sought. She knew she'd dressed well. "You're mighty pretty, Miz' Shield," Ned greeted her. Awkward in his black country-cut suit, fingers as clumsy as bananas gripping the delicate stemware, his simple, rural manners attracted her even more. His eyes devoured her, but he glanced toward Shield as though seeking approval.

"Why thank you, Ned," she said, deliberately using the southern drawl of her childhood. "That's very kind of y'all to say."

Shield grew expansive with the food and wine and Ned became a little tipsy. Reyna gloried in her ability to enchant these men. Enjoying their congeniality, she began to doubt her plaguing suspicions. It seemed impossible that either of them could be involved in subterfuge.

She smiled faintly, arched her back, bosom thrust forward. Ned's look riveted there. "Tell me," she purred, "how do you get away with it?"

Ned and Shield exchanged a guilty look. "What's that?" they chorused.

"You say you're with the railroad, but I've never seen a single passenger."

"That's the point," Shield said. "You're not supposed to."

"Let's talk about me," Ned interjected. "I knew I just had a hour before they'd light out after me with the dogs. I ran till I got a stitch in my side so bad I couldn't run no more, but then I heard the baying of the hounds and so I picked myself up and ran some more. Y'all can't begin to know how scared I was."

"I think I know," she said, remembering the horror of her own flight.

"Excuse me, Miss Reyna, but it's simply not possible for a white woman from San Francisco to understand."

Reyna smiled inwardly at how her disguise had fooled them; but for a reason she didn't fully understand, she still did not dare to trust them with the truth.

"Oh!" she said. "So, now that you're an overseer, you think you know it all."

"*Overseer?*" Shield exclaimed.

"Yes, overseer," she said, confused by his angry tone.

"Oh, child," he said patiently. "We don't use that word. Ned is the foreman at Fairfield *Farm*. *Overseer* suggests something very different. Fairfield is a *farm*, not a *plantation*. *Plantation*, like *overseer*, has bad memories attached to it."

She looked stricken. "I see," she said, then lowered her eyes. "I understand."

Ned's big, rough-knuckled hand instinctively flew to comfort hers on the table. "I'm sorry, Reyna," he squeezed her trembling fingers gently. "I'm sorry if I upset you."

"No. No. It's all right." Her small fist drew away from his and fell quiet in her lap. "It's quite all right."

By the end of the evening, Reyna had made no progress in her knowledge of the railroad or what she was to do. How would the strength she'd known as Mamaloi, Queen of Voodoo, reveal itself in this northern country surrounded by strangers? She lay in bed a long time, her mind flitting about like a hummingbird, unable to fasten itself onto any one thing.

Then, she rose from her bed with a greater sense of purpose than she'd had since she left San Francisco. She slipped on shoes, threw a shawl over her nightdress, and closed the door of her bedroom behind her.

Clad only in her nightclothes, Reyna chose the servants' back stairs for modesty. Her temper flamed higher with every step as she cautiously made her way by the dim moonlight leaking through the stained glass ceiling of the hall.

She had suffered three months of posing as a student, a convent-educated orphan, niece and ward, as a passive observer aboard ship, and as they visited railroad stations along the way. She'd been treated like a child among adults, had sat quietly listening to insulting, coded conversations at the dinner table in Boston and this night had been chided for her inability to understand the hardships of slavery. Finally, for all his desire to "protect" her, apparently Mr. Shield would not give her details about the work in which he wanted her help. Having lived as a free woman for eight years, Reyna refused to return to humiliation.

"Call me stupid," she muttered under her breath, "but I'm nobody's fool and I'm not just another female to be set aside. I know how to get things done. My laundries employing uneducated slaves compete with Johnny Chinaman and my stable is the best in town. My saloon is crowded every night and try running parlor houses if you think that's easy. Look at my stock portfolio if you want evidence. And, I'm Mamaloi, the Queen of Voodoo in San Francisco. My mama promised me that I've got the power."

Her temperature had cooled somewhat by the time she reached the back porch — at least lowered to the heat of smoldering coals. She'd regained control enough for careful calculation. Now she must proceed with caution.

Ahead of her, under the arms of an enormous catalpa tree, a stone building rose from the ground. Save for a door and two tiny windows, the ivy-covered rock might have been a pile of stones or an Indian burial mound. That single room afforded just enough space for a bed, a chair, and a chest to hold a few personal items. It had begun as the farm's dry vegetable storeroom until Ned claimed it for his home.

When Reyna approached, Ned's shadow was so intertwined with that of the catalpa, she felt his presence before she could separate it from the tree. He stood gazing at the stars spattering the night sky. A comet plummeted toward earth, etching a trace of its fiery path on their vision.

Reyna stood quietly studying him for several minutes before advancing. Now that she'd audaciously come hunting him, she wasn't quite sure how to begin. What could she ask of this simple farmer? How could he help? She reached out and took his sleeve.

He jerked to attention, the swift, automatic reflex of one who'd been in hiding a long time. Just as quickly, he calmed himself and seemed to absorb her presence with the night air.

At last, he said, "Miss Reyna, please don't do that."

"Do what?" she asked quietly.

"Sneak up and scare me half to death."

She grinned in spite of herself. "I need to talk to you."

He attempted to pull back the wrist then, but she held on tight. She stepped closer, her body near enough for him to feel the warmth of it through her nightdress. Still, she clung to his sleeve.

Reyna could see him staring down at her, the moon reflecting silver on the shawl waterfalling over her breasts in the thin chemise. His stare probed her cats' eyes in the moonlight and she could sense his desire like the wanting she'd observed at dinner. Taking another step, then another, Reyna pushed him back to the tree.

She fought back the insane impulse to laugh. At just a little over five and a half feet tall, she had forced the big man up against the trunk of the catalpa. Now, she meant to press even further. Railroad or not, north or south, east or west, lover or slave, she was still Mamaloi, high priestess of voodoo, a woman of power.

She asked coldly, "Are you happy?"

She paused for his answer but still gripping his cuff, she put her hands behind her and thus drew his arm about, the back of his hand against her soft buttock. "Tell me, are you happy, Ned?"

"Yes," he said. "but what's happy? I guess I've had more than my share of happiness."

She said nothing but refused to let go as he tried once more to free his hand. Looking up, her lips level with his chest beneath his open shirt, she casually directed her hot breath lightly there. He shivered, but not from cold.

"Are you sure?" she asked. "Have you really had your share of happiness?"

Reyna could feel him want to pull away, but she also felt his lack of will to do so.

She exhaled again, slowly, hotly.

Now, she could feel his hot stiff sex throb against her abdomen; and knew he was as powerless to prevent its spastic pulse as to stop the beating of his own heart.

"We can't do this. It ain't right," he gasped.

"Ain't right? Who says what's right?"

"Well, it ain't right because it's wrong against Mr. Shield, the best fren' I ever had."

"He'll never know."

"An' it ain't right because you're white. Do you know what would happen to me . . . to us?"

Reyna paused a moment, then took Ned's arm and led his hand down her back, across the corded adhesions left from her near-fatal whipping as a slave.

She felt his sudden recoil as he recognized the cruelty unveiled beneath his fingertips. All who had been slaves knew the language of the lash and its written record on the body.

"Now, we understand each other, Ned. I ain't no rich, spoiled white girl. No one ever give me nothin'. I took everything I ever got." She paused a moment to gather herself and added, "And since you're the only one who knows about this, I'll know who told if word gets out. If that happens, I promise you, you'll wish you'd died at birth."

"Well, I . . . seems to me y'all are in a terrible hurry, Reyna."

"Did I say that?" she asked, a huskiness in her voice. "Did I say anything about time?"

Ned said nothing, stood there breathing hoarsely; still, she could feel his obstinate resistance. She imagined the tree trunk, rough bark against his back, as she leaned forward pressing her breasts against his ribs, forcing her pelvic bones into his groin. The strong, man-smell of him filled her nostrils.

Rearing her head back, she gazed up at him, whispered, "No, I ain't in no hurry, Ned. Are you?"

"No," he breathed, staring down at her upraised face.

He remained quiet awhile, then stepped aside, away from the tree. "Why'd you come here?" he asked. "Why here?"

"Because of the railroad," she said simply, and moved to close the distance between them. "All of us who *can*, MUST help black people. Mr. Shield has gotten it in his mind that I'm a defenseless child. You must help me help."

Chapter 6

Reyna slipped out of bed at first light. It was chill and damp and her shadow leaped on the walls when she struck the lucifer to light the candle. Her movements were swift and purposeful as she dressed herself without calling a maid. Defiance flashed from her eyes and a hard line etched across her lips as she donned the straightline gown of a Boston Brahmin in the newest color, Continental Brown.

While nothing had been truly resolved by her encounter with Ned last night, she felt a thousand pounds lighter just for having shared the secret she had carried alone for so many years. Furthermore, the mere telling of it seemed to make Ned an ally if not a friend. A more precarious step lay in convincing Shield that she was not a helpless child.

Well, then, she thought, *there is a cure for that. I can show him a woman if that's the proof he needs. My figure, my face, my lips, those are not the unformed parts of a child. I was the most famous cook and housekeeper in San Francisco No one else had ever been paid so well for managing three of the finest guest houses in the city. Mr. Shield, bless him, has a lot to learn.*

The kitchen at Fairfield was a few steps off the back porch of the main house, a wondrous place of well-seasoned brick and gleaming copper pots. A fire had been started in the beehive oven and a big iron coffee pot over the embers of the fireplace filled the room with its enticing odor. A large, cinnamon-colored woman at the far end of the room paced back and forth among the kettles and skillets like a tigress in the space that was clearly her domain. Reyna entered and stood quietly for a moment.

Shield poked his head in the kitchen door.

"Oh, Edward," Reyna called out brightly. "I was just about to prepare breakfast. What would you like?"

"What's the matter, Hattie?" he asked. "Aren't you feeling well?"

"Oh, you know me, Mister Shield. I'm right as rain. Nothin' ever wrong with old Hattie."

"Well, then . . .."

"Miz Shield, she say she want to cook breakfast, sir."

Shield paused a second, appeared to try to comprehend. "You won't have time for that, Reyna. Besides, it's Hattie's job.

"But . . ."

He stopped her with an arm about her waist. "You are not the cook, Reyna," he whispered. "Hattie's the cook. You stay out of the kitchen."

"But Edward . . .."

Uncharacteristically, he snapped, *sotto voce*, "The work is unsuitable for my ward. Remember, we have introduced you as my niece." Tell her what you want, then go change."

"Change?"

"Yes. Riding clothes. I want to show you the farm."

Not far from the road, beneath a stand of walnut trees, a settlement of a dozen houses gathered in a rough sort of village where the workers lived. There was no particular pattern to their placement; the shacks were built as they were needed. When a new worker was hired, he chose a site, and the others pitched in to help raise a house. The little dwellings clustered in a semicircle like a tiny, ramshackle town about a communal area. Only a handful of women and children were in the village when they rode through that morning. Women waved, smiled, and sang out greetings. Children left their play and gathered to stare, big-eyed with wonder at the owner and the lady.

Then, Reyna realized what it was that lent an edge to her feelings.

In a crazy sort of way, Virginia and Fairfield Farm brought back shades and shadows of her childhood as a slave in Georgia at Riverview Plantation. They were not at all alike, of course; that was cotton and slavery, this was tobacco and free people. The hundred employees of Fairfield numbered among the fortunate 3,000 free Blacks of the state where 40,000 others still labored in bondage. The concept of this venture, a farm run for wages by free black people, made her proud. But, still, an uncomfortable similarity between bondage and paid workers bothered her.

A hundred yards from the knot of tiny houses stood a padlocked drying shed. How odd, she thought, to place a barn so far away from the nearest field. A pretty little fresh water well, encased in brick, a new rope to the bucket, sat just to the side of the sliding doors of the shed.

"Let's stop for a drink," she called out. "I'm thirsty."

"No! Don't ever go near that place," Shield answered darkly. "Stay away from there. There's a well just up ahead where we can drink."

"Why? What's wrong with this one?"

"Poisoned," he said. "Water's poisoned."

"Oh, Edward!" Then, as an afterthought, "Don't you think you ought to seal it off?"

"They all know to stay away."

"Well, I think the least that could be done is to take the bucket away if it's dangerous."

"I'll speak to Ned about it," he agreed, sounding cranky at her interference.

It continued to intrigue her, a barn clear out in the woods with an unprotected well of undrinkable water; all the more odd considering the efficient orderliness of the rest of the farm.

When Shield and Reyna rode in from their tour of the farm in the early afternoon, Ned stood in the doorway of his little stone cottage.

Remembering their encounter of last night Reyna focused on Ned's behavior, watching his every move. Unable to ask, she was eager to determine what effect the information about her color had produced. Instead, he appeared to be almost too calm as though he'd forgotten the incident. In a wry sense, that was almost worse than exaggerated secret keeping.

She could see now, too, the physical source of his attraction. His blue-green eyes fairly dazzled against his beige flesh in the afternoon light. Not handsome in the usual sense, the man had a good-natured wholesomeness that appealed to men and women alike. Some unique combination of black and white, free and slave, allowed him to persist in spite of the adversity of slavery. That persistence was his strength, perhaps the greatest strength of all Negroes who survived.

Ned spoke to Shield in a way that included her in the conversation. "Everything's going well, sir. When you've got time, I'd be happy to go over the accounts with you."

"I've been looking at some of them, but there's no hurry for the rest. We'll be staying awhile."

That night, toying with her food, a heavy oyster bisque with fresh baked bread and new churned butter, she gazed at him, intently studying his features in the flickering candlelight. He'd begun to age in the short time they'd been here, dark crows' feet now lined his eyes and his lips, turned down, made him look sorrowful more often than not.

It had taken time, but Reyna had come to realize she'd sorted out her relationship with Shield. She looked at him then, and a genuine fondness for him moistened her eyes. On impulse, she reached across the table and patted the back of his hand.

He brought his eyes to meet hers. "I'm sorry, my dear. My mind seems to be wandering. It's just that I've something I need to say, and I'm jittery about how to say it."

"Oh, Edward, You don't need to hold back. What is it? Is something wrong?"

"No, it's nothing like that, but . . ." Shield bent over to the side, then shuffled around under the skirt of the tablecloth, and finally came up holding a parchment scroll of some sort. "It's this. It's taken my solicitor too confounded long to work it out, but it's here at last. I want you to keep this copy."

He drew himself together and sighed, a deep exhalation of sound and air. "It's the formal paper proclaiming you to be my niece and only heir."

Her thoughts scattered like buckshot. He was giving her his fortune. He was risking his reputation for all time if her true heritage were to become known. But, most of all, he had just handed her the keys to the underground railroad.

"Why?" she asked. "Why me? Why now?"

His face fell, looked ten years older in repose. "There's no one else I know who is better qualified to lead. A person of color wouldn't last a minute in this country."

Her face turned dead white at the words. She had never suspected the depth of his trust in her, his appreciation for her skill. Still, there was the unanswered question that she could perhaps never ask: *would he feel the same if he knew of her African roots? Clearly, he had said the opposite. A person of color wouldn't last a minute.* It was not until later, when her joy at his expression of trust had cooled, that she discovered the poison in the apple: accepting the inheritance committed her to continuing to hide her heritage.

Then it was his turn to reach across the table and pat *her* hand affectionately, "I'm not trying to alarm you but it makes such good sense to be prepared for the worst."

Speechless at the enormity of what he'd done, she could only croak out, "I'm flattered by your trust in me, Edward."

"I've thought about that . . . thought about all of this a great deal. I know you, Reyna. You're a woman of principle. I trust you to do the right thing when I'm gone."

Shield began to act more oddly. Inexplicably, he often left the house in the middle of the night. She first noticed it after one of their long evenings together, an evening complete with a fire, a book, long pauses between unhurried sentences of conversation. When the warmth of a good dinner, followed with sherry, had drowsied them, he saw her upstairs to her door. There, as usual, he pecked at her cheek by way of good night.

Later, sleepless, she left her warm bed and drifted across the room to the window. In the side yard, lighted by the clear, new moon, a caped figure stood shrouded in the dark of a large oak tree. A short while later, a murky shape she guessed was Anatole, the stable groom, led Shield's horse out under the tree. The waiting figure heaved itself to the back of the stallion and galloped away.

She learned to recognize the signs preceding his leavetaking — a restless uneasiness, a mood more than any words he uttered. He kept precisely to the schedule she had memorized, and by a choreography equally imprinted on her brain, she rose to see him go.

But that night was not to be the same. Not one, but three figures stood beneath the tree. They moved about, not in celebration as might three rogues riding off to visit whores, rather more funereal, using hand gestures so as not make a sound. It was Shield, Ned, and a man Reyna had never seen before. Anatole held the reins of three steaming horses with hooves clad in sacking to still their noise. Shield rode away in the company of two others.

    Reyna watched from her station with a moth and candle fascination of wonder and dread. The probability of their involvement in a smuggling ring terrified her. The classic smuggling was accomplished by a triangle that began in New England with maple sugar. They traded the maple sugar for slaves on the coast of Spain, and then traded the slaves for rum in the Caribbean Islands. Moving the liquor inland from off shore boats had become a major industry on the coast. "Oh! in the name of Vodu!," she prayed. "Don't let Mr. Shield be involved in that!"

Chapter 7

A heavy object struck a wall. A table tipped over. Thumping and bumping noises roused her from sound sleep. In the first few minutes, unsure of the sounds, Reyna lay there disoriented and then frightened. Not even the moon lighted her pitch black room. Rough men's voices swore in the front hall. It seemed that burglars had attacked — no, invaded — the mansion. Her body stiffened. "*In the name of Vodu,*" she prayed. "*Don't let them come upstairs.*"

Suddenly, a keening wail pierced the air as Hattie cried out, "Oh, Lord a' mercy! Oh, sweet Baby Jesus! Oh, Lord a' mercy, would you just see what's happened here!"

Then, Lessie joined the commotion, shrieking, "Oh! Mista', Mista'! What they done done to y'all? Oh! Mista', Mista'! Save us Lord Almighty!"

Reyna leaped from her bed, threw a robe around her shoulders, ran out into the hall and down the central staircase.

Coming out of the darkness of the unlighted front hall, Ned and Anatole half carried a crumpled and disheveled figure that she gradually made out to be Edward's. At sight of her, Ned turned his head away, seeming to stare hard at the jumbled bundle of clothes, arms and legs all pretzel-twisted between them. The stable hand, Anatole, a muscular, dark brown man looked away, too, as though ashamed to be found inside the big house. Absurdly, Reyna's first thought was how much Edward would resent the dirt on his immaculate riding pants.

"What happened?" she asked. "Have you sent for the doctor?"

Most of what she'd first thought dirt was blood, caked and drying; still more of it bubbling through his shirt from a wound somewhere on his torso.

"What's happened?"

"We'll tell y'all about that when we get him settled. First, let's get him to bed."

As her wits returned Reyna ordered, "Lessie, heat some water! Hattie, bring clean cloths and towels!"

Her voice was stronger than she felt. Shield's injuries were desperate; anyone could see that. On a second thought, she raced to her own bedroom and returned with the traveler's desk containing her herbs and ointments.

The men gently carried him up the stairs and placed him upon the bed in his cavernous bedroom suite. The massive, square four-poster bed swallowed Shield like a rag doll. His office and sitting room were no less foreboding. Outsized mahogany furniture, upholstered in wine-red velvet, sat about on maroon Persian carpets. The gloomy space was further darkened by mahogany wainscoting from floor to chair rail. Ned wrung his hands anxiously, a useless gesture he couldn't seem to stop making. Anatole glanced about nervously as if fearing sudden intruders.

Shield lay there comatose. She could hardly make out the slow rise and fall of his chest. His face was a bloodless mask.

"Help me," she commanded the servants. "We'll have to cut his clothes off. Try not to move him any more than you must."

Using paper shears from his desk, Ned and Anatole went to work on Shield's shirt and undershirt. As they cut away his garments, Reyna could see a series of deep-scraped abrasions, the worst of which ran from his right shoulder to his waist and had raked away the top layer of skin as it went. The wound, already an evil-looking purple, now wept clear, sticky liquid. She fought back the nausea rising in her throat.

Hattie came with cloths and towels. Reyna ordered, "Anatole, go downstairs and help Lessie. Bring two buckets of water, one hot, one lukewarm. And, bring some clean lard for these hurt places. We can't allow them to stick to the bandages."

The open mouths of a half dozen short, thin slits in the left side of his rib cage bled profusely, pumping with his pulse. While she waited for the water, she held the openings shut with her fingers, temporarily stanching the flow of blood.

As she did so, she sang the ancient mantra of her voodoo healing ritual under her breath.

"Heron mande! Mande heron!"

"Mande heron! Heron Mande!"

Out of the corner of her eye, Reyna saw Ned go slack-jawed recognizing the voodoo chant, but she had no time to attend to his squeamish memories. She'd put his anxieties to rest when this crisis had been managed. In their midnight meeting, she had settled *who* she was; now, the voodoo chant told him *what*.

Ned opened Shield's belt, then paused before cutting at the trousers.

Noting his aversion, Reyna barked, "Oh, for heaven's sake, boy! Do you want this man to die? Cut his trousers off! We've got no time for y'all's modesty about a naked body!"

Nodding to Hattie, she said, "Thank goodness, you're here! Men are next to worthless in an emergency."

Hattie and Reyna worked well together, washing and poulticing the man's body, bandaging the wounds to arrest the flow of blood. Reyna noted that Ned blanched again when she reached into her reticule for spider webbing to close the wound, lambswort to ward off infection, and a healing unguent she'd made of ground castor bean.

Sitting on the bed, both hands holding together the lips of a cut, blood welling through her fingers, Reyna caught Ned's eye and said, "Now, I want to know what's happened here."

The foreman shot a look at Hattie, answered, "It's not my place to tell you nothin'. Mr. Shield tell you his ownself when he wake up."

"At least, honor me with one answer," she said. "These aren't just the marks of a fall from his horse, are they?"

Ned looked away, clamped his lips shut in a pantomime of silence, but shook his head in the negative.

"Knife?" she asked.

He nodded assent.

At last, when they'd finished, Reyna washed herself from the same bucket of water they'd fetched for Shield. She brought a chair from across the room and planted it firmly alongside the bed. Sighing deeply, she said, "You can leave now. I'll call you as soon as there's a change. Hattie and Lessie will sleep on pallets in the pantry and we'll come for y'all as soon as there's something to tell."

Hour after hour she sat staring at the gray face with its closed and darkened eyelids. As she watched his suffering, she prepared herself for the confrontation she must have with the three conspirators, Edward, Ned, and Hattie.

As time passed, sometimes the patient's flesh seemed to jerk of its own will, his head to rolling back and forth on the pillow. Now and again, delirious with fever, Shield thrashed bolt upright, glared about with sightless, red-rimmed eyes and railed at her. "No, no," he cried out. "Leave me alone." He suffered unquenchable thirst, called for water again and again, but when she held the glass to his lips he drank no more than a swallow. Several times, struggling against shaking tremors, he shuddered, "Reyna, child. I must talk to you."

"Not now, Edward," she said, firming him back to the pillow. "Later."

An hour after midnight, Shield began to perspire heavily. He soaked the bedding and pillows, yet his hands and feet remained cold to her touch. Reyna changed the wet blanket three times for fresh ones heated in front of the fireplace before drenching sweats broke the fever and eased him into unconscious sleep. She stood, arched her back against the ache of constant bending, then resumed her vigil.

She remained there, steadfast, long after the spring moon, blotched with yellow-green, climbed past the bedroom window. The anxious caring, the tense, minute-by-minute assessment of his condition turned her to her own plight as well. The stillness, broken only by his throaty breathing and occasional fits and starts of pain or fever, reminded her how empty her life had become. She now had every creature comfort but lacked the sense of achievement that had once been so important to her. She had been made to feel useless here. Resentment about that rose like acid in her throat. Incredibly, too, at that moment, she hated his dying for making her feel guilty about her *wants*, her *needs*.

She must have nodded off a minute — later, she swore to herself it could not have been more than a few seconds — for when she looked up his eyes were open, the irises yellowed and watery, but looking directly at her.

"Lean closer, Reyna, I must talk to you and I've not much strength left."

"How do you feel?" she whispered. A ridiculous question under the circumstances.

"Not well at all."

"I'm so sorry, Edward." Again, the words rang hollow, so trivial alongside his pain.

He fixed an eye upon her. His pathetically thin fingers fluttered over the coverlet.

"I won't trouble you much longer." He held out the feeble hand that had fallen back on his chest.

The hand she took felt like an icy claw. She thought she saw tears wetting the corners of his eyes.

"You know too much about the spirit world to be superstitious about death." His voice trailed off to a vaporous whisper. "They've killed me this time."

"Who? Who did this to you?"

"Wait. I want to apologize. I've come to know that we all have a right to choose for ourselves what we do — that includes what risks we take with our lives.

"When you agreed to join us I was pleased. Then, as I got to know you and to care about you, I discovered I couldn't bring myself to let you risk your life. . ."

"Edward! Wait! Later . . ."

He rambled on, ignoring her interruption. ". . . denied your right to make your own choices."

A stillness settled over them then. What he had said *was* true, of course, but she could not bear his assumption of guilt.

She leaned to rest her head lightly on his chest, clung pitifully to the feeble hand.

His voice was weak, more breath than sound. "I've risked my life and yours, too."

At first, guessing he was delirious and she was numb with fatigue, she gave little importance to his drifting sentences, but he continued to talk of a mysterious threat. Finally, she sat up, drew back to study his face. "What danger, Edward?"

"I never wanted to involve you. This house. Boston. The warehouses. All of it's a sham. You're in great danger."

"In danger of what? Tell me."

"This is a station. You've been living in a station of the underground railroad. Not just those stations I showed you along the way. But, Boston. And, here, too."

Although unsurprised, she asked, "What?"

"I was caught by villains masquerading as Federal Marshals. They were looking for abolitionists. I've been stampeding slaves."

She looked up, bewildered.

"Getting slaves to run away or revolt."

"But, that's wonderful, Edward!" Reyna said, once more in awe of this gentle man she had come to admire.

"No!" He jerked up in the bed, quaking and bug-eyed, straining as though fearing *someone* listened, "You could be hurt."

"But, Edward, remember, I came here to help." Despite herself, Reyna couldn't keep some of her bitterness about the past few weeks out of her voice. "Have you forgotten that? That's the only reason I'm here!"

"Don't argue with me now, child. I must tell you all of it. Under the law, slaves are chattel. They belong to someone else. Slave owners say we steal property. The least thing that can happen is arrest. Some are lynched and tarred and feathered. Look at me. I'm an example of their justice."

She stared at his wasted face, saw the destruction there and felt only pity for him. "I'd never let that happen," she said with a force that seemed to startle him.

"I recruited you because of your extraordinary abilities. You're a very talented leader. I recognized that quality instantly in San Francisco. It's just that I didn't want to endanger you." The thin, reedy voice weakened again. A dry cough hacked in his throat. "Oh, you almost caught us when you heard them in the house in Boston."

A great fit of coughing wracked him then, darkened his face and bobbed his head furiously against the pillow. Pink flecks brightened the spittle at the corners of his lips. When it passed, he continued feebly, "Reyna, child. I don't have much time. They know me and this house. They attacked me in the dark because they don't have enough evidence to have me arrested."

"Tell me, who are the others? I'll go for help!"

"No. Never. Damn it, woman, how many times must I say, 'What you don't know, you can't be forced to tell'?"

"But, then, what can we do?"

"Absolutely nothing. They've chosen this way to stop my work."

Despite her lack of sleep, Reyna sat wide awake, wondering, picturing gentle, kind Edward conducting secret, after-dark missions, smuggling slaves out of the country.

"Who did this to you, Edward?"

He lay quietly, seeming to struggle to regain the strength drained by the long conversation. "I don't know who it was. It was dark on the road and they wore hoods. That's why I've been careful not to involve you. They must suspect you are involved, but you have never been implicated."

"All the servants, the people in this house, are black. Surely . . ."

"Reyna!" He chided her, "Excuse me, child, but believe me. We can trust no one."

"But black people, surely . . ."

"Black people, hah! No one! Last month I helped a black family. A man, a woman, and two children. We fed them, gave them clothing, a passage to Canada, and a note to buy land there. Later, I discovered ours was the fourth station to do so."

"What do you mean?"

"They were frauds. They were free black people who make a handsome living pretending to be escaped slaves. Once they collect money, clothes, food, they move on to the next station where they are unknown and do it again."

"Is it possible?" She was aghast.

"There are many others. Black people as well as white. Black people who pretend to act as guides north in order to fleece runaways of their money. White and black seamen who charge exorbitant prices for passage on rafts and barges. Remember and learn from that. Never trust anyone based solely on appearances."

His head lolled back in the pillows, sinking deeper into the softness. His big eyes closed, draping his vision with the gray lids of the mortally ill.

At last, his labored breathing announced that he had again fallen into a deep sleep. The household had long since retired when she closed his door and an eerie, unnatural calm gripped her. To light the way, Lessie had left a guttering candle that reflected the maroon carpet like dried blood splashed upon the gray walls. She entered the little pantry where Lessie and Hattie shared a single pallet and blanket and heard herself, her almost expressionless voice, as she sent Lessie to get Ned to come to Mr. Shield's bedroom and Anatole to alert the workers in the village. The rush of her own thoughts refused to let her rest. Hattie followed her upstairs to the sickbed

The three of them stood close about the bed silently watching for his awakening. Hattie and Ned, heads bowed, prayed quietly. Ashen-faced they had apparently expected the worst when they responded to her summons, but relaxed during the vigil waiting for Mr. Shield to wake up feeling better. Conscious of their new knowledge of the mistress's devotion to voodoo they also hoped her power would protect their employer.

At long last, Shield's eyelids fluttered, uncovered his milky eyes which blinked a couple of times then settled and focused. A faint smile indicated that he recognized them.

"Good morning, Edward," Reyna greeted him softly. "Look who's come to see you."

A slight nod of his head.

Reyna cleared her throat and moved closer to the stricken man, asked calmly, "Do you remember, sir, our conversation last evening?"

Ned slowly wagged his head in grateful acknowledgment of his employer's recovery, no matter how slight. A stream of tears flowed down Hattie's freckled, dark brown cheeks.

Another frail nod from Edward.

Ned and Hattie bent forward, clearly taken aback at the idea that anything could be important enough to cause Miz Shield to mention it in the sickroom.

"I've been thinking these last several hours about what you said, Edward, and I, too, have something I must tell you. I hardly know where to begin . . . It's so difficult to tell . . . I guess I never truly trusted you until you confessed to those things I could only guess at . . . Now, if I am to stay here with you, it must be without secrets between us. "

Shield rolled his head over on the pillow to face her, his cheek resting against her soft hand on his shoulder. As ill as he was, Reyna could still read the troubled concern in his eyes.

"I guess I may just as well say it aloud, but please let what I say stay among the three of us here."

Hattie and Ned nodded vigorously, curiosity written in their faces.

Reyna inhaled a deep gulp of breath, said, "I was born a slave. . . I — "

She noted that Ned turned away, perhaps to hide the fact of his previous knowledge of her race. Good. A sign that he'd not revealed her confidence. He could be trusted.

Hattie stared down at the carpet. She swayed a little on her feet, absorbing news she found shocking.

"No, wait," Reyna continued, controlling her voice to say the words so long withheld. "I was born a slave in Georgia, but my father was a white man in Virginia. He sold my mother before I was born."

"Who done it, Miz Shield?" asked Hattie, unable to restrain the astonishment showing in her face.

"I don't know. It was so common in those days. My grandfather, my mother's father was also a white man. My mother told me my father was related to the president, President Jefferson."

Shield beckoned her to bend down, put her ear closer to his mouth, a voice more breath than sound. "Is this true, child?"

'Yes, Edward. It is."

"Be careful, Reyna," Edward whispered. "The patrollers would be even harder on you if they find out." The effort of offering even that small speech apparently exhausted him and he slipped back into sleep.

By evening, Shield had worsened. He babbled incoherently and complained of simultaneous chills and fevers. Exhausted, Reyna sent Anatole racing to Charles Town for the physician. She ordered warm soup from Hattie and positioned herself like a sentry at the foot of the sick man's bed.

Hattie crept through the door with the shuffling gait peculiar to people visiting sickrooms. Exaggeratedly steadying the food tray, she grimaced at each clink of spoon against bowl.

"Miz' Shield," she whispered. "Miz' Shield, I brung the soup."

"Thank you, Hattie."

At the sound, Shield sat bolt upright, sightlessly staring in their direction. "What's that?" he cried out. "Who is it?"

"It's your soup, Mr. Shield. Fresh made just for you. You just get some of ole' Hattie's soup down you and you'll be right as rain."

After all that had been said about treachery, Reyna eyed the soup suspiciously. Pretending to taste a spoonful for warmth, she carefully swallowed, watching the cook's face, before crossing the room to Shield. The broth seemed hearty, mildly seasoned, nothing unusual in its flavor. Hattie appeared unmoved by the act.

Reyna had dozed off when Shield stirred fitfully. Ned and Anatole waited in the hall. The workers from the farm knelt praying in a semicircle on the lawn off the front porch. The doctor from Charles Town was due momentarily.

Suddenly, Shield cried out and clutched his chest in fierce pain. "Reyna!" he gasped. His dark eyes bulged in their sockets and went white.

Springing from the chair, Reyna ran her arms under his back, clutched him close, rocking gently. "Don't worry," she soothed. "The doctor will be here any minute. You're safe now."

The body in her arms stiffened, shook with spasms.

"It will be all right. Yes, Edward, we're right here with you."

At the end, he opened his brown eyes and mumbled indistinctly, "Yours. Everything is yours. All I ask . . . use some of it for the railroad."

Part Two

The Station Master

Chapter 8

Lessie, the second floor maid, sat on a stool in Hattie's kitchen kingdom watching as the cook prepared a chicken pie for lunch. Hattie, her cinnamon complexion flushed from cognac she combined with the thickened roux, tried to ignore the pitch-black maid whom she regarded as feeble-minded. Not an ungenerous woman, though, each time she supped a sample of cognac-flavored soup she brought a spoonful over to pour an equal amount on Lessie's pink tongue. It amused her to observe Lessie, unused to spirits, grow tottery on the stool as the morning and the cognac wore on.

"Oh, ma'am," Lessie declared after one such spoonful, "that be as good as God's own crawdaddy stew."

"Hmmph!" shrugged Hattie, unconvinced that the black teenager knew the difference between pole cat and 'possum.

Still, the talkative maid continued. "I think Mr. Shield's send off was the most beautiful thing I ever did see."

Although she knew for a fact that Lessie had never attended a funeral in a church before, Hattie let the remark pass. "Yes, the coffin was beautiful, like a giant jewel box."

At the word "jewel box" Lessie's hand flew to her collar where she wore the gold and pearl gift brooch from Reyna

"Made special for him . . . and brought all the way from Boston. I never saw nothin' like it in my life." Lessie closed her eyes a moment as if harvesting the memory. "But, I thought it was sad to see Miz' Reyna sittin' all by her lonesome downstairs in the white section."

Hattie winced at her own mendacity, but offered, "Well white folks are different from coloreds. They don't . . . well they just don't seem to have much heart. Then, too, Mr. Shield didn't have a whole lot of white friends out here, if you know what I mean. Did you ever see Miz' Reyna cry? You know, her in her room in private. Did she cry the night Mr. Shield died?"

The maid squinched her eyes up tight trying to remember. "No, I don't rightly think she did." She thought another moment, then exclaimed, "Oh my God! I never thought about it, but Miz' Reyna didn't cry a bit. What I saw her do was turn her face real mean, as mean as ol' satan. Them yella' eyes of hers was shootin' lightnin' bolts around the room and her looking like a bull ready to charge somethin'."

Picturing the scene in her mind, Harrie poured herself another cognac, and gave Lessie a dollop, too. Tossing it back in one gulp, she said, "She's changed somehow. It was like Mr. Shield's death done turned her old before her time. She walks all tall and uppity like, lookin' down her nose. Not like she was afore."

Lessie put in, "Yes, ma'am. I used to think we was friends." She patted the brooch. "Now, she scares me, the way she is all turned inside and hateful."

As if she'd been listening and had heard it all, Reyna poked her head in the door. "What are you two up to?".

Hattie recovered first. "Oh! Miz' Reyna, we were just sayin' how pretty Mr. Shield's service was, the flowers, the coffin, and all."

Lessie furtively turned her collar over so her brooch would not be noticed.

"He was a great man. He deserved the very best," Reyna said, then scrutinized Hattie. Her remark stirred fears shared by all the people of Fairfield. *What would they do? Would Miz' Reyna sell the place and send them away?*

"Mr. Shield, he say . . ." the cook began.

"Mr. Shield is no longer with us, Hattie," Reyna interrupted with the sharp edge they'd come to fear. "There will be no changes here. We'll go on as we always have because I want it that way."

She was gone before they could react. Lessie shuddered as though facing an icy breeze.

The transfer of ownership had been simple. It required no more than half an hour with an officious, nervous-acting, white solicitor from Richmond. Everyone had been introduced to Mr. Edward Shield's ward and knew Shield had no other heirs. Still, certain other persons in Jefferson County were relieved to be spared an investigation into the man's death that had been reported, uncontested, the result of a fall from his horse.

Although Ned suspected that Shield was her guardian only in name, Ned's unrequited romantic interest, not to mention his fear of her voodoo at Mr. Shield's bedside, bought his silence.

As she set her course on this maiden voyage through the dangerous straits of the underground railroad, Reyna understood that Ned held the keys to her success. She needed his experience and strength, his knowledge of the station and the roads and trails leading in and out of it. What she did not need was a man falling in love with her — one clipping her wings as Mr. Shield had.

"Wing clippers, " she said to herself. "All men are wing clippers. Let them fall in love, they put you on a shelf to gather dust. They're all alike."

After the funeral Reyna had returned to Fairfield and summoned Ned to the office alcove of the dead man's bedroom suite. Despite her sadness at Shield's death, she felt glad to be free of his restrictions on her activities.

Perversely, the risk-taking that had cost Edward his life convinced her more than ever of the need for bold action. Although she'd suppressed her grief, the rage she felt demanded reprisal. The fire that had made her Queen of Voodoo flamed in her breast.

She would have liked to have made a show of doing something; but there was nothing left for her to do. The farm in Virginia and the brokerage in Boston were as orderly as Shield's life had been. The estate moved along at the same pace without him.

When Ned whisper-stepped into the room, Reyna lay her head back in the chair and lifted the heavy veil. She'd not been alone with him since Shield's death. *Did it matter?* She wondered. *Did he care?* The line of upraised chin above her slender neck, the high cheek bones and the solemnity in the oddly-colored eyes — everything about her bespoke commanding dignity.

Reyna knew Ned had been deeply shaken by his employer's death. She'd seen his handsome face collapse with grief at the funeral. More than once she'd spied him blowing his nose into an enormous handkerchief when he thought no one could see. Now, standing there in Shield's bedroom office, he lowered his head, locked his eyes on his feet.

"Ned," she asked. "Can you manage the farm alone? "

He looked up. "Yes, of course I can."

"The books? The accounts? The schedule of planting and harvest?"

"Of course. Mr. Shield always did the managing, but I know it as well."

"Good," she said. She turned her head to gaze out the window at the rolling hills of tobacco, knee-high in mid-growth. "That's exactly what I'd like you to do. If you're certain you can do it, I'd like you to take over."

Having thus settled the overt business affairs, Reyna turned to the matter uppermost in her thoughts. In all the necessary encounters with the servants since Shield's death, she hadn't dropped the smallest hint of his final, revealing confessions.

"I'd like you to assume complete responsibility for Fairfield Farm."

"Oh, Reyna," he cried out. "For y'all! Anything!"

Irritated by his obvious enthusiasm, she said, "I will review the accounts, of course. But, the bulk of the responsibility will be yours."

"Thank you, Reyna, Y'all won't regret it."

"I must return to Boston . . ."

The big man recoiled. She was leaving.

"I must return to Boston. I've written ahead for a memorial gathering to honor Mr. Shield's memory."

"How long will you be gone?"

"I'm not sure. There are other arrangements to be made . . . things that must be done. And, then, there are the other matters of Edward's — of our — work."

The foreman avoided her eyes, carefully considering the implications.

"I intend to see our work go on. One of Mr. Shield's last wishes was that his *work* should continue. I intend to see that wish carried out. You will prepare the railroad for passengers as always."

He peeped up at her then and a jubilant glow spread across his face.

"But, first, before I leave I want to have another service, the *real* service to help Mr. Shield on his way to the other world." Leaning back, she raised her hand to her throat as if casually, but lifted her favorite voodoo amulet by its leather thong from her bosom to dangle outside her gown.

An involuntary gasp escaped Ned as his eyes fixed on the talisman.

"Oh, for pity's sake, stop it Ned. I saw the look you gave me when I sang to the loas, the gods at his bedside. Have you forgotten?"

"I remember, but when I thought about it, I was sure I was wrong. Even now . . . you can't be a believer?" His mind reeled; to know that she was of African descent and now to confirm her voodoo worship.

"Oh, yes, I can. And am. I am descended from a long line of religious women. I saw your response to my prayer when Mr. Shield was brought in sick. How many of us are here at Fairfield?"

"No one really knows. Thirty. Maybe forty."

"And Lessie and Hattie?"

He nodded, tongue tied by what he'd heard.

"Good. that will do nicely. On your way out have Hattie and Lessie come up to the office. We have work to do. Now, go tell the believers to be at the front gallery at 11:30 tonight. Remind them they must wear no clothing that is crossed or tied. Now, please leave me. I must prepare for the ceremony and the journey back to Boston."

A hoot owl in the pawpaw tree below her window cried out its haunting question as Reyna dressed for the ceremony honoring Edward Shield's passage. Tonight she would release his sacred *emi*, his spirit, from his body so that it could find peace.

She debated for a long time about whether to wear white or black. White was the color favored by Oduduwa, Angel of Death; but, she had a surprise mission this night and chose the black. Opals were special to Oduduwa and she pleased the god with a rich necklace of the stones strung on lacy, sterling silver filament and a form fitting belt of the same costly materials. A band of white silk tied back her luxurious hair in a ponytail. She painted her face a ghostly white and a black death mask surrounded her eyes. Then, she stood back to admire her handiwork.

When she had finished, Reyna crept quietly out onto the second floor gallery to watch the congregation, *her* new congregation, arrive on the lawn spread out before the mansion, now a sanctified site of worship. She leaned back against the wall so her silhouette would not be seen. On one hand, she was anxious about performing for an entirely new group, people whom she guessed had no idea of her power; on the other hand, she found the challenge exhilarating. It had been too long since she last worked with the magic. She felt starved for the thrilling connection with the serpent, a need as demanding as the sexual hunger in her loins.

Lessie and Hattie had been surprisingly cooperative that day as they followed her direction in preparing for the ceremony. With no more than a minute's discussion, they accepted, even rejoiced in having a religious queen among them. Her announcement had answered many of their unspoken questions. The way she'd kept her own counsel in her months of inactivity at Fairfield. Her command at the bedside with her own herbs and poultices. *What white woman would travel with those things?* Finally, of course, there had been the talisman, the powerful scapular of Vodu that she wore around her neck. Putting those facts together, the two of them had simply swallowed hard, looked popeyed for a moment, but accepted her for what she said she was. Vodu or not, she was their one tie to the life they'd come to enjoy. Reyna guessed they'd wondered about her all along. Obviously they'd also missed the fulfillment of Vodu in their lives.

This day, the three of them had "doused" the front lawn with the purifying smoke of *jirrijirri*, a rank odor of rotten meat and mesquite. Reyna had directed the building of Mr. Shield's effigy, ironically a suit of his riding clothes, a broad brimmed hat and riding boots. They stuffed the costume with cotton batting, shaped to his form as though his body filled it. A napkin draped over his face and neck gave the startling appearance of a living, masked Mr. Shield.

After creating a thick carpet of redolent pine branches and needles in the center of the lawn, they dragged an antique oak chair with ball and claw feet and armrests to place in the middle of the pine mat. In that chair, no doubt the possession of some forgotten ancestor, they placed the lifelike effigy dressed as they had last seen Mr. Shield. Then they beheaded a half dozen young *gallo*, two-year-old cocks from the farm's flock of poultry. With the blood of those fowl who'd crowed their last at dawn, the trio drew a giant Pharoah's Circle about the chair.

At the foot of the stairs to the main gallery they placed a six foot parson's table to serve as an altar and precisely twenty-nine sacred Look-to-Heaven candles and covered pots of mamaloi's oils for the blessing. After a brief moment of mutual congratulations for their effort, the three went inside to prepare themselves for the celebration.

That night, as the moon rode high above the big house, the devotees of voodoo began to gather, solemnly trudging in from the forest about the cleared front lawn. Holding candles, they looked like a flight of fireflies among the dark bodies in brief white shifts and loin cloths, hushed for the occasion of Mr. Shield's death and the presentation of a new queen. Two coal black fellows, up from the Carolinas, brought hand carved hickory wood drums, lighter in weight and higher toned than the traditional bamboula of the deep south. Squatting on their heels at either side of the parson's table altar, they began to caress the skins of their instruments lightly, sending a throbbing pulse into the night and the gathering. Evanelle and Maryann, who played finger cymbals, the *zells*, of North Africa, added the melody to the rhythm of the drums. Ned had built a roaring fire in a wine barrel a few yards in front of the altar.

Awed by the sight of the figure in Mr. Shield's clothes, the worshippers paused outside Pharoah's Circle of blood to gawk, to respect his *emi* in the presence there. Only their fear of violating that circle kept them from rushing forward, close enough to touch the phantasm.

J. P. and John Henry came forward to distribute gourds of sweet *gala,* a blend of rum and filtered pear juice. As the night, the spirit presence, the sweet *gala,* and the anticipation lifted them up from the weariness of a day in the fields, Reyna sensed their restive readiness. Here a hip swayed, there a finger snapped, a longing look in the direction of the musicians and the multitude began to move a little, to find with their bare feet and naked bodies the rhythm in their souls, a music that wanted to come out, to express itself. In tune with that mood, too, the musicians played a little louder, a little faster, joining them in their need.

J. P. and John Henry returned with helpings of sweet *gala*. The dancing became more frenzied. A tall island woman, hair braided with cowrie shells, twirled like a human top while a coterie of young males counted the turns, one-two-three-four to a total of twenty-five at which point she stopped, staggered off to the side to catch her breath, and accepted another gourd of sweet *gala* to moisten her parched throat. Big Tom, a man with the thick jawed look of the African Kingdom of Gaboon, began cartwheels from the altar to the furthest reach of the lawn and back, a distance of two hundred yards. Couples had paired up to dance, eyes closed, arms and legs flailing with the rhythm, feet slapping it out on the short grass. From her promontory on the upper gallery, Reyna knew when it was time. She raised a hand to catch Ned's eye in the crowd. At the sight of him, butterscotch-colored skin shining in the moonlight, she imagined his aquamarine eyes, yearned for his touch. At her signal he left the sanctified site.

When Ned returned, struggling under the weight of a woven, dome-lidded straw basket, Reyna pushed open the double doors of the mansion and glided out onto the main gallery, and stood at the top of the stairs. Some among the gathering saw her there, elbowed their neighbors to look, to hush, to give Mamaloi their attention. They melted forward to stand in a semicircle about the porch.

"My brothers and sisters!" she cried, raising her arms, hands turned palms down, calling for their attention. "My neighbors and friends, all of us are related by our community . . ."

A hush fell over the crowd as they gaped in awe at the woman they'd known as Mistress Shield. This night she had become a goddess — no, a Queen — radiant, beautiful, commanding. Her black silk sheath, background for the fortune in opals and foil for the white streamer in her hair, the white platform shoes that elevated her to tower above them. By common acclaim, a cry escaped their lips, "Mamaloi! Mamaloi!" *The voodoos had found their queen.*

Again, she raised her hands, palms down, commanding silence, then kicked off the platform shoes and, barefoot, slowly made her way down the steps to the altar. She nodded to the drummers for a tempo, low and slow.

At the altar, she removed the high top of the basket and withdrew a copperhead snake. Its sleek, flat face, bronzed in the light of the Look-to-Heaven candles; forked tongue licked at its scaly lips. Beady black eyes darted around in the candlelight after the sudden release from the confining darkness of its woven prison.

Holding the creature aloft, she cried out, "Vodu has told me to tell you, 'Be not afraid.' We will see the end of the evil ones who beat us and starve us and sell our children away. All this Vodue has promised . . . "

She looked out among the faces and told them what she knew they wanted to hear, "All this Vodu has promised because Fairfield will continue the struggle begun by Mr. Shield."

Tenderly replacing Vodu in his basket, she covered it with the lid, then took a Look-to-Heaven candle in each hand and raised them like beacons for her disciples to follow — *how good that sounded in her ears, her disciples* — led them to the bloody trail separating Pharaoh's Circle, stepped over it and strode to the chair with its man-like burden. Reyna turned to face them as the forty or more filed in, shuffled about, quieted, nervous and expectant.

When they were all still, waiting for her word, Reyna said, "The answer to questions about why I care so much is *because I am one of you*." She paused. Someone coughed. Many stared at their bare feet. "Let me show you what they have done." For the first time as their voodoo queen, she snatched a piece of the shoulder of her black silk gown, tearing it off her arm, let it drop to her waist caught by the opal and silver belt. The congregation gasped, stared at the incredible beauty of her perfect figure, nubile breasts, milk-white flesh. Before their minds had stopped reeling, Reyna turned her back to them, shouted over her shoulder, "Now see what they have done!"

Now her subjects cringed at the sight. Tears flashed to the eyes of many. Across the light of the sacred Look-to-Heaven candles playing on her back, lay a mass of ugly adhesions, welts, criss-crossed like railroad tracks rutted in the lovely flesh. They were staring at the work of a dozen vicious beatings, souvenirs from the hands of her former owner, Mistress Suzanne.

Reyna fell to her knees as the confusion of her worshippers filled the air. On her knees, she lay her head in the lap of Mr. Shield's effigy, stretched out her hands to hold the cotton filled sleeves of his jacket across the chair's armrests. "Oh, my brothers and sisters!" she intoned. "See what my master . . . no, it was my mistress . . . who beat me so when I was but a child. Do you see now, my brothers and sisters, why I care so much? Now, please, for Vodu's sake, touch my honorable scars. Be not afraid of my body. Touch me and take the healing of the snake from him to me to you . . . and there to the *emi*, the spirit of Mr. Shield on his journey."

Entranced by what they'd seen, single file, one by one, her followers came to her, touched her wounded back, the old, knotted scars like hardened ropes under the milky flesh, and felt the power surging into their own fingertips. Reyna rose, then, formed them in a circle, holding hands, outside Pharaoh's markings. J. P. and John Henry returned with sweet *gala*. The drums commenced again, a dirge, a quick step, a two-four time, a danceable rhythm with *zells*.

Once more, Reyna entered the magic circle with the Look-to-Heaven candles and lit the pine boughs under the seated figure. Surrounding the burning pier, the worshippers, hands linked, closing their circle, an entranced ring watched as the *emi,* rose like a puff of smoke, a tiny cloud and vanished in the midnight sky.

Chapter 9

The elaborate rubber-tired carriage that Reyna hired for the trip to Boston resembled a mobile coffin. Black satin wreaths adorned the doors and black leather rosettes knotted black swags that swooped from corner to corner. Wagons, lone riders, and other carriages gave the vehicle a wide berth as if the death it carried were contagious. They would not have come even that close had they guessed the mind of the woman inside.

Hidden beneath a dark tent of funereal veils, Reyna sat motionless, mind and heart as cold as graveyard stone. A piercing look hazed her strange, cat-yellow eyes, the penetrating stare of a hawk seeking prey. The marshals' cruelty brought back her childhood when the white man knew not even a scintilla of human restraint. Master had lashed her mama's back to bloody ribbons. Mistress Suzanne, Master Hamber, and Mistress Maria had beat her body and used her like a dog in rut. Hour after hour in the darkened carriage moving toward Boston, Reyna tasted the bile of hatred brought to her mouth with the memory of white men's abuses. And, she vowed to Vodu to avenge Edward Shield's murder.

Mr. Shield's memorial service was held at the home of his friends, Captain James and Mrs. Phoebe Gardner, on Pemberton Square. Phoebe prepared the guest list and sent the announcements. When the first of the guests arrived, Phoebe went down to greet them.

The Gardner house on Pemberton Square intimidated Reyna. Like its owners, there was a cold formality about the cavernous rooms. It was as though their effort to maintain an air of social acceptability had sucked all the warmth from the place. While they were never less than gracious and civil, and outwardly sensitive to her grief, Reyna was not certain that the couple felt anything at all.

At this moment, she'd have given a great deal not to have come here, indeed to have returned to San Francisco. But there was no turning back. This first public appearance gave her the opportunity to take her place among a gathering of the most important abolitionists in Boston.

The big double parlor was banked with the tribute of flowers that had been arriving for two days. Gardenias, carnations, and prim arrangements of waxy calla lilies, in florist pots and floor-standing urns, leaked the sick, sweet smell of death throughout the house. Ironically, even funeral bouquets relieved the brooding melancholy of the dark-stained wainscoting, trademark of the designer, Rene de Puis.

Reyna did not intend to be seen as a pitiful survivor. Changing silk for watered silk in the shroud-like dress of mourning, clever stitching converted the square bodice to an empire line, brought attention to her figure and gave an incongruous sensuality to grief. She kept the necessary triple veils, but exchanged one of the black ones for gray, cinched at the back of her head with a ring of blue white pearls. A great deal depended upon this memorial service.

The guests, in knots of hushed conversation, became silent when she appeared at the head of the stairs. Reyna stood for a moment acknowledging the upturned eyes of Shield's friends before majestically sweeping down. Her years of conducting voodoo rituals had perfected her gift for theatricality, and she never lacked for imagination in exploiting that talent.

Phoebe waited at the landing, while Captain Gardner, chewing nervously on a strand of his mustache, bustled forward to hug her briefly and take her other arm.

Two portly men in dark, pinstriped jackets, stood just inside the door.

"May I present Mr. William Lloyd Garrison, the publisher and public lecturer." Gardner beckoned to one with a mass of shaggy, graying black hair and mutton chop sideburns. "And this is Mr. William Morris, an attorney and, from time to time a member of congress. Gentlemen, Miss Shield."

And both of them abolitionists, Reyna added under her breath.

Phoebe reached out to touch their fingers familiarly.

Reyna said, "Thank you for coming, Mr. Garrison, Mr. Morris. Gentlemen, it's good to see you." Now that she had need of them, her pleasure was greater than they realized.

"I'm happy to meet you, Miss Shield," the mutton chopped orator intoned mechanically. 'This is a sad day . . . a tragic day if I must say so myself. Edward was a true friend, the noblest of men . . . the truest . . . truer than an arrow . . ."

Knowing Garrison's tendency to overwhelm himself with his own rhetoric, Morris intruded to take Reyna's hand. Hawk-faced, with iron-gray eyes bordering upon rudeness in his study of people, he pumped her hand as heartily as he would a man's. "You have our deepest sympathy for your loss. In a way, it is all our loss. Edward was a fine man."

"Thank you for saying that."

The designer, Rene DuPuis, rushed up breathlessly to take her hands. The Gardners gathered closer in their circle.

"Ahem," Gardner cleared his throat. "Shall we greet some of the others? There's Mr. Phillips and Mr. Parker. Reyna, you must say hello to them."

"Yes, of course. Lead the way, Captain. I'm afraid there are so many of Edward's friends I never had the opportunity to meet." Over her shoulder to the designer, she added, "I hope you'll be in town a few days, Mr. DuPuis. I must talk to you seriously."

The heavy-set men, Wendell Phillips and Theodore Parker, stood in an area formed inside the bay window. They had similar, penetrating brown eyes; and, each of them gave Reyna the strong impression of absolute self-certainty with unchangeable opinions.

Phillips said, "We all share in your bereavement, Miss Shield. Your loss is ours."

"That's kind of you to say."

A half dozen Quakers knotted together against the wall in the second parlor. The men held broad-brimmed hats under their arms and pale-faced wives at their sides. Their muted conversation hummed like a hive of bees. They introduced themselves.

"I'm glad to know you all, happy to have you with me today," she said simply.

Of all the guests, one stuck out in her mind. There was nothing particularly interesting about him physically, nor did he say anything overtly curious; but, beneath the surface, something lay hidden, something like a hammer in a velvet glove.

Gardner introduced them hesitantly. "Reyna, this is Mr. Charles Pilar. Or, should I say Monsieur Pilar, Charles?"

Fixing his sky blue eyes on Reyna, he said, "Monsieur or Mister, it doesn't matter. We Canadians travel quite easily between two languages and two countries. Edward has told me about you and I'm sorry that our meeting has to be on a tragic occasion. Your guardian was a very great man."

"That is always a good thing to hear."

"I do not say that lightly, Miss Shield." At a nervous cough from Gardner, Pilar's eyes darted in that direction.

"I'm just beginning to learn that," Reyna responded. "In the last few days I seem to be getting an education. It's strange how you can come to truly appreciate someone only after it's too late."

"We shall all miss him a great deal."

"Thank you, Mr. Pilar, but just how did you know my guardian?"

"He was my employer and . . ." Gardner coughed again, more insistently. "He was my employer and my friend."

"What kind of work did you do for Edward?"

"I guess you could say I helped your guardian in his freight business." His voice slid over the word *freight* easily; yet, a slight nuance suggested merchandise more important than ordinary commerce. "As a Canadian and as a fur trader, I know the countryside, all the trails from the northern United States to Canada. Many of them are unmapped as yet."

"Really, Pilar!" Gardner put in gruffly. "This is hardly the time to talk about business!"

"No, Captain, please. I'm interested in anything that has to do with Mr. Shield."

"Well, I've told you all there is, Miss Shield. I simply helped him in the transport of goods under uncertain conditions of weather and roads."

Gardner took her arm and steered her away from the Canadian. "Come. Let us greet a few more of your guests."

"No, James. No more today. In the days to come I want to seek out each one of these good people to thank them individually. I want to ask them all to more private gatherings where we can share my guardian's memory. Now, I'm fatigued . . ."

"Of course, dear. Whatever you say."

"I'm a little weary, but I want to speak to Mr. Shield's friends as a group. We didn't want a boring sermon. Mr. Shield would have hated that, but I do want to say a few things to everyone here."

"Are you sure you feel strong enough? These people are his friends. I know they'd understand if . . . ."

"I'm certain, Captain. Please get their attention."

Clearing his throat, Gardner stood up tall to call out, "Ladies and gentlemen! Please give us your attention. Thank you for coming today. I know Edward would be pleased for the honor you do him. Before we part, Miss Shield would like to greet you personally."

The room quieted, expectantly awaiting tearful words from Shield's ward and heir.

Reyna slowly raised a delicate, long-fingered right hand and swept the veils away from her face. An involuntary shush of air escaped the guests. The face they expected to be grief-stricken was not that at all. Their eyes were met by hers, an imperious scrutiny. Her haunting golden eyes swept over them.

"Friends," she began, clear and cold. "I truly want to thank you for your presence here today. I know he would be as proud of your friendship today as he was the day he passed on."

The crowd shifted nervously, looked right and left.

"I simply wanted to let y'all know how much I appreciate that."

An audible sigh of relief escaped the crowd.

"And, I want to let you know, too, that my last hours with Mr. Shield were an inspiration to me. During those last hours, he told me of his work and of its importance."

Her glance about the room grew more piercing. "I want you to know that work *will* go on. I intend to continue it in his memory, to pursue it even more vigorously than he did."

A stunned silence greeted the strength behind her words, as if for fear of betraying a secret never publicly aired.

"That's all I have to say, friends. I intend to see his work continue. To that end, I will need your help and for that I will be speaking with each of you soon."

When she left the room and regally mounted the stairs, she was startled by a sudden, spontaneous outbreak of applause. A wave of excitement at the thought of the new adventure washed over her.

Chapter 10

Pacing around and around in an agitated circle, Reyna perspired from more than August heat. In spite of the warnings of the dying man, she had been clever but her cleverness put her at risk to be sent to prison or back to slavery.

At her direction, Charles Pilar foraged throughout the south to find, and sometimes recruit, escapees, and then guide them to the locked barns at Fairfield. From Fairfield they went to the house in Boston, then to King Hawk at his tribal village in Nequasset, Maine, where they were again met by trapper Pilar who led them to Canada. Once her scheme was in place, Reyna doubled the number of escapees they helped and tripled the amount of Shield money used in the effort. But, her boldness had depleted her fortune and her name had become known to the authorities.

This night, marshals stood on the road outside the entrance to her drive, questioning all who came and went to her house. Considering the volume of her trade and the almost public way she went about it, it was surprising the end to her operation hadn't come sooner. Her solicitor in Richmond, having suspected the nefarious work, had washed his hands of her, then smoldered with fury when she calmly transferred her financial affairs to a non-Virginian, Captain James Gardner, in Boston. Earlier this day, police officers had brazenly searched the mansion under the sneering scrutiny of a local slaveowner. At the moment, with the locked barn down by the worker's village full of human cargo, the marshals had posted a twenty-four hour watch on all her properties.

Now, the sultry summer air added to her despair and kept her mind from working. Like a combat general, Reyna had called for her lieutenants, Charles Pilar, Ned, and Rene DuPuis. She needed a strategy before they arrived. Yet, the harder she thought, the more blank her mind became. She was acutely conscious of her own footsteps and the drone and blip of a Junebug crashing insanely against the netting at the window.

A knock at the door announced Ned. The man's adoration had grown hopelessly out of proportion. Once revived, their affair had mellowed since that first night; but there was the work of the railroad to be done, and while she might hate herself for it, she could not desert her fellows still enslaved to seek her own happiness.

"Reyna, I came as soon as I could. It doesn't look good out there."

"I know," she mumbled, drawing away from his embrace. "They searched the house today and went back for a warrant to search the barns tomorrow. If they open the barns and the freight's still there, we're lost."

He said simply, "Y'all will go back to slavery and they'll kill the rest of us. Killin'd be the easy part. Maybe sell off the kids if they're lucky."

"Sell off free people? Even with papers?"

"Free niggers that stampede slaves ain't free no more."

"Don't say that," she said. "Don't even think it."

"Won't make it go away to play-act like it ain't so." Ned shook his head, clearing away the image. "I've been tellin' y'all, Reyna, and y'all still don't seem to understand. We've not talkin' law! Why, you'd be lucky to live long enough get to town, let alone to court!"

"I understand very well, Ned. They were pretty disgusting when they searched the house. Said things to me in front of a sheriff that they'd never dare say on the street."

His big aquamarine eyes turned as dark as the bottom of a well. A cord worked in his jaw as if he wanted to say something but couldn't. Drunken voices from the road rose and fell on the suffocating air as a reminder of their helplessness. Reyna put out a hand to calm him.

"I heard that," he said when he'd regained control of his voice. "They went through the farm worker's houses, too. Looked at everybody's free papers."

"How many are there? What are they doing down there?"

"Six or seven of 'em. Ain't doin' nothin' just now but standing around, getting drunk and mean. Making everybody show free papers. Took Hattie a quarter of an hour to get past them on her way to the Tolivers."

"That's a bad sign." Worry creased her forehead. "Give southern boys a holiday and they get into mischief. How'd Hattie take it?"

"Oh, Hattie's fine. She's been a southern nigger too long not to know how to treat Ol' Massah."

"Is there a chance they'll do more than insult us tonight?"

"There's always a chance, but I don't think so. I know some of these boys from town. As long as they've got a bottle and company and as long as they're being paid by the day, they're usually happy to wait."

"Ned, I do have a plan, but it's dangerous."

He smiled grimly, looked toward the road, and said, "I know all about danger."

"If you can get them away from here, Pilar can take over and get them on to Nequasset."

"Straight to Nequasset without stopping? No one's ever done that before. Why not to Boston like always?"

"I didn't mean to tell you, but we can't go to Boston because the house there is being watched, too. Besides, I've got four people to get out of there now. What's important right now is whether they can walk to the outskirts of town."

"Oh, Lord!" He banged a fist against a palm in exasperation. This new information, sealing off Boston as an escape route, compounded the dilemma. "Four more!"

Her calm voice masked her fear. "Don't you worry about that. I'll take care of it. As it is, they've got such a tight watch on the house at Louisburg Square, we have to smuggle in the extra food for the folks there. So Boston is out for this group. That's another reason we've got to act fast. As soon as we decide here, I'll go back to Boston and see what I can do."

"Damnation!" he grunted incredulously, getting used to the risky plan.

"Y'all just forget about that, Ned. I said I'll take care of it. Right now what you need to think about is how to get the freight out of the barns tonight. Rene is coming and I'm depending on him getting them to Bolivar on foot."

"I don't know whether anyone could do a thing like that. Have to do it in the day. Have to stay off the road. It's a long ways to walk and the whole county's watching. Don't expect a body could make more'n six or eight miles a day on foot. Come across one hunter in the woods and the whole thing'd come apart."

"But," she said, agonizing with him. "There isn't really any choice. We can't use wagons and can't use horses. They'd be noticed . . . Rene's coming. If you can get them out, we'll have to let him figure out how to get to Bolivar. Then, when things calm down in a few days you could take a couple of wagonloads of tobacco to Bolivar where Pilar can meet them for the trip to Nequasset. It'll work, Ned, I know it will. Right now, we've got to do something before the sheriff gets here with the warrant to unlock the barns. It's just a matter of time. The best we can hope is that you can sneak them out of the barns, one by one."

"Oh, Reyna, I don't know." He shook his head. "Six or eight miles a day is all they can make. Without papers. They'll never be able to travel during the day —"

"Ned! Don't you worry about that part!" Her voice snapped with impatience. "That's none of y'all's nevermind! Leave that up to Rene! Can you sneak them out of the barn? You'd have to do it quietly. The slightest noise and that bunch on the road would be on you like a pack of dogs."

"If I get 'em out of the barn, then what? We don't dare ask the workers to take them in."

She laughed dryly. "Why not? Marshals wouldn't know the difference. They all look alike."

"The marshals can count," he said, ignoring her bitter humor. "First thing they do is ask to see ever'body's papers again."

"The workers have got to help. There's no other place to hide them till Rene gets here. Oh, Ned." She edged closer, put a hand on his waist, and implored him with her big eyes. "You're the only one I can depend on. You know these people and they trust you. If each household would take just one.

When Rene comes, I'll send him down. He can get them to Bolivar by the cow paths across the fields if you can get them out of the barns with no noise. How many of them are there?"

"Last count, we had thirteen."

The unlucky number was more frightening than the plan she suggested. It was an omen that made her stomach queasy.

"I'll try, Reyna," he answered solemnly. "I'll do my best."

Ned did not say it lightly. He knew the consequences. He also knew he could never refuse her anything.

She threw her arms about his neck and kissed him. His lips mashed against hers; his tongue came forward. She felt the tremors begin in the muscle of his back, hips grind against her as his arousal grew.

"Not now," she rasped, breathlessly pulling back. Still, her index finger traced a little circle on his chest.

"Yeah," he grunted in reluctant agreement, trying to calm his desire for her.

"When we have more time, it'll be better," she promised. "You won't regret it. You'll see. Now, go. And be careful. I want you safe."

After he had left and silence wrapped about the house again, she resumed her circular pacing. Rene, the effeminate little designer, was the key. He must be persuaded to play his part. Pilar, too, had yet to learn his role.

Chapter 11

Tension crackled in the air as Ned crossed the lawn toward the road. The marshals and the workers' village lay ahead. He ambled along as though nothing was out of the ordinary. He could have gone around the livestock barns and through the fields and kept out of sight of the so-called marshals, but that might arouse their suspicions later. It was better this way, he decided, better to pretend his errand was innocent.

Ned knew these temporarily deputized "marshals" served at a judge's order in a quasi-legal capacity to solve petty or troublesome civil disorders. If the stakes, reckoned in human lives, were not so high, he might have considered the entire charade of slave escape and capture to be no more than a monstrous national sport.

This night Ned faced the worst of southern crackers. All black people knew this dirty business paid only a dollar a day and expenses. Legitimate tradesmen and farmers were too occupied to take time out to hound a scraggly bunch of runaways. Slaves patrols were mainly composed of small town, unemployed hooligans empowered to act out sadistic compensation for their own powerlessness.

The cluster of marshals bunched together at the road outside Fairfield Farm passed a jug of distilled corn between them. Fragments of their conversation reached Ned before he was close enough to see them.

"Whooee! It sure is hot!"

"Gimme 'at 'ere bottle, Jake. You've hogged it long enough."

"Sure as hell is quiet out here. Think it'll be much longer?"

"Hard to tell. That nigger-lover is smart, gotta hand that to her."

They all stopped talking and turned at the scrunch of the foreman's tread on the roadside.

"Who goes there?" one called out officiously. "Who goes?"

"Its only me. Ned."

The men surrounded him. They scrutinized his features and looked mean even though most of them recognized the free Black who managed Fairfield Farm. Corn liquor was strong on their breaths.

"What y'all doin' out, nigger?" Jake demanded.

Ned answered quietly, loathing himself for showing respect. "I ain't doing nothin', sir."

"What you doin' up at this hour?"

"Well, boss, I'm up this late a lot. On a place this big, there's a lot of work to do. Seems like it's never done . . ."

"Well, don't you go prowlin' 'round at night no more, nigger. You just better git back ta home."

"I'm not prowling, sir." To control his temper, Ned dug his fingernails into the palms of his balled-up fists. "I'm not doing anything like prowling. What I got to prowl for?"

"Don't you know this place is under surveillance?" The man jabbed an index finger into Ned's chest, accenting the word as three, *sur-veil-lance.*

"I do know that, sir, but there ain't nothing here. We ain't doing nothing against the law at Fairfield."

"Don't lie to me, boy. Everybody know that nigger-lovin' bitch you work for is stampedin' slaves."

"Pardon me, boss, but you got her wrong. Miss Shield is a lady. She don't have a bad bone in her body. She'd never do nothin' wrong."

"Well, nigger, Judge Autry thinks different. And, we'uns is here to prove it. We'll do it, too. Come tomorrow morning, all of y'all will be in jail. That includes y'all as well as y'alls nigger-lovin' mistress."

"But, you ain't said, boy. What you doin' out? If you ain't prowlin', where you goin'?"

Like Hattie, Ned had been a southern nigger too long not to know how to treat Ol' Massah. It disgusted him, but he knew how to use the stereotypes to stay alive. What he could get the white man to believe was more important than truth.

"Well, I'll tell you true, sir. I ain't up about official business at all. I got me a woman down 'cross the road. That's where I'm goin'. To visit my gal."

A guttural chuckle greeted the information. "So! The buck's got hisself a gal!"

"Yes, sir, I 'spect I do."

"If'n that's it, why didn't y'all tell it straight out in the first place?"

"Well, sir, that's a problem. Seems like Lindy, Lindy's the gal's name; well, it seems like Lindy's pappy don't take no shine to me. If he was to find out I'm sparkin' his girl, he put a stop to it."

"I don't know, boy." The leader jabbed at Ned's chest again. He shook his head. "I'm probably a fool to take a chance on you, but we'uns are gonna do it. Just this one time. Tell you what we'uns is a gonna do. We're gonna let y'all off to go see that gal of y'alls. Now, git. Git on down there."

"Oh, yassuh, boss. Thank you!"

Ned turned purposefully toward the workers' village. The stares of the marshals followed him down the road, prickled the back of his neck, but he dared not hurry.

A nervous wakefulness infested the houses of the farm workers. It was so still the foreman could hear his own breath whistle in his nostrils, but the serenity was a fraud. With the events of this day, not a soul slept inside the twenty-five houses. The workers lay rigid in their beds, speechless and silent, afraid that even their own thoughts would give them away.

Walking tall, a piece of shadow broken off one of the little buildings, Ned mounted the porch of the first resident he meant to see. He wisely chose to call on the oldest of them, one with the status of age, a priority among the black people. An ancient yellow dog lying in the yard raised its head at his familiar form, then flopped back down again, thumping its tail in the dirt.

Ned didn't need to knock. Old Mattie, an aged field hand with skin as thin and wrinkled as putty-colored parchment, opened the door before the foreman reached it. At his signal, Ned's finger across his lips, the old woman slid the door open wider and they went inside without speaking. The two of them huddled at the far side of the living room of the cabin, far from the open windows where their voices might carry.

"What is it? What is it, Marse Ned?" the old crone whispered. She'd never shed the language of slavery.

"We need help, Mattie. They're out there. The slavers. It's only a matter of time."

"What do that be to me? What it be to me how much they stan' aroun' in the middle of the road, drinkin' an' cursin'?"

"It's only a matter of time, old girl. Only a matter of time 'til they get a warrant to open the barn."

"Shoot! That still ain't none of my affair. I ain't got nothin' to do with it."

"Mattie! There's thirteen people in the barn at the edge of the village. We . . . they need help."

"Oh, Marse Ned! Don't I know it! But, I dassn't get involved." The old woman's thoughts sped to the bedroom where four grandbabies lay on a ragged pallet. "If something happened to me, what would happen to them? I can't get into this mess."

"I know it's hard, Mattie and I know you're worried about the kids. You and me, we don't matter. We can take our knocks with the best of them. But, the kids. That's different. They don't know, and God willing, they'll never have to learn. As for us, we don't have a choice. In a way, y'all could say it's for them. So there won't be no more of 'em born or living in slavery. They's nine of 'em, nine kids, up the road in the barn. What happens to them, Mattie? "

"Don't Marse Ned. Please don't." Ned could imagine her red-rimmed, yellowish eyes, the ache she felt inside. "I knows y'alls right. I knows it, but I'm too old. "

"You can't!" he said angrily. "You can't take a chance even when you know very well if Mr. Shield hadn't . . . if Mr. Shield hadn't took a chance, y'all'd still be a slave in Mississippi on old Marse John's place. You'd still be there, that is, if you wasn't dead of the way he treated you. Mr. Shield, God rest his soul, took a chance and now . . ."

He quit talking then, let the silence speak in the sweltering room.

"Besides," he said at last. "No matter what happens, we're all in it. If they find those people, who's going to believe that we weren't all in it?"

"Oh, Laws, Marse Ned, everything I know tells me it's a mistake, but y'all are right. I'll take just one."

He was tempted to whistle when he stepped off the porch on his way to persuade the rest of the baker's dozen he needed to house the slaves. Mattie's consent would go a long way with them.

Chapter 12

Those crouched in the locked barn at Fairfield were the most frightened of all. They knew what would happen if they were captured. Ironically, the two families hidden in the barn had not been particularly mistreated: they had simply wanted to be free. Now they feared being caught and taken back to greater misery.

Freedom had been no more than a vague idea to Adam when his friend, Luke, suggested the escape. Most of the freemen they saw around the plantation in South Carolina didn't seem any better off than slaves. In some cases, the living that freemen wrested from their scrawny farms was harsher than slavery. Luke continued wearing away at him with talk of a new dress for Lizzie, school and shoes for the kids, and, maybe, a horse for himself. Gradually the idea stuck. Freedom came to mean a horse of his very own.

The two families, Adam, Lizzie, and their three children along with Luke and Ruth and their brood of six, struck out one night after the evening horn. They'd have liked to say goodbye to the others; but, not daring to call attention to the escape, they settled for backward looks at the cabins of their sleeping friends. Walking in the dark was rough on the kids, yet the band made seven miles that night following the snaky bends of Fish Creek and the light of the north star. During the day, they hid under a thicket of branches and brambles carefully gathered as camouflage.

Master John and the dreaded hunting dogs never got close and that somehow made it worse. Once, they heard the baying of hounds far away and they congratulated themselves for being so cunning as to double back and forth across the creek in order to leave no scent. When the good feeling of freedom died down, the fugitives began to feel depressed and lonely, away from their friends and the only home they knew. In a peculiar way, they felt bad for Master John, too; felt bad about the faithlessness their act displayed and what the loss of property would mean to him. They would have felt better if they had endured the run-and-hide of pursuit, because then they could have felt they'd won a fair fight. As it was, they'd simply sneaked away.

The four adults took turns carrying the two youngest, Adam's daughter, Effie, and Luke's Rose Ann; but the feet of the others were a mass of blisters and cuts from briars and sharp stones as they stumbled on and on, guided by the north star. All of them were half starved and near dead with dysentery from eating raw, green corn, the only food there was to steal.

They had spent the morning in an abandoned corn crib on a deserted farm. Cautiously covering themselves with straw and old corn husks, they had not quite dropped off to watchful sleep when a noise, the unmistakable tread of a human foot, alerted them. The thirteen were instantly awake and holding their breaths.

The footstep sound was followed by a man's voice. "All right, folks. C'mon out. Nobody's going to hurt you."

No one moved so much as an inch.

"I said, 'nobody's going to hurt you.' Now, c'mon out. All of you. The kids, too."

Adam slowly opened his eyes to peer through the chaff that covered him. The hair rose on his arms. An intense itch set up in the nape of his neck. A short, wiry, white man with sandy-colored hair stood motionless in the entrance bay of the corn crib. A long barreled rifle pointed skyward from the crook of his elbow.

"You'd better c'mon out. I won't hurt you, but the 'trollahs,'" he pronounced the word *patrollers* in Black dialect. "The trollahs, now, they sure as hell mean to hurt you."

Adam stirred a little, hesitating.

"They're only about a half hour behind me down the road, so you'd better move. We don't have all day."

At that, Adam sat up sharply, emerging from the straw and chaff like a trout out of Fish Creek. "Ah ain't done nothin' mast'! Hones' and fo' true, I ain't done nothin'."

Ignoring the transparent protest, the short Canadian waved the rifle like an extra arm at the rest of the lumps under the husks. "I'm not here to harm you. I'm here to help. Get out from under there and let's get going."

"How you know we was here, mast'?" Adam asked as the other twelve rose from the hay. Bits of dried grass clung to their faces and hair.

"Well, first there was a sign posted in town. You people are fair game with a price on your head. Every slaver in the county wants a chance at the reward. Second, with as many of you as there are, you left a path as big as a plow. If the patrollers were better trackers, they'd have found you before me. I've got a wagon. You'll be crowded aplenty, but we've got no time to waste."

Pilar, walking full ahead, signaling caution with his hands, led the two families to a wooded knoll alongside the country road. Beneath a tree at the roadside, a long, wide-bodied wagon stood loaded high with baled cotton.

"If'n any of you need to take care of necessaries, do it now," Pilar bawled. "There won't be another chance before nightfall."

The trapper unhooked the tailgate and lowered it to open a hidden compartment beneath the floor of the wagon. A little more than five feet wide and fifteen inches deep, it ran the length of the conveyance. By slithering on their stomachs and twisting their legs around, the adults barely fit in the space. After the children squirmed in, the secret vault was literally crammed full of black flesh. Once the thirteen runaways were all loaded, he slammed the tailgate shut again and locked it in place.

"I know it ain't going to be comfortable-like," the trapper called out from the plank seat behind the team. "In fact, it will be mighty sore, but there's too many of you and we gotta get you all in one trip. One more thing. There must be absolutely no talking. We're sure to be searched and if there's a single sound, they'll likely kill us all. You for running and me for helping. One word from you and we're all dead."

The phrase, 'it will be mighty sore,' was a masterpiece of understatement. Lying on their backs, so close that the ceiling of the compartment touched their noses when the wagon stood still, was nothing compared to what happened when the Canadian slapped the horses with his whip. The wagon lurched forward, raking its human cargo across the rough-hewn floor. Scratchy, cotton fibers filtered down through the floor boards from the bales above and drove them mad with itching in the heated chamber. Dust, sprayed up from the road by the horses hooves and wagon wheels, drifted through the tiny breathing holes to fill their lungs and noses, and muddy their perspiring faces. They tried lying stiff and rigid, but that simply increased the scrapes on their skin when the wagon swerved. They tried relaxing, letting themselves go limp, swaying against the soft bodies of their neighbors, but that failed, too, when bone cracked against bone with the wagon's sudden jerks and jounces. They were miserable and helpless, unable to move or shift about, and too afraid even to groan with their discomfort. 'It will be mighty sore,' didn't begin to describe the agony of that journey.

As the 'conductor' promised, before long they heard the rapid clop of nearing horses. Inside the box of the wagon bed, they couldn't tell how many riders there were, but they felt the drumming of many hooves on the earth and the crazy jerk of the wagon slowing to a stop. Adam and Luke, Lizzie and Ruth reached out automatically in the stifling dark of the coffin-like container to touch the children to remind them of the command to silence. Eight riders on steaming, lathered mounts surrounded Pilar and the wagon.

A man Pilar guessed to be the leader, reined up in front of the wagon and impertinently grabbed the harness of the lead mare. A greasy black, down-turned mustache drooped below his chin.

"Hey, stranger," he demanded. "Y'all see a passel of niggers on the road?"

"Sir?" Pilar asked calmly.

"I said, did y'all see a bunch of niggers on the road?"

The other riders eased their horses closer, studying the wagon driver's face, watching the interrogator for a clue to action.

"*Mais, non*," the conductor answered. "I saw no Negroes come this way."

"Are y'all sure? We seen a crib where they was ahidin' a couple of miles back. This is the only way they could a come."

"But, I tell you, monsieur, there was nothing on the road."

"Y'all sure talk pretty, mister. Ain't nobody 'round these parts talk like that. Where y'all from? You a Yankee?"

"I am from Canada."

"Oh, that's it. A Canuck. That's right near bad as a Yankee. Y'all 're gettin' all our niggers and they ain't a thing we can do about it. Canada must be a pretty poor place! Livin' with niggers! But, say, mister, what y'all doin' down here any how?" The man's eyes, drifting to the bales on the wagon, were followed by those of his equally scruffy companions. "What you got there?"

"Cotton. As you can see, it's cotton. I'm a trader. Buy cotton here, sell it to the mills in New England."

Suspicion darkened the leader's eyes. "Bales that big could hide a lot of things."

"But, it is cotton, monsieur. I give you my word."

At his lead, the eight slave hunters circled the wagon, searched the bales, occasionally put out a fist to pound one of them. Inside the false bottom, the huddled runaways lay still, praying their thudding heartbeats would not betray them.

Pilar fought the temptation to turn to watch the inspection.

A pitchfork used to load and unload the bales hung from iron toggles on the wagon bed. The inquisitor bent low in the saddle, snatched the implement, then rode up to face Pilar.

"If'n it's only cotton you got, I am sure y'all won't mind my using this."

"Monsieur, I am a legal trader," the Canadian answered, feeling with his heels for the rifle on the floor beneath his feet. "You have no right — "

"Rights! Don't y'all tell us about no rights when you'uns come down here rilin' up our Nigras, stampedin' our slaves." He thrust the pitchfork like a jousting lance, punctuating the words, "Don't y'all come down here tellin' us about no rights."

Wheeling away, the man slowly moved around the wagon, plunging the sharp fork into each of the bales, repeating with each thrust, "Goddamn! Damn Yankees and furriners! *What about our rights?*"

In the hiding place beneath the bales, the slaves winced with each lunge of the tool. At last, satisfied there were no runaways concealed in the cotton, the patroller slung the pitchfork back into its brackets and sailed forward to confront the foreigner.

"We can't prove anything this time, mister, but there's something about you that I just plain don't like. Take a look around you. You got eight good men who knows your face. Now, you git! Git outa here and don't come back! It'll be a sorry day if any of the eight of us ever catch you around here again. C'mon boys, we got work to do! Gotta catch us some niggers and lookin' at this white trash is makin' me sick to my stomach!"

When they had gone, a cloud of dust and whoops of bravado, back down the road toward the deserted corn crib, Pilar climbed from the plank seat and walked with wobbling legs around the wagon to inspect the cotton for damage.

"All clear. They're gone now," he mumbled at the side of the wagon. "All clear."

On and on, farther and farther north and more than a week, the load of cotton traveled. They stopped in the evenings at hospitable barns and wooded areas, places marked by a faded rag knotted about a fence post or a scarecrow whose broken, tree-branch arm drunkenly pointed out the direction of shelter. In the cover of night, the Blacks, doubled over from cramped muscles and weeping abrasions from the splintery lumber of the compartment, crawled out to fresh air and to wolf down whatever their anonymous hosts had left in the wayside hideouts. Before the first light of every day, they packed themselves back into the suffocating sepulcher until, at last, they reached the locked barn at Fairfield.

The tobacco barn at Fairfield, not unlike others of its type, was simply a loose-boarded shed with an open, center aisle between two rows of wide shelves to hold drying leaves. A thin stack of tobacco leaves was layered against the walls so that it was all that could be seen through the cracks. Other than that single stack, there was no tobacco there. There never had been. The 'drying' shelves had always been used as rough, off-the-floor bunks for fugitive slaves. After the misery of the wagon, the dark, closed-up barn was a palace.

No one in the village of workers ever knew exactly who occupied the building at any one time. It was safer not to know. Adam and his family and Luke and his were slipped in after dark. Unknown hands had spread out a sumptuous welcoming meal of cornbread and fried chicken and clabbered milk on the shelves. Used, but clean and presentable clothing lay on another. When they were fed and toileted and settled, the door was sealed again. The free workers prudently remained in their own houses so as to be unaware of the activity. But all those within as well as those without the locked structure knew the risk they took.

A conductor on the railroad usually led a group of runaways only the distance of one station. At each station, another conductor guided them to the next where they were housed until it was safe to travel on. Most often, neither passengers nor crew of the railroad knew the details of the line's inner workings. Reyna Shield had defied that convention when she organized the trunk line with a terminal in Richmond and stations at Charles Town, Bolivar, Philadelphia, Boston, and Nequasset on the route to Canada.

The two families Charles Pilar brought to Fairfield moved into the barn without knowing where they were. They ate the food and put on the fresh clothes, heeding their guide's directive to keep still while they rested a few days before continuing the journey. Lying in family groups on the bunks, they breathed easier for the first time in days.

Adam with Lizzie's head on his shoulder, his muscled arm about her body, cuddled little Effie on the other side. Steady breathing on the bunk above noted the sleep of his nine-year-old son and eight-year-old daughter. Lizzie sighed and closed her eyes, giving herself up to wonder at what they had seen and done. The big man lay still, wide awake with his own thoughts. He knew neither where they were nor how far they had to go. It seemed he'd given up all control over his destiny the minute they ran away. That thought struck him as stranger still. In seeking freedom, he had sacrificed his independence. How odd it was to derive a sense of self-determination from the familiarity of things, even slavery. Yet, here he was totally dependent on the good faith of others. An involuntary sigh escaped him as he pondered the mystery of that.

"Daddy?" his little girl whimpered in the dark. "Daddy?"

"Sshh, chile. Sshh."

"But, Daddy, ah wants to know sumpin'."

"What is it, chile?"

"Is we free yet, Daddy? Do we be free?"

"Not yet, baby. Not yet. Maybe tomorrow. Now, y'all go back to sleep and don't think about it. Maybe tomorrow."

The two families lived in the barn three days awaiting the chance to continue their journey. On the third day, the trouble started. Loud shouts carried through the slats in the walls. They heard women crying in the distance and the violent slamming of cabin doors. Huddled in a quaking throng in the center aisle where they could not be seen, they heard angry voices, white men's voices, demanding entrance to the locked shed. The words were indistinct, but a low voiced murmur assured them that someone with authority was refusing to open the door. Hours later, that same murmur, a cultivated, black man's voice, close to the exterior wall, warned through the cracks, "They've gone on down the road apiece. But, be quiet. They'll be back."

Trembling at the news, the thirteen refugees climbed back onto the bunks to lie still and tense and afraid.

Chapter 13

The marshals' shouts on the roadside grew louder as they filled in the idle time with coarse humor and foul language between deep draughts from a passed around jug of home brew. Their bravado and boisterous laughter reached as far as the nervous households where Ned stealthily went about canvassing residents to shelter the thirteen refugees. It carried as far as the mansion where Reyna continued to pace the floor and it seeped terror into the barn containing the runaways. Everyone recognized the men for what they were, a pack of cowardly brutes.

The rowdies hushed at the hoofbeats of a horse on the road. They parted and fell back in awe at the sight of a sleek, blooded gelding. Its rider wore a tan, Prince Albert suit and carried an elegant, ebony walking stick. Astonishment turned to chagrin when the torches disclosed a black man.

Rene DuPuis, boiling with urgency, slowed his mount to a halt.

"Where you goin', nigger?" the man called Jake demanded, grabbing the bridle. "What y'all want here at this time of night?"

"I have immediate business with Miz' Shield. She sent for me."

"What's your name, boy? Who the hell are you? Mighty fancy, y'all dressed up like a white man."

Not even the citified Black dared give himself the title of 'mister.' "My name is Rene DuPuis, sir. I manage some property for Miz' Shield in Richmond."

"Y'all better just turn around and go back to town. You got no sense, boy? Niggers can learn to call at respectable hours like ever'body else." Addressing the querulous faces of his comrades, Jake finished triumphantly. "Damned niggers! You gotta learn 'em everything."

Rene said simply, "But, Miz' Shield has sent for me, sirs. She said the matter was important. Told me to come right away."

"Miz' Shield didn't say no such thing, boy," an acne-scarred white man put in. "You a liar, boy. Ain't no white woman call for a darky in the middle of the night. Less'n you smile real purty, how she even gonna know you there in the dark?"

The whole gang of them stepped back, doubled over, and slapped their knees in drunken laughter. It seemed they'd never heard anything so funny and they repeated it over and over to each other.

Rene DuPuis waited patiently for the inane amusement to cease. "I don't understand, gen'lemens." The designer rolled easily into Virginia dialect. If he could make himself sound like one of them — well, not exactly one of them, but one of *theirs* — perhaps they'd let him go. "I . . . I don't understand just what's happenin' gen'lemens. Back home in Richmond, they ain't no — "

"What's happenin', boy," Jake broke in, "is that your Miz' Shield is 'spicioned of stealin' slaves."

"That can't be true. I swear it, master. I know for a fact that can't be true. Since Ol' Marse Shield passed, she just trying to keep this place goin', but she'd never break the law. She ain't from here, so she does things funny sometimes, but that's only 'cause she just don't know our ways." The accent, the submissive tone of the black man, washed over them, comfortably deferential. "Now, please gen'lemens. Please let me go to see Miz' Shield. Mebbee I can clear all this up. I'm sure it's some kind of mistake. Miz' Shield is a good woman. She never ever cause no trouble."

Jake staggered forward, elbowing the acned one aside, and leered up at the man on horseback. "All right, nigger. We gon' let you pass this one time."

Rene's relief didn't make its way to his face. "We gon' let you by, but not for what you think. We'uns goin' let you by so you can give your little, nigger-lovin' missy a warnin'. Tell her that her and her kind ain't wanted in Charles Town."

The others grunted 'yeah' like a response to a church litany.

"Tell her she ain't wanted in Virginia."

"In fact, you can tell her she ain't wanted in the whole southern United States."

"Now, you get gone, boy. Go on up to that 'ere house. We got a fancy suit of tar and feathers for all of y'all. An *un - lim - it - ed* supply of tar for everybody what wants it. Now, git, boy."

"Thankee, mast'. Thankee," the Richmond man mumbled between his teeth as he nudged the gelding forward. As he turned in at the driveway, the noise of the marshals returning to the jug and loud boasts of what they'd do to nigger lovers rang in his ears.

Reyna stopped pacing and called out, "Come in, Mr. DuPuis," to the rap of the walking stick on her office door. She had heard the lull in the raucous carousing on the roadside and guessed the men had intercepted the designer. She prayed they wouldn't hurt the little man and when the shouting resumed, she speculated he'd been allowed to pass. His stylish clothing and effete mannerisms disturbed her not so much for the deviation they revealed as because they cast doubt about his strength to do what must be done. Rene DuPuis, in the velvet-collared Prince Albert, appeared as soft as a woman in the doorway.

"Rene," she said simply, drawing herself up to full height. "I'm glad you could get here."

"I came as quick as I could, Reyna."

"I suppose you know there's trouble."

"I do now," he remarked acidly. "I just met it on the road."

"They've searched the place, this house, and the workers' houses, too. Now, they've gone to get a warrant to unlock the barn."

He pursed his thick, pouting lips. "What can we do?"

"We've got to get the freight out of here." She studied him carefully, searching for a sign of steel behind his languid manner. Then, in a gesture strange for her, she crossed over to take his arm, as though he needed reassurance. "We've got to get the passengers away. For now those men have only suspicions. Tomorrow they will have evidence. We cannot allow them to get that evidence."

His slender cane behind his back, Rene stood, legs apart, examining a design in the carpet, a black Napoleon lost in thought. "What can we do?" he asked again, calmly appraising his employer. Though he had no taste for women, Rene had an uncanny ability to understand them. Since the death of his friend, this one, Reyna, whom he had once considered no more than a lovely girl, had captivated him with her boldness. Apparently, she was as fearless as she was beautiful. "How can I help?"

"Ned is down at the workers' settlement," she said. "He's trying to get some of the workers to hide them. He'll sneak them out of the barn, one by one, until the barn is empty. Then the patrollers can search to their heart's content. They'll find nothing. There'll be no evidence."

"But, it seems your problem is solved." The yellowish eyes, bulging beneath the prominent brow, remained passive. "What do you want of me?"

"When the marshals find the barn vacant, they will surely search the cabins again asking for free papers. We need to get the passengers out of here before they come. We can't take the chance of stopping in Charles Town. We need to take them straight to Bolivar where Charles Pilar can lead them on."

"I see. You want me to conduct them to Bolivar."

Reyna tightened the grip on his arm. "You'll need to start before daybreak and you'll have to travel during the daytime with the whole countryside watching for them."

"I know this country like the back of my hand."

"You know what will happen if you're caught, Rene. It will go hard on the passengers; but, for you, it'll be worse."

"Pardon me, madam," he said, yanking his arm away. Taking a small, jeweled box from an inner pocket, he paused to pat a pinch of snuff into one flat nostril and sniff, then repeat the gesture in the other. The tobacco made his eyes water. "You'll excuse me, Reyna; but, I know these things better than you ever will. After all, I'm a Virginia nigger. There's also my private life which you suspect, but which I will not discuss."

Her face registered surprise, then pity for his twice-plagued condition.

"No! Don't look at me that way! It's true, I belong to two hated populations. My point to you is that for both of them, I pay with personal danger every single day of my life."

When he left to find Ned in the village, Rene DuPuis took the back way, the circuitous route through the west field away from the guards on the road, aware that the debauchery of the guards grew more violent with liquor in their guts and time on their hands.

Chapter 14

The white lightning burned the throats and gullets of Jake and the pockmarked white man. Their companions staggered about in an alcoholic haze, but evil sharpened the emotions of those two. The first swallow of liquor led to gamecock-strutting and loud talk. Next, weakened powers were shored up with lies of sexual conquest. Finally, when most men became happy or sleepy or sentimental, Jake and Weasel grew morose with self-pity. It was then, unable to shake the feeling that they had been wronged, they became driven to uncontrollable violence.

A big, heavy-set man with oily hair straggling over his ears, Jake threw a beefy arm about the bony shoulders of scar face. Of the two, Jake, the more obnoxious, was the more dependable: his meanness was consistent. His companion, Weasel, was justly named. A thin, night-prowling creature, he was known for quick, phlegmatic shifts in temperament. One minute quietly brooding, the next he lashed out, striking with the bite of a sharp-toothed rodent at whomever was closest. Whereas Jake held out a tiny bit of fidelity toward his low-life comrades; Weasel had no loyalties.

"Let's us mount up and ride down by the darky cabins just to let 'em know we's still here, " Weasel said.

"Weasel, you got a real mind. I gotta hand it to y'all for that," Jake grunted. "Mebbe give that fancy, free nigger somethin' else to think about, too, whilst he's pumpin' on that gal a' his."

Enthusiastic about making serious mischief, the reveling patrollers grabbed torches to light the way and half-ran to the ring of tethered horses.

Charles Pilar, the third of Reyna's lieutenants, left the road 300 yards before the posted guards. Dismounting, he led his horse across the gully and through the fields to arrive unseen at the back door of the mansion. It didn't take his trapper's intuition to tell him there was trouble on the road. Without knocking, he stole silently into her office. Only that lack of his usual courtesy revealed the tension knotted in his gut.

"Miss Shield, there is much trouble — "

"I know that. That's why I sent for you. The men outside are deputized and they're getting a warrant to search the barn. We've got to get those people out of there."

Accustomed to long, patient hours observing every nuance of the forest and its wild game, Pilar was well aware of her beauty, but he was even more attracted to her iron self-possession.

"Forgive me, Reyna, but there's more to it than that."

"Such as?" she snapped, irritated to have her authority questioned.

"You must get away from here."

"Me?"

"Even if you succeed in emptying the station, they'll never believe you. Have you met those men?"

"Of course not! Why should I?" She flashed back to the piggish, slovenly police who had searched the house.

"Because they are the type of men who will stop at nothing. They are crude and coarse. Stupid, yes, but they have a kind of cunning it's best not to underestimate. And they are drunk. Such men, even at the best of times, have no respect for the law. When they find the station empty, they will want to smash something . . . anything . . . perhaps, even you."

Her eyebrows arched. "They wouldn't dare harm a woman."

"Ordinarily, no," he admitted. "But they will be angry for their loss. And anyone, especially a woman, who sides with Negroes is an enemy. Such a woman is lower than a Negro in their eyes."

Revealing no fear, Reyna nonetheless saw the logic. "Ned is down there now. Rene will get them to Bolivar. As soon as Ned reports back, I'll return to Boston."

"You don't have time. Beside, they'll never let you pass on the road."

Down on the roadside, the shouted obscenities of the men on horseback drifted up to them, stirring tension and fear and a painful awareness of the futility of their situation.

"You know the back country, Charles. Can you take me?"

"It is too risky for a woman. You would be spotted."

"We'll set that to rights at once." Before his startled eyes, Reyna snatched the neckline of her dress, ripped it down the front, then stepped free of her petticoats.

"Reyna!" the Canadian exclaimed "Are you mad?"

The pile of torn, brown satin on the floor was abruptly joined by a cloud of corseted petticoats and she stood bared to pantalets and camisole. She greeted the man's stunned embarrassment with a crooked smile.

Although accusing her of the defect, a kind of madness took Pilar in the presence of his scantily clad partner. He had known women solely in the extremes of formality or fornication. The former he met clothed and unapproachable. The latter he took in mildewed back rooms or on animal-skin pallets in the woods. Now, he was alone with a wealthy and beautiful young woman whose breasts pushed hard against a thin layer of undergarment. The shadows of her breasts, the triangle of her pubic hair, showed dark against the filmy cloth. He dared not look there and, still, he couldn't look away.

"Good Lord, man, have you never seen a woman?" she asked imperiously.

"It's not that," he stammered.

"Bring me the water pitcher," she commanded. "And the basin."

When she grabbed a pair of scissors from the desk, Pilar thought the unbalanced woman intended to commit suicide and he could do nothing to prevent it.

By the time he reached her with the basin, Reyna had loosened her hair and cut a long strand of it from her head. Dropping the hair unceremoniously into the basin, she reached back to shear away another and, then, another. Horrified, Pilar watched powerlessly. When the basin lay full of her hair she stepped back.

"If it's a man you want to travel with, you've got one. Mr. Shield's trousers will fit me. I can wear one of my own riding jackets. Don't you see, Charles? If anyone spots us, they'll see two men out riding. There! Hand me Edward's riding crop."

Minutes later, two figures crept out the back door of the mansion to slip through the shadows to the stables. Below them, in the settlement of workers, the marshals were raising hell.

Chapter 15

Rene DuPuis and Ned lay flat on their bellies under the stoop of the Tolivar shack. There had not been time to transfer the refugees from the barn; indeed, Ned had just persuaded the last of the free workers to provide shelter when he found DuPuis searching for him in the dark of the communal lane between the houses. They had barely a moment to confer about the plan to rescue the families before the commotion broke out. At the first loud cries of the marauding patrollers on horseback, the two men wisely dove for cover under the little porch.

Jake and Weasel in the lead, the horsemen raced around and around the group of houses, shouting threats and curses at the residents. Ned heard his name called out, connected in vile language with the fictitious Lindy. One of the men took up a popular tavern song comparing Africans to apes.

Throughout the furious raid, the clutch of occupants in the shacks cowered in terror. The Shield cook lay rigid on her pallet in the home where Rene and Ned crouched under the stoop. Tears gushed from her eyes as the ugly shouting went on and on. Old Mattie folded her grandchildren in her aged arms. Hands clapped over the youngest one's ears, she moaned again and again, "Pay'm no mine, chile. They go 'way soon, God willin' it."

The intended victims in the barn huddled together in the middle of the cavern between the shelves. Luke offered up a simple prayer to which the others whispered 'amen,' too afraid to speak out loud even to God.

The marshals had circled the workers' village a dozen times, shouted and sang till their voices scratched, when Jake held up an arm to halt in front of the locked barn. Sweat streamed from the lathered horses in the hot night air and Weasel wiped his face on his sleeve. Under the porch, Ned strained to hear the words.

"Boys," Jake bawled out. "Let's us call it quits."

"Whatever y'all say, Jake," murmured among them.

"After all, they's no more drinkin' liquor left."

Someone sniggered, hiccuped, then went silent.

"And they's no more for us to do here. We can come back tomorrow with the sheriff and the warrant."

"Just a minute, Jake," Weasel spoke, clear headed again after riding in the air. "Let's not be in such a hurry. If we leave now, y'all know damned well they gonna get away with it. Tomorrow they ain't gonna be no evidence no how."

"Aw, Weasel. I just don't see no use to hangin' around here half the night. Let's go on home. Come back tomorrow with the sheriff."

"Ain't gonna be no evidence tomorrow. Ain't gonna be none tonight." The wicked ferret smile lit up his pock-marked face. "What say we help Miss Shield get rid of the evidence tonight!"

A confused mumble from the others greeted him and man looked to man for an answer.

"Ain't no use no how, boys. Let's help all we can." With that, Weasel threw his torch directly to the roof of the barn where it lay smoldering, then flared up again.

Blue tongues of flame ate their way along runnels of tar to ignite the seams and joists and outline the building in murderous light. The tar, once heated, ran down the roof, dripped molten fire onto the dry, wooden sides and exploded the thin layer of tobacco leaves. As the idea became clear, the marshals rode closer, one by one, to add their lighted torches to his on the roof. In a matter of seconds the barn was a blazing inferno searing the grass a yard around its perimeter, singeing the hair of horses and riders, and scorching the clothes of the hidden ones under the nearby porch.

When the last torch had been flung, the heat intolerable, the marshals took off at a gallop to watch the fiery tomb from a safe distance and continue the vigil of Miss Shield. They didn't hear the short-lived cries from within the barn.

Reyna and Charles Pilar had reached the second field of Fairfield crops before the sky flamed crimson from the burning barn. The two lone riders in the dark reared their horses to a jolting halt to look back. They knew what they saw. Her great eyes drenched with tears at the horror, Reyna gaped at the Canadian. She leaned dizzily in the saddle and vomited. "Oh, my God, Charles!"

In that instant of horrendous tragedy, too, a single thought cut her to the quick. She'd left her altar in Boston on their last trip there. If she'd had it here, perhaps — just perhaps — she could have enlisted Vodu's intercession. The power of the serpent could have prevented this.

"Oh, my God!" she cried aloud. "What have I done? How could I be so stupid?" The agonized sob on her lips was nothing alongside the white hot fire surging through her guts.

No less tight-lipped and ashen-faced than she, the Canadian dumbly nodded.

"We must help!" Her shriek bubbled with despair. "It's my fault. Those people are innocent. We must make the marshals see reason!"

"No, Reyna, no! It's too late for that. There is nothing you can do here," he roared, slashing the rump of her mount with his stout-handled quirt. "There is much you can do as long as you remain free. But, there's nothing at all that a prisoner can do."

When he laid the riding crop across the flank of her golden mare, the animal leaped and sped forward, away from the inferno of Fairfield and the burning tobacco barn.

The two black shadows raced against the dark horizon until the lunging beasts could gallop no more. Sweat pouring down the Canadian's brow was whipped away in the wind. In the distance, a pale strip of dawn lit the sky.

Seeing her contorted face, when they'd come to a brush-filled gully alongside the trail, Pilar had grunted, "Let's stop here. We're still too close to risk traveling by day. Better hide out now and go on tonight. We can stash the horses in the woods."

Ironically, he had chosen a hiding place in the underbrush not unlike the ones used by the slaves they'd just tried to save. Reyna and the trapper sprawled out, side by side, to close their eyes till nightfall.

She woke first, late in the afternoon, groggy from intermittent snatches of sleep. Her cheeks felt numb and she was mildly conscious of hunger pangs. Without moving her body, she rolled her head sideways to observe the sleeping Canadian in the light freckling through the concealing twigs. His chest rose and fell, light and easy, with untroubled dreams.

Shoulder to shoulder, arm against arm, her face was not six inches from his. Splashes of sunlight bounced with the leaves overhead and flecked his sandy hair with gold. At such close range, his features were surprisingly delicate. A collar of flesh inside his shirt at the base of his neck was pale peach and his ears like small, pink-lined shells. In the middle of her examination, he stirred and opened the eyes from which he got his Indian name, Ochoaka, sky-blue.

"Good morning . . . or, rather, good afternoon, Miss Shield," he whispered. "How long have you been awake?"

"Not long," she murmured.

"Did you get any rest at all?"

"A little."

"Well, lie quietly," he yawned. "Perhaps you can go back to sleep. We can't leave for a couple of hours yet."

"I want to thank you, Charles." Her hand, on the ground next to his, crept over to grasp his wrist, then moved down into his palm.

"It's nothing," he muttered. "Don't think about that. We're not clear of trouble yet."

"But, I want you to know, no matter what happens, I'm grateful. Thank you."

He pressed her soft hand reassuringly. "*Au contraire*," the man demurred. "It is we who are grateful to you. For a man and a Canadian citizen, it is different. There is not so much to lose. But, for you, a woman, an American woman, you have much more at stake. Thank you."

Pilar squeezed the fingers still in his. "Thank you for your kindness, Miss Shield."

Touched by the compliment, Reyna rolled over and leaned to peck at his cheek, but abruptly changed her mind and placed her lips firmly on his. Startled at first, Pilar pulled back, then lay quietly to receive the kiss that began as gratitude, then changed. Close together there, her full soft lips were on his mouth.

She pulled away and let her head fall back to the ground. Neither spoke. Tension crackled in the silence between them. Several minutes passed before either of them moved, and then her hand again found his.

She didn't pause to consider whether it was curiosity or craving or simply a way to pass the time in the underbrush on a sultry Virginia afternoon. She guessed, too, that her spontaneous desire might be an involuntary response to the proximity of death. Once more, she reflected upon her own adage: *Men were after all only grown up boys.* And, if anyone made advances, Reyna knew who it had to be.

Her hand moved like a land crab, out of his and across the front of his coarse brown denim trousers. Her long, thin fingers seemed so clumsy, all thumbs, fumbling with the stubborn, leather buttons down the front of the denim.

Pilar made no more than one little gasp, a quick intake of breath sucking what was left of his lean belly up behind his ribs. He didn't even move his head. His eyes looked down the length of himself like a patient watching a surgeon.

There were so many buttons! An infernal nuisance! Reyna had undressed with Ned in the dark and in the light, but had not before considered how many buttons men must contend with. Her own breath caught as she loosened the cotton drawers and reached in to extricate the thick erection.

The short, thick length of the man stood free then, thrusting upward from a surprisingly copper colored mat of hair. It angled outward, free from his body.

He was no match for Ned in size. Perhaps it was so with all white men. The swollen head of his penis appeared an angry, brick red. As she watched, a pearl of clear liquid bubbled to the opening. She touched it with her thumb, smeared it across the strained cord at the base of the head, a gesture she had learned to please Ned. The Canadian squirmed, groaned and thrashed his head from side to side.

More by instinct than thought, Reyna yanked free the buttons of her own trousers, then rose to crouch and slip them below her knees, and moved to straddle him, lowering herself onto the short but very hard penis. The legs of her trousers, tight across Pilar's, manacled her ankles. He grunted as if in pain, then gave in to the sensation.

A touch of madness overcame her then; she had to satisfy her desire.

Twigs and branches scratched at her head and back; his penis thrust deeper and deeper into her, moving more quickly each time.

Maurice in San Francisco, Ned, and now, Pilar, had been simple conquests. Despite the crescendo groans of the man racing toward his climax, she remembered other times. There, in that secret copse in a fallow, Virginia field, the memory of Maurice's lusty cries rang out in her mind. *"Oh, Sweet Jesus! Sweet Jesus, I'm spending!"* It was all so easy.

It happened in the same way for this one, too. Pilar suddenly arched his back and went rigid. Inarticulate cries gurgled in his throat. He thrust hard, harder, harder still, his face flushed, strained muscles stood out from the hollow of his throat. He groaned loudly, climaxing with a scream, then a gasp of release. When Reyna was certain he was done, she dropped forward, moved down, flattened on his chest and held him until his breath returned.

Later, when they got up, straightened their clothing to mount up and leave, that special look of devotion had come into his eyes. Cynically, she thought, *The trapper, trapped in his Puritan ways, could justify his behavior only by falling in love.*

Chapter 16

The leaves of the Japanese maples behind the wrought iron fence in Louisburg Square had turned dark red and were just beginning to drop into skittering piles on the ground. At the entrance to the cul-de-sac, three tall, black-coated men paced back and forth keeping watch on the house. They could not search private homes in free States; but temporary constables could stand guard to inhibit the unlawful passage of wanted property. Their presence at Louisburg mortified the neighborhood and shattered the Shield household.

"You've no one to blame but yourself, Reyna," Captain Gardner snapped. "I've warned you and warned you, but you were never one to take advice. "

Although it was midday, the drawing room was as dark as night. The heavy velvet draperies had not been open for a week and the candles streaked the walls with shadows. The jumping candlelight made Gardner's blustery admonition seem all the gloomier while Phoebe slumped back as pale and unspeaking as a ghost against the horsehair upholstery.

Reyna sat upright in a side chair, determined and unrepentant. "I know what it means, James," she said. "But it's my money and I can do with it as I like. "

"Your money or not, you've no right to jeopardize the rest of us this way."

It was then that Reyna first saw Gardner as he would always be. *I pity James and Phoebe*, she said to herself. Her eyes widened at the insight. *I pity the stinginess of their souls. What if they knew of my childhood slavery? What if they knew that I own three laundries, three parlor houses, and maintain two private residences? What if they knew me as a Queen of Voodoo? I pity this overfed mouse of huff-puffery, but I know, too, that I need his cooperation because he is also an influential Boston Brahmin.*

Despite the danger, or maybe because of it, a shiver washed down her back. A rush of overheated blood, a prickling on the surface of her skin, had overcome her during the hideous torching and frenzied escape from the farm. There had not been time to speculate about the source of the excitement, but Reyna could not deny the pleasure of hunt and chase. It was as familiar as the snug wig covering her cropped head.

At last, she said flatly, "James, I want you to sell the farm."

"This is not a good time. I've told you that."

"Good time or not, I want to do it. For God's sake, James, it's not even safe for me to go there. Sell the farm and with the proceeds I want you to buy places in Canada for the workers."

"Reyna! Haven't you done enough? You'll ruin yourself and the rest of us with you. Do you have any idea what that will cost?"

"A great deal, I suspect. But still, it's what I want to do. Mr. Shield would have wanted it that way."

"Edward?" The man stopped in his tracks to wag an accusing index finger. "Edward Shield would not want any such thing! The man was certainly high principled, but he was not a fool. Remember, thirteen people have died. Burned to death in that barn. No one would want that. Now, you want to sell the place and give the money away."

Reyna clamped her jaws tightly together to keep from responding. Gardner could never know what the tragedy at Fairfield Farm had been like and his self-righteous admonition was all the more offensive because he couldn't know.

At that moment, her attorney-friend seemed very tedious and tiresome, his wagging finger an intolerable impertinence. A streak of irritation flashed through her. In the two years since Edward's death and her control of underground activities, it had become increasingly difficult to be patient with persons she suspected of cowardice or lack of imagination.

"I'm sorry that you don't agree, James," she said bluntly. "Believe me, I know you think you act in my best interest, but ultimately each of us must do what *feels* right. In this case, the decision is mine to make. Get whatever you can, but sell it. Pay off the workers with land in Canada."

In extreme annoyance, the captain chewed violently on the end of his mustache until he seemed about to bite off the right side. When his face calmed, he announced blandly, "It will cost you more than thirty thousand dollars."

"Is that so much?" she asked, a voice as controlled as his. "For the freedom and happiness of loyal and true friends?"

Gardner sighed. "It shall be as you say, Reyna. But . . . " he paused to shake the finger again. "Don't ever say I didn't advise against it."

"Good! Then, it's done." Reyna stood abruptly to meet him eye to eye. "I'm a grown woman. I can bear the consequences."

She turned away from him and went to his wife who sat glumly staring into her lap. A wisp of straw-colored hair fell over her temple and Phoebe refused to meet Reyna's eyes. Any sort of boldness seemed to terrify her.

"Don't worry, it'll all come out all right in the end," Phoebe said as she accepted Reyna's consoling hugs while Gardner began to make ready to leave.

"Oh, and Captain," Reyna added at the door. "When the farm is sold, have Ned come here. I can use him. There is much to be done and he's too valuable to me to lose. Tell him I can use him if he's interested in continuing to work under the same conditions as before."

She was glad when stern-faced James and faint-hearted Phoebe had gone,. The time alone without being forced to justify her decisions afforded an opportunity to think. Something had to be done to get the passengers now concealed in the house past the mercenaries on the street.

In the drawing room, Reyna edged the draperies apart to spy on the guards as if to assure herself the danger was not imagined. She poured a glass of sherry and reached for the butler's pull to summon Marvin, the houseman and chauffeur. By the time the servant's coal-black face appeared in the doorway, Reyna had regained command of herself again.

Reyna found the man extraordinarily appealing, an attraction that confused her somewhat for she'd not found herself drawn to men of such color before. But, this man was different. He had qualities she imagined in an African prince. So tall he ducked under doorframes and as lean as a greyhound, Marvin had great black eyes that were perfect circles in their sockets and an ivory smile that gleamed behind his ebony lips. His kinky hair divided almost naturally into corn rows. Most enchanting to Reyna was the man's deep baritone, a sound as calm as ocean waves.

"Marvin, Mr. Charles Pilar is in the guest suite. Please tell him I'd like to see him."

"Yes, ma'am."

"And, when you've done that, go to the residences of Mistress Stork and Mistress Justice. Ask them to come to tea tomorrow. Tell them it's important."

"Are you sure, ma'am?" He cast his eyes in the direction of the guards outside. "Are you sure it's safe for them to come here?"

"Of course, I'm certain! What a strange thing to ask! The Society of Friends has been dealing with Crackers for years. Go now, Marvin. Tell Mr. Pilar, then go to the Quakers. Be sure to tell them it's urgent."

It amused her to arrange herself artfully on the sofa while she waited for the Canadian to come downstairs. She lay one arm along the mahogany arm rest, then decided sitting primly to the side best displayed the sensuous line of her leg. Her rust-colored dress wasn't the most fetching against the dark upholstery, but it would have to do.

"Charles," she greeted him, widening her eyes, deliberately softening her expression. Some devilish inner spirit possessed her then. Strangely, even with danger all about them, she found it exciting to toy with him, her falcon to his field mouse. "I hope you've rested well."

"Quite well, Reyna." His glance took in her pose on the sofa. "At least, as well as one can with those men outside."

"Don't let them bother you," she muttered. "Leave them to me. I have a plan for them."

"Reyna!" he urged with an intimate look that was at once tender and lustful. She was astonished at how easy it had been to make him fall in love with her. "Again, you seem not to understand. Or, you still seem to ignore your danger. Please be careful. I don't want you to take unnecessary chances."

They had arrived at the Louisburg house at dusk, dead weary, wanting only a bath and supper in their rooms. Eighteen hours later, Pilar answered Reyna's summons. He appeared to be awkward, as though afraid that here in Boston, their relationship would be only a business one.

"Charles," she said slowly, tempting him to look at her; she was posed suggestively on the sofa. "Will you do me a favor?"

"Of course."

"Well, then . . ." She settled back. "Please go to Nequasset. Wait for me there with King Hawk."

Pilar had not expected the request. Crestfallen, he asked quickly, "What about them outside?"

"Don't worry. I told you, I have a plan. Besides, your fears are foolish. This is Massachusetts. If they become a problem, I can call the police."

"And — *them?*" He looked toward the hidden entrance to the secret passageway below the stairs. "Can you call the police about *them?*"

"Charles!" she raised her voice, exasperated. "Stop fretting! You're behaving like an old mother hen. Edward taught me well when he told me, 'The less you know, the better off you are.' All you need to know is that there is a plan. Now, please go to Nequasset. Stop at King Hawk's and wait for the passengers. They will need a conductor across the border."

"But . . ." His sky-blue eyes were misty and confused. He could not understand how she could have used his body, given him such pleasures, but she had not loved him. *What kind of woman was she?* His eyes asked the questions he could not utter.

There was no easy answer for Reyna so she said simply, "Arrangements have been made. And that's that."

"Reyna." He leaned forward, his desire to approach her obvious.

"No," she said firmly, in the same tone she earlier used with Gardner. "There's nothing for you to do here. We'll need you in Nequasset. Wait there. I'll join you when I can."

Chapter 17

The Quaker ladies Reyna had met at Edward's memorial gathering arrived at Louisburg Square in a carriage as closed and black as their garments. The good women looked neither right nor left when they mounted the stairs to the Shield house. Well aware of the temporary constables at the corner, but armed with the obstinate passivity common to the sect, they glided along serenely as though unaware of the scrutiny of the deputies.

Tension within and without the house had heightened in twenty-four hours. Apparently, to relieve the boredom of the watch on the inactive residence, the men on the square had grown bolder and began to march past in military style glowering toward the windows. A hundred times, Reyna had crept close to the veiled windows to steal furtive peeks down the street and came away shuddering. Once, in an outpouring of impotent rage and despair, she shook her fist at the draperied casement and then cried bitterly over her defenselessness. Her knees shook with relief at the appearance of the Quakers.

"Good Mistress Stork. Good Mistress Justice," she said warmly, controlling the emotions ready to burst from her throat. "How very nice to see you after such long a absence. And, so good to have your daughters with us. Come. Let us go into the drawing room for our tea."

Her personal maid, Carmen, had laid out a pretty feast of sugar cakes on gleaming silver for the ladies. Linen, starched stiff with edges paper crisp, lined the places. Only the candles, guttering against the dim light of the dark curtained room, augured anything more auspicious than five well-to-do-women enjoying each other's company on an autumn afternoon.

Following pleasantries about the weather and the delights of tea and cakes, Mistress Justice dove into the topic. "Thou art in trouble, Goodwoman Shield."

"Nay, no more than any of us," Reyna replied, gripping hard to her teacup to stay the trembling. "It seems to me, we're all in trouble. The entire nation's in trouble."

The Quakers stopped toying with their cups and saucers, poised like children caught in a game of *Freeze*. Their severe black gowns, draped about the chairs, accented their solemnity. Reyna guessed at the thoughts behind the long-brimmed bonnets shadowing their faces.

Charity Stork broke the silence with a rapid nod to her daughter's bonnet. "You're probably correct in that after all. Feneuil Hall's no more than a debating society these days. And the subject of the debate's always the same, 'What to do about the south's peculiar institution.'"

"As if that were truly a question, Mistress," Reyna offered, forcing round-eyed innocence to her face. "None of us truly believe there is a question in that, now do we?"

"No. Never a question when God's will is being put aside," came the muttered chorus from within the black bonnets. "Never a question at all."

They grew silent and returned to meditative sips of tea. Constance Justice, redirected the conversation. "How can we be of service to thee, good woman? We are ready to help. Thou needst only to tell us how."

The simple, plainspoken overture humbled Reyna. She had planned to persuade them. The offer, coming so direct and unadorned, brought her to the edge of tears.

"Thank you," she mumbled. "I do need help and I thank you for being good friends. As you know, there are constables guarding the square."

Four bonnets dipped and four bonnets turned fearfully toward the draped window.

"I have been forced to sell the farm in Virginia. They burned a station and killed thirteen passengers there."

The bonnets jerked back, involuntary gasps escaped them.

"Now they are here because they suspect this house."

The dark heads bowed down, gazing at their knees.

"Unfortunately, it's true. I have four passengers hidden in the station and although those men outside cannot come in, they can make it impossible for the people to leave."

The women leaned forward and Reyna found herself whispering, "Can you stay the night? I can get word to thy husbands?"

"Yes," they breathed as one.

"If thee can stay the night here, it will give us time to be well away before the constables know."

"But, who will take thee away, Goodwoman Shield?" Charity asked. The others also looked up for an answer. "Who will lead thee?"

Taking heart from their willingness, Reyna leaped to her feet and snatched the bonnet and false hair from her short-cropped head.

"I will," she cried out, eyes flaming with defiance at the guards outside. "I can drive and I can ride. I arrived here dressed as a man and I can leave the same way. I will be the conductor on the line this trip."

Dramatically emphasizing the speech with a burst of courage, she raised a clenched fist. "Come, ladies. Quickly! If we're to outfox those villains, we must make all haste!"

"Marvin!" she shouted as she led the women up the stairs. "Marvin! Get our guests, the passengers! Take them to Mr. Shield's room. We must make ready! The train is about to depart! Carmen, come with us! There's work to do."

In her bedroom, the Quaker women looked about, apparently nervous and confused. Reyna herself wondered whether her bravado frightened the meek women as she rummaged through the contents of her armoire. The shuffle of men's feet in the hall announced Marvin leading the fugitives. Suddenly Reyna whirled around, only then appearing to remember her guests.

"I'm sorry, good friends. I forget myself. Please remove thy clothing."

"What?"

"Oh! I'm sorry. I forget myself again. I didn't tell you, good ladies, that I escaped from Virginia dressed as a horseman. Our fellows, the passengers in the next room, will leave here dressed as a group of Quaker ladies if you will lend them your garments. When you've disrobed, Carmen will take the clothing to Marvin for them. Choose whatever you want from my wardrobe. I promise I will see your gowns returned to thee in good order. In the meantime, your husbands can bring thee fresh things when they call for thee tomorrow. By that time, the 'ladies' and I will be safely far away."

Kevin O'Toole and John Conaghan, two of the three watchmen at the entrance to the square, pounded their fists together not so much to dispel the chill as to create the illusion of activity at a very dull job. Patrick Conaghan, John's younger brother, the third man of their afternoon shift, had gone to the public inn to relieve his bladder and fetch hot coffee. Kevin and John hardly looked up when the band of Quaker women, covered head to toe in the funereal garb of their community, guided by their youthful driver, returned to the carriage and drove away.

Chapter 18

Reyna could not relax until they reached the city limits and turned off toward the coastal route to Maine. If four runaway slaves dressed as Quaker women in a carriage driven by a lady in man's clothing were captured, the best they could hope for was swift justice in the courts. But outside the city, the law was of little interest to slave hunters: not even free men were safe. It felt good, somehow, to have her altar under her seat against the forward bulkhead of the coach.

In addition to the danger of capture, the road to Maine was hazardous. Rutted and pot-holed, it sometimes dropped away from firm ground to track along the rocky shoreline, jolting the horses and the carriage through the lapping waves of the Atlantic. At night, the uncertain roadway forced Reyna to dismount and lead the way with a lantern in one hand and the team's bridle in the other.

The entire four day trip was without respite. She didn't dare call attention to herself or her passengers by racing the horses or by stopping at an inn for food or rest. She paused only long enough to change horses, always in the hazy, half-light of dusk, and remained high up on the driver's box grunting monosyllabic commands to wayside stable hands. More than once, she feared discovery, but she maintained a cool exterior despite the dread knotted in her chest. After a look or two, and a kick at the carriage wheel spokes to test the axles, the stable men went on about their business. They growled more about the late disturbance of their routine than suspicions about the untalkative driver.

Days spent high atop the driver's seat with a clear view of the road beyond the horses were more frightening than the exhausting nights. The route to Nequasset Village in Maine at the mouth of the Kennebec river was jammed with travelers, most of them wild-eyed boys and men, rootless adventurers with empty purses. In the company of those hapless poor were genuine villains, smugglers and blackguards of every stripe including bounty hunting slavers well aware of the easy access to Canada across the border.

As the carriage rumbled by with its fleeing burden, there was no way of knowing which of the strangers they passed was dangerous. A man seeking work to provide for his family had the same beaten, droop-shouldered slouch as a cutpurse searching out a victim. Hungry eyes watched the passing carriage and sent a shudder up Reyna's spine.

To complete her disguise, she looped a thumb inside the waist of her trousers and pulled the corners of her mouth down in a scowl as she had seen men do whenever she overtook them. At the sight of riders approaching in the distance, she looked off to the side of the carriage and, although no amount of twisting her tongue around produced enough saliva, she imitated spitting. She tched the brim of her hat in passing and croaked "howdy" from the back of her throat. Once, she braved chewing the end of a small black cigar, but the sty weed brought such a nauseating taste it was all she could do to avoid miting. Miraculously, throughout the long journey, no one paused to ask rections or to exchange conversation with them.

At the bend in the river just past Brunswick, three men suddenly burst out from behind the brush alongside the road. Scruffy and unkempt, wearing filthy farmers' overalls, the costume of the middle south, they were not the typical hunters, trappers, fishers, and lumber men of Maine. They wore identical tall crowned, wide brimmed, soft felt hats, and they carried new long-barreled Winchester rifles. Crackers. She knew instantly what they wanted. Bounty hunters, looking to capture runaway slaves. The woods of Maine were as full of them as ticks, low life renegades who made a living from other people's misery.

The largest of the fellows, George, weighing in at 250 soft-bellied pounds, came racing toward the carriage, then abruptly stopped, spat a great mouthful of tobacco juice, and shouted up at Reyna, "Get down outta there, boy. This here's an inspection station, and we're a posse on the lookout for smugglers and runaway property."

Reyna froze, trying to decide whether to confront the men or to acquiesce; but her immediate problem, more than being discovered to be a woman, lay in finding a way to get her passengers to safety. Pitching her voice deep in her throat, she said, "We're not smuggling, sir. My mistresses are on their way to visit relatives in Nequassett."

"Are you really as dumb as you sound, boy? I didn't ask if you wanted to come down. I told you to git down."

Reyna straightened on the high buckboard plank, felt with her heel for the reassuring side of the altar.

"Now you can do it easy . . ." He fondled the butt of his Winchester. "Or you can do it hard. Suit yourself."

She decided she had no choice. She'd play her hand out, see where it led. As she made her way down from the high seat, George said to his fellow thieves, "You men check that storage box on the back."

When she'd alighted, Reyna walked around the coach where his fellows were stripping the large coffer at the rear where the baggage and tools for the brougham were stored. She caught her breath as she — and they — noted that there was no baggage. An awl for repairing bridles, extra wheel spokes, mallets for tightening the axles loosened by the rocky carriageways, the usual lot of replacement parts for a coach that size soon lay strewn about the roadside. The disappointment at finding no smuggled goods showed in their faces. God help them if they discovered her altar. Reyna grew even more tense as their frustration was certain to give birth to anger. Her heart sank when she considered the encounter that loomed nearer when they searched the carriage and its passengers, four black men dressed as Quaker women.

The big man poked her in the ribs with his blunt forefinger. "Who you got in the carriage, boy?"

"Four ladies from St. Charles," she croaked in the huskiest voice she could muster.

"Well, haul 'em out here, boy. Let's have a look." His companions stopped throwing tools out of the locker to pay attention then, eager to see the passengers. They'd never heard of runaway slaves riding *inside* a coach, but anything was possible in these days of abolitionists and nigger lovers running around all over the place.

"I'm afraid, I can't do that, sir," she croaked.

"You can't . . ."

"No, sir, I can't." An idea had begun to blossom in her mind. "You see the ladies are too weak to walk."

"Why would that be?" the bounty hunter asked, skeptically. The fresh greed behind his doubt spread over his face.

"Have you heard of St. Charles?"

"No."

"Oh," she said. "That's why you don't know what happened."

Reyna could see the slaver's patience running thin with her stalling. "What's St. Charles? And what does it have to do with anything?"

She took a deep breath, pretended to swallow some personal sadness, before she continued. Her slowness of speech was only partly to give her time to think ahead; she also could not control the deep voice when hurrying the words. "St. Charles is just outside Boston. The Ursuline Convent is there . . .and there's a community of the Society of Friends. Quakers."

George's henchmen leaned closer to the low voice because they, too, had not heard much news and were intrigued by Quakers, a strange group of people that everyone knew taught Indians and pickaninnies to read.

"I'm sorry to take so long, sir, but what I've got to tell is too important to leave out details." She cocked her head to one side, at last asked, "Have you heard of Black Tongue?"

"No, of course not," he bellowed. "Get to the point boy an' if you're funnin' me you'll hear from the business end of this here rifle."

"Well, sir," she said, beckoning them to come closer, as though sharing a confidence. "Black Tongue is a common name for a rare kind of influenza like the one that killed half the city in '28. The disease begins like a tired and weak feeling, like when you're working too hard and not getting enough sleep." She paused a moment to observe, rubbed her own eyes as though scratchy from lack of sleep. The trio of villains nodded, acknowledging the feeling. "The next thing that begins to happen is that your mouth feels dry like you're always thirsty." Again, the nods. George even ran his tongue around the inside of his cheeks, creating saliva for moisture. "A coupla days of that and your tongue begins to swell up and your eyes start to bulge out."

The leader of the bandits interrupted angrily. "What's all this malarkey got to do with us? You've got exactly three minutes to finish up, before we haul those gals out of there and see for ourselves."

Reyna chose to play stubborn then, crossed her arms over her chest. "It's fine with me, sir. I'm just a driver; but these four ladies are the last ones alive out of 125 people in the community. All the others died of black tongue. Oh, it's a terrible way to go, sir." The big man began to sneak anxious glances at the coach. "When you die, your tongue has so swole up, it forces your mouth open and it sticks straight out all full of some kind of black blood and mucous. Your eyes bulge out till they look like they're about to pop."

Like a sail out of wind, the bounty hunters visibly shrank as they contemplated the death that could wait for them in the carriage.

"Worst of all," she added. "The disease is airborne, it spreads by breathing the air that *they,*" she nodded in the direction of the carriage's compartment, "breathe out. You can do as you like, sir, but don't ask me to help you. I would rather stand here and let you shoot me with that there rifle than open that door. At least a bullet's clean. Just don't ask me to open those doors and windows and take a chance. And, God knows, I'd rather die than get into that carriage." A dry chuckle shook her then, as though she enjoyed her own graveside humor. "Rather die, I would, sir."

The three men couldn't resist staring at the dark windows of the coach doors. The leader slowly shook his head, clearly unable to decide whether or not to risk exposure. Reyna held her breath.

At last he commanded brusquely, "Get that death wagon outta here, boy! Have you no sense at all in bringing the plague down on all our heads? Get gone and heaven help you if I hear that the disease spreads account of you."

Reyna forced herself to carefully replace the tools in the box, then cautiously walked the length of the brougham and climbed up over the wheel to the buckboard. She looked down solemnly at the trio of would-be thugs, gave them a thumbs-up sign in parting, and cracked the whip over the team to get them moving.

In the last mile of the trip, a spasm of trembling shook her when it seemed they would arrive safely. She had accomplished what was thought only men could do. She was proud of her feat. It chased away the self-doubt from the shambles left behind in Virginia and in Boston and grateful tears rushed to her eyes. True, she could not go back as stationmaster in the underground railroad. In fact, she couldn't go back at all — she was just beginning to realize that. However, she could go on, and a new plan had begun to hatch. There was something she had to do.

Nequasset, an Abnaki word meaning "at the pond," was a town of more than half-breed — a mix of Indian and white; it was many breeds. Europeans, Americans, Canadians, and the surviving few of a dozen Indian nations gathered by the sea at the mouth of the Kennebec River in Maine.

Half-naked children, big-eyed and shivering in the autumn chill, came to the doorless openings of the huts and houses to stare at the carriage as it drew near the settlement. King Hawk's cabin, the last building, opened onto the waterfront. By the time the horses reached it, dark shapes of adults could be seen behind the children, as curious as the youngsters yet feigning nonchalance. When the team halted, the old man himself appeared outside, blinking his good left eye in the light.

The mere sight of her old servant eased Reyna's weariness. "King," she called down. "It's so good to see you."

Confused by a familiar voice coming from a stranger, the Indian squinted in puzzlement. Pilar stepped out of the cabin and stood grinning behind him. She nodded to the trapper, acknowledging that he'd arrived safely to wait for her here.

"It's me!" Reyna cried out again, jumping down to the ground. "Is that any way to greet a friend?"

Recognition slowly crossed Hawk's face. "Miss Reyna," he cried, scooping her up in the strong arms that once had hurled harpoons. "It's good to see you, Young Miss."

Pilar glanced about fearfully, nervous that the joyous greeting might arouse undue interest among the neighbors. Then he set to caring for horses so starved and tired they looked about to drop in the traces.

"Come. Come into my lodge, Miss Reyna."

"Yes, I'd like that. I'm very tired. But first let me assure my passengers." Reyna went to the side of the coach to tell those within they must wait patiently until nightfall to disembark lest they excite suspicions among the villagers.

It took a few minutes to adjust to the dark interior of the lodge before she could find a place to sit. Other than a scattering of poles and nets, fishing implements necessary to living, the only ornamentation was an old harpoon from Nantucket, a bitter souvenir of young manhood. Despite the starkness of the Indian's cabin, the dim light dispelled the gloom from her mind. The smell of cold ashes in the fire pit blended with the odor of oily fish; but a warmth and abiding calm filled the humble place. No one could find her *here*. In a few hours, the freight in the waiting conveyance would be spirited away. Her mission was ended.

A silence descended upon the odd trio as they settled in Hawk's lodge. Reyna felt a sadness to the marrow of her bones. This was their last time together and she didn't know how to say goodbye.

They sat for several minutes, the three of them crosslegged on the ground around the fire pit, before Reyna spoke. "You know I must give up my work now, friends." She strained to see their faces in the dark.

"Yes, I hear." Hawk nodded toward the trapper sitting as still and unmoving as stone. "Mr. Pilar has told me of the trouble."

"There is nothing I can do," she said bitterly. There was no hope that she could ever return to Boston or Virginia. "In fact anything I do now is worse than doing nothing." A pause, then her voice pleaded, "It is so bad, I must sell my properties."

A slight tic pulsed at the corner of Pilar's eye. Reyna was surprised by what she read in his clear blue eyes. Her retirement from the underground seemed to affect him no less than Hawk. Apparently, he had no better idea than the Indian of what he would do without the railroad. Without her enterprise, they were both unemployed, nowhere to turn.

"I can't go on as stationmaster," Reyna continued. "I've become too well known. Now, they will never leave me alone. They'll watch my every move. This, then," she waved at the open door toward the carriage. ". . . is the end of the line."

There was nothing they could say to that. It was true.

Then the inspiration struck. "Charles," she said. "You will be able to take this group north?"

"Of course, Reyna," Pilar nodded slowly. "*Mais oui.*"

"Take them in the carriage. Not the wagon. When you've the opportunity, return the carriage to Marvin at the house in Boston. Don't worry, I won't need it for awhile. I have other plans."

"Oh?"

She drew herself up. "Before I quit I want to be a conductor. Like the trip from Boston. I want to lead others to freedom."

"Reyna! You don't know what you're saying!" Pilar pounded a fist into his palm.

"Miss Reyna!" The Indian was no less startled.

"Listen! I am here, am I not? You, yourself, did not recognize me, King. I can ride. I can drive. I'm not some kind of pretty flower to sit back and do needlepoint all of my days. I can do what any one . . . any man . . . can do."

The trapper's face reddened. "Reyna! You don't know what you're saying. Do you know what they'd do if they caught you? Do you have any idea? Do you think they'd spare you because you're a woman?"

"I expect no sympathy. Nor do I have any . . . for them."

"This is different. This is not a carriage ride from Boston."

"I have friends. I know the trunk lines of the railroad. Don't argue with me, Charles. The distances are short from station to station. I know the people in between."

"Yes," he spat back. "You know the people. You know too many people. That's precisely what's to your present difficulty. It's time for you to retire. If you persist, you will harm yourself . . . and you will harm the rest of us as well."

A gloomy quiet settled about them. She knew Pilar simply meant to dissuade her from risking further danger. He couldn't bear the thought of her coming to harm.

She patted his knee. "Look, we've known each other a long time. I took to this work freely, of my own free will. I know you don't agree with me. You never have. Not from the beginning. But, tell me, honestly, have I ever let you or anyone else down?"

"No," he muttered.

"Well, then, what's the matter? I mean, other than your rigid standards for women?"

The Canadian sighed deeply and straightened his back, glanced down at the hand warming his knee. "Reyna, you do everything to such an extreme. After Mr. Shield's death, you took over with a vengeance. It wasn't just our trying to help some poor unfortunates anymore. All at once, you were single handedly fighting a war with the whole south."

"Is that so bad?" She pulled her hand back. "Is it so bad to be the way I am? Let me assure you, mister, I cannot be other than what I am. You know me. I can't do anything half-heartedly."

The two of them sat as stiff and uncompromising as enemies, eyes focused straight ahead.

At last, Hawk broke in, "Listen to him, Miss Reyna. Listen to him. This man, he cares for you."

"Then, wish me well in this new thing that I must do."

It was Pilar's turn to extend a comforting hand. "Reyna. Reyna, dear, please hear what we're saying. We will help in any way we can, but the life you propose is not a life for either man or woman. It is not just unsuitable for women. Only a homeless, prehistoric species who've outlived their time — like fur trappers — are fit to be conductors."

"That may be true." From some place within herself, a source whose origin not even she understood, a bold new strength filled her. She raised her head, her eyes cold and unblinking.

"If you are my friends, let me find these things out for myself and in my own way," she said.

Pilar was first to offer, "All right, Reyna. I've seen that look on your face before. If there is no convincing you, have it your own way. But, please let us know what you have in mind." He thought: *If she went on with the underground, it was possible he would see her from time to time.*

Reyna slid down to the floor to sit facing them. The whites of her eyes, shadowed in the dim interior, narrowed to those of a wary cat. The dominating quality she had not learned to control returned. Strength flowed from that force voodoos called *the power*. It charged the dim space.

"I hope you're not planning a trip to Georgia," he remarked.

"Georgia! Why on earth would you think Georgia?"

"Well," Pilar palmed his ponytail. "Pardon me, Reyna, but I've noticed you always get a special look on your face when the talk gets around to Georgia."

"This time, you're wrong. Maybe some other time. This time, I want to go to Tennessee."

"Why Tennessee?"

"I want to go to the slave pens in Memphis. It's one of the major slave markets south of Cincinnati. They furnish the entire south with their disgusting 'business.'"

She swept away their gasps with an icy laugh. "I have an old score to settle with a man who operates those pens. I mean to settle that account before I quit."

"Please, Reyna. Couldn't you satisfy this insane urge by helping lost runaways find stations? We've never done anything else. Sure, we've convinced a few timid plantation people to leave, but to go to a market. Couldn't you help with something easier?"

"No."

"We have a lot of people who need help between here and Philadelphia."

"No. I said, 'no,' Charles."

Hawk's face clearly reflected his concern that his beautiful friend would attempt such a dangerous scheme. Finally, he spoke. "Take me with you, young Miss. Please. Please let me come along to Memphis."

"You?"

"Yes, me. Ochoaka is needed here to help our new passengers across. And, there will be others from other stations. He is needed here. He can stay in my lodge. My people accept Ochoaka as a brother and he is needed, while I . . . I . . . " The old man's voice clogged with emotion. "For me, there is nothing. I could be useful to you on the journey and afterwards. Please take me along."

Reyna turned the idea and its possibilities over in her head.

"Of course!" she cried out. Rushing over to hug his scarred face to her breast, she exclaimed, "It's perfect! Come with me, King, and after we deliver the passengers from Memphis to Cincinnati, we'll go back to Drummond Island to see Grandma and our friends."

Chapter 19

A team of broad-chested, gray workhorses hauled the peddlers' cart over the mountain pass as if the land were flat and the load weightless. Blankets of string netting kept flies off the backs of the beasts. Straw hats, holes pierced for their ears, protected their eyes. The horses' thick hooves sent a continual shower of dust and dirt back over the wagon and its merchandise as well as the peddler and his deaf-mute apprentice.

Roaming from town to town, peddlers crammed everything they owned from bedrolls to cooking stones in the wagon with their wares — bolts of linsey-woolsey, cheap calico, undyed cotton and denim, knives, horseshoes, and fireplace brackets. Strung together by their handles, pots and pans hung from the sides of the wagon and kept up a clanking protest at every turn of the wheels. Layers of mud covered both the merchandise and its purveyors, their perpetual cloud of dust transformed to plaster by rainstorms along the way.

The sight of a peddler drew children to the roadside and country matrons to the front gate for they brought all the medicine and hardware families needed but, most important, they brought the news. Farmers deserted their fields and hurried to stop and jaw a bit with a man who had been someplace else. A genial, gossipy lot, peddlers paid for dinner at the farmers' tables with carefully stretched out yarns from town.

The two behind the big, gray team, however, were not at all like the rest of their kind.

After weeks on the road, the owners of this particular mobile general store were as grimy as their muddied wares. The senior partner, a swarthy, gypsy-looking fellow, wore a black felt hat slouched over a dirty, red handkerchief tied around his forehead. Greasy black hair hung to his shoulders. An old scar, possibly earned in a roadhouse brawl, ridged his cheek and one eye stared blind and white from its socket. His young companion, apparently deaf and lacking the ability to talk, while less obviously disfigured, looked just as mean and shifty. The apprentice wore a billed cap pulled down over his face, kept his jaws tight-clenched, and answered questions with hideous grunts while motioning to his speechless mouth with a twisted forefinger. The disappointed farmers who encountered those two at the wagon gave no more than a minute to their shoddy goods before shuffling back to work. None looked close enough to spot the strange, multi-hooked arrow, a harpoon, on the floor of the wagon.

Involuntary sighs escaped the peddlers as their wagon eased down the western slope of the Cumberland Gap and into the rolling valleys of the blue grass country of middle Tennessee. They breathed easier leaving the regions where slave hunters hunted them; but ahead, at the far end of the State, lay an exploit daring enough to stop a heart.

They had passed an outcropping just beyond a fork in the road when Reyna glanced over at the Indian in time to see him brush a tear from his sighted eye.

"What's happened, Hawk?" she asked. "Is something wrong?"

His face darkened; he wiped his nose on his sleeve. "This is a terrible place, Young Miss."

"Tell me, Hawk. What do you mean?"

It was then that her long-time companion told her of Tennessee; the destruction of the land, the game, and finally the people ending in the trail of tears. Native Americans had resided here as partner in a whole that was earth and sun and water. Then, the white man had come and broken the land into parcels but when the pie was cut, there was no slice for Hawk and his kind in the new scheme of things. Early trappers harvested all the game of the forest and moved on. Fox and mink and muskrat were nearly gone. Once plentiful, beaver had been decimated to provide tall hats for gentlemen in cities an ocean away. Hunched over on the rough, wooden seat, forearms planted on his knees, the Indian grieved for the loss of his brothers.

When they passed the deserted remains of Fort Loudoun, Hawk recounted how his countrymen had fought to hold their own. The Cherokees, having captured the commandant of Fort Loudoun, took special care with him. Scalping him alive, they made him dance a final ceremonial before amputating his arms and legs. Captain Paul Desmere died with his mouth full of dirt and his ears full of their chants, "You want land. We give you land."

Beside Hawk on the buckboard, Reyna was no less aware of the end of things as she knew them. Hawk's feelings matched her own. The menu of inhumanity that had been served the Scotch-Irish in Europe, they had turned around and ruthlessly fed to the Native Americans. Now, it was the daily fare of black people, free men and slaves alike.

"Cheer up, my friend," she said. "It seems that in our own small way, we are about to avenge those who have suffered so terribly."

He said nothing, but after a while he smiled. "You are wise beyond your years, Young Miss. There *is* a joy in counting *coup*."

Reyna nodded grimly. She regarded the price on her head in Boston as a badge of honor, a medal she'd won in the battle for her people, but she also knew that the war she'd waged had left scars, too. Her lip creased with cruelty when she considered her mission to free slaves in a raid on the slave pens at Memphis.

And, there was also that *other* matter: *the man*. While he was only a shadowy memory, she'd come all this way, maybe the length of her life, to avenge a childhood wrong. Her plan was so daring it sent a shiver of excitement traveling the length of her spine. She shook her head, dispelling the dark image that came with the recaptured vision of *that* man.

As they drew near Memphis, the road clogged with riders on horseback, country wagons, and gigantic drays piled high with cotton, pulled by six-oxen teams. The tempo on the road increased, too, quickened with the pulse of life in the town.

Hurry. Hurry. Hurry. Everything hurried toward some unannounced destination. Wagons and buggies, horses and mules surged about the derelict pair of peddlers lurching along Washington Avenue to find their way to North Main Street. At Second Street when they could see the river, it was as jammed as the road. Caught up in its lusty enthusiasm, strangers sang out, "Howdy!" "How y'all!" "Nice day!" Excursion boats paddle-wheeled by with shrieking, steam-driven calliopes and scented the sky with the smoke of their wood-burning boilers. Shouted profanity from sailors filled the air like smutty love songs. Rich planters and their ladies, river boat captains and waterfront rowdies strolled and swaggered shoulder to shoulder on the wooden sidewalks.

Slaves, shiny black as coal, bent under huge bales of cotton and chanted work dirges as they stumbled across tote planks from dock to ship. Seamen off low-lying barges and hard-bitten "bullies" who fought river pirates and brawled in waterfront taverns, ambled among the grog shops and whistled to ladies in second floor rooms. The raucous din of Memphis ignited a spark that Reyna intuitively understood.

Alarmed by the feverish sparkle in his companion's eyes, Hawk leaned close to grip her elbow. He cautioned under his breath. "Be still, Young Miss."

Turning north, the impostor peddlers left the wealthy Beale Avenue district. The new Gayosos Hotel, a Victorian fancy with broad verandas overlooking the river had stolen the respectable guests from the old establishments, the Bell Tavern, the Pefraza Hotel, and old Sam Stodgins' Place. The shifting fortunes of Memphis were as transient as its residents. Unconcerned with the rich and the prominent, Hawk and Reyna headed toward Pinch, named for the poor, pinch-bellied inhabitants of Catfish Bay and Auction Square. There they'd meet their accomplice, Paddy Meagher, gambler friend of Old Hickory and owner of the Bell Tavern.

Auction Square was really no more than a small clearing before a huge barn. An eight foot hickory fence, "the pens," behind the barn, hid the unbecoming sight of the slaves' exercise yard from the possible view of ladies. A massive, squared stone provided a raised platform to view the chattel during the auction. No other block, north of New Orleans or west of Atlanta, was as active as the market in Memphis. Despite being hardened by years with the underground, Reyna felt her flesh turn to ice at sight of the stone monument of Auction Square.

A coffle of slaves, chained ankle to ankle, slow-footed toward the barn as the two peddlers passed. Big-muscled young men with ebony skin shiny as satin, their manacled walk and dejected faces masked youth as they circled the block. A corpulent trader directed their steps with threats from a cracking bullwhip. Their humiliation brought blood rushing to Reyna's face.

She found herself gaping, slackjawed at the slaver who had taken away her mama at Riverview Plantation. The look of his mean little pig eyes had never changed, no less evil after twenty years. Master Thomas's present location had reached her by way of a station of the underground. His coarse, shoulder-length hair had gone completely gray, yet his foulness had not been diminished with age. Adding two decades seemed neither to have decreased the immense belly, nor weakened the brute strength of the man towering over the line of slaves. The memory of him returned to her as fresh as an interrupted nightmare.

As though once was not enough — it never was with slavers — Master Thomas had tried to kidnap her ten years later for bounty money in New Orleans. There could not be many gigantic, southern Master Thomases who were also slave hunters and traders. It simply had to be the same man. Everything she felt about slavery, her own and that of these others, flooded back with the sight of Master Thomas at Auction Square.

This particular group was being sold for obvious reasons. Gray adhesions, scars of multiple beatings, advertised their owner's difficulty in controlling them. Ignorant field hands born not fifty miles from Memphis, none of them had ever been away from Ol' Mast' James' place before. The crime of the young, black giants, the eldest of whom was only eighteen, was mostly mischief natural to their age. Born on the same farm, they had grown up together sharing youth, adolescence, and young manhood. It did not surprise them to be whipped; indeed, they benignly accepted the harshest of beatings as their due when Mast' James laid on the lash for "foolin' aroun'" about their work. Old Master's constant threats to "sell dem down de ribber" had met with indifference — what could he mean? Would anything be different? It was, therefore, amazing to wake one morning and find a trader actually had come to take them away from their families, friends, and homes.

There was no foolin' aroun' then. That chilly, gray morning, the young slaves had been summarily loaded into a wagon, chained, and driven away. More for show than necessity on the trip, Leviticus, the biggest of them, got a tooth knocked out and the slavers notched L'il Martin's ear. By the time they reached Memphis, all six of them understood they had said goodbye forever to the familiar beatings of Ol' Mast'. Master James may have exaggerated their perfidy, but the slavers were taking no chances. To break the reputation for willfulness among the group, the slavers kept at their charges day and night. Each night after rations and exercise, the slaves were locked in separate pens in individual stocks, crude, oaken posts with lateral members to bind hands and feet and wooden yokes to clamp about their necks. Now the auctioneers would sell the most docile bunch of darkies a man could ever want.

Eyes downcast, not daring to look higher than the bill of her cap, Reyna saw it all, saw the welted stripes of pain; but most of all, she remembered the blustering trader. He was the real reason she had come to Memphis.

A shuddering jerk of her head signaled Hawk to move on, to crack his whip above the team and hurry them away from Auction Square.

Chapter 20

Although some folks said he was eighty years old, no one knew for sure. He'd been gray-headed longer than anyone remembered, but his eyes and his body were still big, clear, and strong. He had a voice that boomed like a bullhorn and a great ham of a fist that could split an oaken plank. He had become famous when his friend, Andrew Jackson, became president, but anyone who amounted to much in Tennessee knew him long before that. They said he fought alongside Old Hickory in the war of '12 and managed Jackson's farm on what was called President's Island. That was all over; gone like the respectability of the Pinch; gone with the death of Jackson in '44, the closing of the farm. Still very much there, however, was Paddy Meagher.

Like his predecessors, too, so long as he had a drop of blood, Meagher would never quit. A hard headed original, he had a spirit of resistance that prompted him to join in the plan of an unknown Yankee, Miss Reyna Shield.

Meagher's Bell Tavern on Front Street was both the best and the worst place in Memphis. A decade before, Bell Tavern had gloried in the shadow of westering men on their way to Texas. Frances "Fanny" Wright had drawn plans for the commune of free Blacks on Paddy's pecan wood table, and the window in the bedroom, second floor front, was the very one where Mrs. Trollope had first seen the Mississippi. Now, times had changed. Cotton and lumber and factories had brought a new kind of citizen from the east, a citizen who rejected the rough and tumble of the western rim of America. Elegance had come to Beale Avenue and mannerly people stopped coming to Smoky Row, the main thoroughfare of Pinch. Meagher, the Bell Tavern, and the Pinch District had fallen on hard times.

Reyna and Hawk gaped from the peddlers' wagon as it reared in alongside the weather-beaten porch of Bell Tavern, just in time to observe a body, all arms and legs, hurtle through the open door of the saloon. It struck and slid down a post, finally coming to rest on the porch where the hapless fellow lay inert with a comical grin twisted on his lips. Seconds later, Paddy Meagher's great hulk filled the doorway, inspecting the efficacy of his "showing the gentleman the door."

"An' don't y'all come back, Tim Johnson," the old man shouted, waggling a finger at the unhearing form. "Don't y'all come back till ye've learned some manners."

He nodded to the ersatz peddlers and roared loud enough for those within to hear, "Evenin' gents. Welcome to Bell Tavern."

The main floor of the Bell was a single, cavernous room. Separate additions to the primary space, rude, lean-to extensions along one side and the back of the building, created alcoves for dining, gaming, and private conversation. A long bar occupied the right hand wall at the rear of which were the steps to the upstairs hotel rooms. Hunting trophies, deer, antelope, and the snout of a wild boar were nailed to the plain, wooden walls; otherwise there was not a hint of decoration of any kind.

The occupants of the Bell, three long-boned farmers and a river man at the bar, a fancy woman, showing signs of wear, huddling with a client over an alcove table, hardly looked up as Paddy guided the shabby-looking pair to a table at the rear. An almost undetectable nod of his head brought a jug of his private brew and three short glasses to their table.

Pouring out a drink for each, Meagher took his at one swallow, but held it in his mouth until they followed suit, before letting it trickle down his throat. His amusement twinkled at the tears the liquid fire brought to his guests' eyes.

"Welcome to Memphis, the real Memphis." He filled the glasses again. "At least they can't take our lightnin' from us. Take away everything else, but not our white lightnin'. This is the real Tennessee."

"Mr. Meagher," Hawk began.

"My friends call me Paddy."

"Paddy, then." The Indian toyed with his glass. The heat of the liquor reddened the old scar across his cheek. "Is everything ready?"

"We've done our part." Paddy eyed the peddler's apprentice. "But, I thought there was to be a lady. A lady made the arrangements. Who's this?"

"There is only us. My helper . . . he's deaf and dumb as you can see. He don't speak."

"Just as well." The slow nod, the same greeting as the one on the porch, and then he tossed down another glass. "Too much palaver goin' on anyway. Ain' nothin' to hear but bad times these days. Better off deef."

But the way he stared, told his guests that Meagher was not fooled. The barkeep knew. Reyna looked away.

"The arrangements?" Hawk asked again, emptying the second glass that his host immediately refilled.

Sprawling back in the chair, great arms folded across his chest, Paddy rolled his eyes toward the back wall of the tavern. "Down the road apiece. About forty yards back. There's a pier. It's the onliest one there. Can't miss it."

"But, that's the new Navy Yard."

"Right next of it."

"But — "

"Don't 'but' me, boy, I ain't a fool. Can't help it if the gov'ment did spend a million dollars. It's deserted. A million dollars an' no one'll ever use it.

Anyways, next of it is a pier. And tied up to that pier is a flat-bottom barge. Y'all met Tim Johnson, the gentleman who was jest leavin' when you was a'comin' in . . ."

"That man you threw out on the porch?"

"The very one. He works the barge for me."

"But, how can it be? How could such a man go on working for you? After the way you treat him, can he be trusted?"

"Oh, that. Well, boy, Tim's been hangin' around the Bell till midnight every night for right onto twenty years. So folks wouldn't get 'spicious if'n he left early, we had to find a way to send him home early."

"Seems like the hard way!"

"Not really. Tim's a good friend. A real tough 'un, that'n." The innkeeper wheezed with restrained laughter, his vast middle shook violently with it. "But, then y'all don't know the half of it. To make it even more believable, I been throwin' him out like that every other night for a month. Folks thinks we got a real mountain feud goin'."

"Must be some kind of man to put up with that."

"Yessirree Bob!" Tears of repressed mirth squirted from the old man's eyes. "'Zactly like that! Anyways, that's none of your bees wax. Tim and me's good friends and I pay him well. When you get your cargo to the barge, he'll get it to the farm on President's Island."

"Is it safe?" Hawk insisted.

Their host leaned forward, rigid with anger at the question. He motioned to the newly filled glasses before them. "Mister, it seems to me, y'all are askin' a lot of unnecessary questions about things that ain't none of your business. Besides, it seems to me, two Yankees in my territory ain't got a whole lot of choice but trustin' my way of doin' things."

When an answer didn't come instantly he repeated, "They don't have no choice a'tall now, do they?"

"No, I guess you're right, sir. They don't have much choice at that."

Meagher relaxed. "Now, then, now that we got that settled. We'uns understood there was the matter of somethin' else, let's call it reciprocal southern hospitality."

Reyna's hand jumped to touch her waist. The barkeep just as quickly noted the gesture.

"Tell your deef friend not to feel for a money belt that way. It's a dead giveaway that any old river rat would spot in a minute."

The big man got to his feet curtly, holding a glass of what was left of the molten liquor. "I think we understand each other now, gents. Now, it's probably time for y'all to retire. Your room is the one in the back, right next of the outside stairs. That way you can just go down the stairs if you need to use the necessary or somethin'. Before you leave your room, put the, ah — the room rental — under the pillow. Now, shall we have a drink to your successful business in Memphis?"

The peddlers rose.

"Oh, and one more thing." The owner of the Bell leaned toward Hawk confidentially. "Tell your apprentice to take bigger steps. Walks like he's wearing a dress. Wouldn't want folks to get the wrong idea, would you?

Chapter 21

Three hours later, after the last of the carousing patrons had staggered into the night, Reyna and the Indian stole down the exterior stairs at the back of the Bell Tavern. A money belt containing $2000 for "southern hospitality" lay tucked under the pillow in the room they left. Hawk moved with the liquid grace of a stalking hunter. Despite the slight nip in the autumn breeze off the river, a line of perspiration surfaced on Reyna's forehead.

The mist-draped moon had just begun to swim out of a cloud when the two arrived at the corner of Auction and North Main. An eerie, gray-green shadow of the auction block spilled onto the ground around it and the closed and bolted maw of the infamous barn kept speechless watch over the street. Too late in the year for crickets, the only sound sputtered from the oil lantern at the door of a log cabin guardhouse outside the slavehold.

Touching his sleeve as a sign, Reyna left the Indian to guard the street and to keep an eye out for sentries. Because of her size and agility, she could more easily slip through small openings. In an emergency, his hoot owl screech would give warning.

A dozen heart-pounding strides carried her to the edge of the structure where she turned to face the street. Hawk's fuzzy silhouette didn't move, nor was there a stir from the guardhouse. Hands behind her back, she edged along the rough, plank wall, cautiously scissor-stepping to find the door. There, slowly, with excruciating care, she drew back the bolt, and slid the panel ajar. Still, no sign of movement from the guardhouse; no alarm from Hawk.

Reyna eased the door closed, then sank back against the frame to gulp long, slow breaths to calm herself. Her face, numb in the breezeless chamber, felt clammy.

It took a few minutes to adjust, to make out the shapes in the dark. Like any barn or corncrib, the slavehold had a broad center aisle faced with individual cells like animal pens. Prospective buyers, walking down the central promenade, inspected the merchandise just like other stock at a county fair. Strangely, there was no sound; no respiration or snores, no rustling of straw on the floor. Absolutely nothing stirred.

Rather than a lack of life, the absence of sound signified precisely the opposite. The six petrified black men locked in the pens waited, fine-tuned to the most infinitesimal change in their environs.

The first muffled sound of someone sneaking about outside had instantly alerted them. The traders had taught them well the penalties of inattention. Leviticus' tooth and L'il Martin's ear had been only the first of the symbolic punishments to bring them in line. One after another, each of the men had been singled out for special treatment to teach them to mind their manners. When Levi spoke out of turn, the masters "planted" him, buried him in a hole up to his chin, for two days. The torment didn't stop. Night and day; the slaves never knew when the traders would want more entertainment at their expense. Now, stooped in the stocks, the harnesses about their necks prevented their turning toward the whisper of the opening door, but they heard and their every faculty strained toward the front of the barn to investigate the danger.

Creeping along the far wall, Reyna made her way to the gate of the first cell, the one holding Levi. Feigning sleep behind narrowed slits of eyes, the big Black studied the approaching apparition. The ghostly figure unlatched the bar of the gate, swung it wide, and entered. He made no sound at all. Dropping to his knees, the shabby-looking peddler boy worked feverishly to untie the leather-thong knots binding the captive's ankles.

At last, the prisoner could bear it no longer. "What you want with Levi, mastah?"

No louder than a croaking whisper, the sudden eruption of the bass voice in the silent dark sent her heart skipping in her throat. "Sssh!" she hissed as low as she could muster. "Sssh. Don't be scared. I'm here to help you."

Disbelief colored Levi's, "How you gon' help this boy, mastah? You gon' buy me?"

The knots fell loose about his legs and Reyna stood nose to nose with the great head ringed in the stocks. The ferocity behind the smoldering eyes of the little white man, dressed as a beggar, stunned the young Black who sensed something very odd about his rescuer. Levi felt a surge of power.

"Better than that," she grunted softly. "We're going to set you free."

"Oh, mastah, don't. Fo' pity's sake, leave Levi to his own self."

"Hush, Levi. We're going to take you north to freedom."

Head firmly clamped in the yoke, Levi stared dully at the nimble fingers undoing the knotted wristlets. "What they want with Levi in the north? Don't nobody, north, south, east, or west, want no mo' niggers."

"Listen to me," she said. The malevolent power returned to her voice. "We're helping you, fool. We're taking you to a place where there are no slaves."

"No slaves?" Doubt and scorn swept over him. "Mus' be a pretty poor place where everybody's too poor to own nobody."

Irked with the ignorant field hand, she hissed, "Stop messin' with me, boy.

Help me get your friends out. I don't have time to stand here listening to your chin music."

Still not quite believing, or not quite understanding what there was to believe, Levi followed her out of the cell. Slinking from pen to pen, they noiselessly freed the captives. An index finger motioned for quiet and the assembled men stealthily headed toward the door. The line of slaves behind the peculiar white man had not quite reached the front of the barn when the faint cry of a hoot owl pierced the stillness.

Hawk had lurked as motionless as an obelisk in the shadows for nearly an hour. The building that had swallowed Reyna lay quiet, shrouded in mist from the river. From the outside, there was no sign of the anxious drama taking place within. The streets, jammed with carriages and wagons by day, now rested without as much sound or movement as a beetle rubbing a pebble. For the lack of anything else to watch, the Indian concentrated on the jumping flame of the coal oil lamp bouncing shadows off the open guardhouse door. A sentry appeared in the doorway from time to time to throw a quick, inspecting glance toward the slave pens.

Some time after three in the morning, the shape filled the opening again and shouted back to another, unseen in the cabin.

"Master Thomas!" The call rang out as clear as day. "I'm gonna have a look around. Need to stretch my legs anyhow."

A guttural assent rumbled inside.

Hawk froze as the dark shadow, a tall man swinging a nightstick, broke away from the light to stroll toward the slavehold.

Two, three, four steps the guard took, seeing nothing unusual outside the building. He paused at the barn door, scratched his head, then went on. Four more steps put him at the corner of the barn. He stopped again, listening. At that point, the roving sentry whirled about and strode back to the barn door where he bent to examine the hasp and the loose, drawn bolt. Shaking his head, the guard halted to listen again. Then, moving determinedly, he hurried back to the guardhouse to rouse a hornet's nest of incomprehensible rumbling from his partner inside.

Cupped hands about his mouth, the Indian hooted before inching forward across the inky Square toward the entrance to the slave pens.

Reyna and the newly liberated slaves huddled just on the other side of the door when they heard the measured tread and the rattled bolt. Grouped about the peddler, six young men, frozen statues, expectantly listened to the deafening silence. When the rapid footsteps carried the man away, a relieved sigh escaped them. Not a sound betrayed the return of their captors. Nor did the breathless slaves, only the width of a door from freedom, hear Hawk's swift advance. Satisfied there was no one outside, Reyna cautiously pushed open the big barn door.

There, face to face, stood Master Thomas and his fellow. She hadn't calculated the revulsion the man could generate after so many years.

In that instant of indecision, struck by something momentous, Master Thomas's ham fist reached for his trademark bullwhip. "What's this?" he raged. "What's this, Master Frank? Looks like we found ourselfs a fox in the hen house. We done caught ourselfs a thief."

Another half step and the immense belly would have knocked her down. He stood so close she heard the breath whistling through his nostrils, smelled the sour accumulation of filth on his clothing. It was not just disgust and fear that buckled her knees and made her flesh crawl. No matter how she tried, her lessons in slavery had led her to believe she was inferior even to the loathsome mountain of degenerate white flesh. Not intellect, not courage, not years of disguise could wipe away thirty-four years of that. A kernel of sand in the heart of a pearl; inside it all, Reyna felt ashamed of her color and recoiled from the glare of the slaver.

"What's this?" he roared again in a bestial snarl. "What you boys doin' outa yo' stocks?"

Reyna frantically sought a way around the hulk blocking the doorway. The six men behind her set up a chorus of groans.

"Naw, y'all ain't goin' no place a'tall." The whip uncurled and teased before them. "Now, just be getting' back to yo' stalls. He'p them find they way, Mast' Frank," he grunted to the tall assistant at his back.

They wavered for a moment. It appeared the frightened gang would roll back like a lazy wave and docilely return to the cells. Reyna put up her hand, a signal for them to stay. After all, it was she who had brought them to this point.

The arm and the whip reared back, ready to strike. The slaves howled afresh in terror, "No, mast'. We ain't doin' nothin'. Don't mean nothin', mast'" Reyna, still standing her ground, eyes clinched tight shut, waited for the lash.

Instead of the stinging whip, there came a great thump, the thwack of an ax in a hollow log and a dead weight crashed past her. Then, as she opened her eyes, the doorway exploded in commotion and noise. Master Thomas lay at her feet, the shaft of Hawk's harpoon vibrating between his shoulder blades. Master Frank thrashed wildly in the grip of strong-fingered hands at his throat. The slaves continued to bawl for mercy. Reyna turned on the six howling creatures and shouted them to silence as the lifeless body of the second slaver slid from the Indian's grip to join Master Thomas on the ground.

"Now, all of you stop caterwauling," she cried, burning them with the awful fire of her eyes. "We have a hiding place, but I don't want another peep out of any of you. We've got to get out of here. Do you know what you get for murderin' a white man?"

Hawk retrieved his weapon, wiping the fish-hooked blade on Master Thomas' grimy shirt.

The escapees, Reyna leading, slid single file down Auction Street toward the wharf alongside the Navy Yard where Tim Johnson kept the barge. They hurried, holding themselves to long walking strides for fear of arousing an alarm from some chance night wanderer. Hawk covered the flank of the column with his one sharp eye.

The docks, a flattering name for the derelict remains of broken down piers floating in riverbank muck, harbored only the boats of outcasts, swamp hunters, snake catchers, and smugglers. Like the lapping, muddy tide of the Mississippi, commercial vessels of any promise had abandoned the Pinch District for the affluence of the city to the south. The unused Navy Yard, costly government orphan, was now another monument to the dashed hopes of north Memphis.

Reyna halted the refugee band at the foot of the concrete embankment of the Navy Yard. The night lay around them, caught in that web of time when its soul is darkest, halfway between midnight and dawn. There was neither the slightest fraction of sound nor light to guide them. For a moment, Reyna panicked. They had been duped. They had murdered two white men, freed six slaves; their money lodged beneath a pillow at the Bell Tavern, but no rescue waited.

A silent figure slipped in from the darkness to touch her elbow.

"Y'all are late," said a gruff voice close to her ear.

When she could speak above the startled ringing in her head, she gasped out, "We need to get away at once. Without delay."

Tim Johnson, shorter by three inches than she, hovered close enough to touch in the dark. An old river man, reduced to earning a living through odd jobs whose legality didn't concern him, Tim was not apt to be ruffled by anything less important than separation from the flask of moonshine in his hip pocket.

"Don't care what kept you. That's your affair," he said in a slow, painfully deliberate way. "Mine's to use the time we got. Y'all are late."

"We've got to hurry!" she snapped. "We've had trouble. They'll be looking for us."

"They be looking for y'all in any case. Can't hurry. Can't make no noise. Gotta use the river current for power. Glad y'all brought a bunch of young bucks. We'll need the help to pole the barge away from the bank."

At last they boarded the flat, open-topped craft and poled it away to join the tide drifting to President's Island. Then there was nothing to do but sit in plain view in the breaking dawn. Reyna's nerves strained with the anxiety to hurry, to get away where they could not be seen.

"Are you sure the island is safe?" she asked. "You see, Mr. Johnson, there was a fight. We don't know what happened to the slavers. They might be in pretty bad shape back there."

No change, no flicker of response altered the man's expression.

"The Negroes will be safe," he answered calmly. "President's Island got lots of free Negro farmers. Nothing suspicious about that at all. Better for them to hole up on the island a mite than to run for it if there's gonna be people out lookin'."

They sat a long while eyeing each other in the first light of day before he added, "An' I'd guess the Injun is safe enough. But, you, white man. You're a whole 'nother matter altogether. Most likely they'll come lookin' for you."

Reyna's hand involuntarily reached to touch the voodoo amulet at her breast.

Part Three

The Fugitive

Chapter 22

Captain Claibourne Van Buren, master of the paddle wheel steamer, the *Joy of Cincinnati*, didn't have to answer the First Mate's rap to know there was trouble.

The captain and his junior officers were in a continual broil. Van Buren made no secret of his dislikes. He didn't like Academy men; his generation learned on the job with the sea as teacher. "Academy boys!" he grumped. They knew new technologies, things like the physical properties of steam and rotors and copper boilers, and owners hired them on as officers at ranks Van Buren had worked years to reach. He longed for a return to the days of keelhauling impertinent crewmen.

At twenty-two, Mr. Bob Barker, First Mate of the *Cincinnati*, had nothing but contempt for the captain who couldn't tell a boiler from a rivet on steam-powered vessels. First in his class at the Academy, Barker had been recruited directly from school as First Mate of the *Joy of Cincinnati* making the trip from New York to New Orleans. To his delight, his classmate, Leander Smith, had won the billet as Chief Engineer.

The young officers' resistance to the old order, of which Van Buren was an example, took the form of underhanded pranks. They passed the time between duty watches playing practical jokes on the crew, the captain, and each other. One night, they released a jar of red ants in the crew's quarters and peeped from a hole in the bulkhead to watch the scratching and slapping before the men fled the infested compartment. Old man Van Buren never did find out why the sorghum molasses he loved on his hot cakes took on the flavor of engine grease. The things they did to each other were a thousand times worse. Barker spent hours carefully ripping the underside stitching from Smith's bunk so that when the engineer returned from midnight watch he'd fall through to the floor. In reprisal, Smith removed the threads from the seams of the seat of Barker's trousers. The two men knew, too, that the worst thing old Van Buren could do was to fire them. Steamboat shipping was growing so fast, there was always another line to take them on.

In addition to the junior officers, Van Buren's trouble on the *Joy of Cincinnati* had begun when they left Chicago. The captain had seen this all before with the California Gold Rush of '49. Now, in '57, the rush to Alaska's gold was simply a repeated refrain he knew all too well. Every ne'er-do-well in the country was rushing there to get some of it. Beginning in upstate New York, the would-be miners jumped aboard anything that moved on the Erie Canal. They followed along till they met the Great Lakes and then crowded aboard steamers to make their way down the Mississippi to Saint Louis. Now, the *Cincinnati* was chock-ablock with the lunatics. When there was no more room in the Gentlemens' Cabin, they took over the Ladies' Cabin, too. Hundreds and thousands of the idiots paid good hard money to sleep on the cabin floor, on settees and tables in the lounge, and finally sprawled out on the open decks. The *Joy of Cincinnati*, built for 300, now carried 500 men and boys in advanced stages of get-rich-quick with little to do but drink and gamble and carouse. The captain thought he'd go mad before the gold seekers disembarked in St. Louis.

Then, a cholera epidemic in St. Louis had forced him to steam on to Cape Girardeau, eighty miles farther south. At Cape Girardeau, the news was worse. Reports from New Orleans declared the port under siege with the same disease. Bodies, they said, lay stacked like cordwood in the streets awaiting time and space for the burying. Stomach churning harder than the paddle wheel, the captain decided to turn around at Cape Girardeau and head back up the river rather than risk it.

As an omen of more bad luck on the return, a young whore and her "aunt" came aboard at Cape Girardeau. Van Buren knew from sailing ship days that women brought bad luck to ships. This kind spelled trouble with a capital "T".

In the shadow of Greene's warehouse at the corner of Broadway and Main Street, on the wharf at Cape Girardeau, Lottie Bremerman waited impatiently to board the *Joy of Cincinnati* bound for Boston. Mrs. Elizabeth Hill, Lottie's traveling companion and chaperone, kept touching the girl's arm as a reminder of deportment. She thought her ward, who had never been as far away from "Cape" as St. Louis, took an unwholesome interest in the horde of males pouring down the gangplank and crushing around them on the wharf.

Mrs. Hill had every good reason to distrust the young lady. Lottie was being exiled to Boston to a "school" for incorrigible behavior. A pretty little slip of a thing with a shoe button nose and pursed lips over flawless teeth, she would make anyone wonder how such a diminutive creature with such innocent demeanor could get in such gigantic trouble. Even openly eyeing the rough and tumble gold-seekers, Lottie looked like a child saint.

Deceivingly so, before she was thirteen, there had been the hired man, Adolph. The family had sent him away in disgrace while the supperless girl watched without remorse from her bedroom window. Next was a traveling peddler of medicated salves. The peddler was banished from the county, but the incident caused the girl's parents to regard their daughter in a new way. Father Evans of St. Vincent's fell, too, in the shadow of his own church at the northwest corner of Main and Williams where parishioners saw him kiss the young temptress in a manner far exceeding Christian care. Finally, Lottie was caught in her own duplicity. The evidence of it was slowly, inevitably swelling under her skirts.

Mrs. Hill, friend of the family, had been chosen to accompany the young woman because she was the only female in town who would. All the others had long since abandoned the vixen who had a vindictive streak as broad as her promiscuity. Mrs. Hill fancied herself a great stone wall, a veritable barricade between the slavering jaws of evil and the child's apparent weakness. The chaperone was convinced that the love of God could defeat the devil in men's hearts and hands. In His name, there was hope, even for Lottie.

Van Buren, resplendent in dark blue uniform and winking brass buttons, flanked by his First Mate and Chief Engineer on the quarterdeck, bowed from the waist to welcome the passengers. The travelers from sleepy little Cape Girardeau did not augur an easy northern trip. He winced at the sight of the woman and her companion, and the too-obvious lasciviousness in the eyes of his arrogant First Mate. The trip north could be as difficult as the one south.

The leers of the First Mate were not wasted on Mrs. Hill and her ward. Lottie brightened noticeably, smiled demurely, nodded her pretty head. Mrs. Hill stiffened as she accurately recognized the latest of the adversaries in the struggle for the remaining shreds of Lottie's virtue.

Rowdy miners, cholera, an aborted voyage, a lascivious wench, and an impertinent junior officer were only the beginning of the captain's problems. Not an hour out of Cape Girardeau, the *Joy of Cincinnati* was overtaken by wild Indians. At first, no more than specks on the muddy river, warrior canoes, each manned by half a hundred braves painted in ferocious, powwow colors surrounded the ship.

The setting sun, swastikas, and mystical symbols of the underworld were painted on the sides of the longboats. The same designs were repeated on the bodies and faces of the braves menacing the big steamer with shaking war rattles and sharp pointed battle lances. An old chief stood in the lead canoe, arms folded across his chest. A double row of feathers from a stately headdress rippled down his back to his feet.

The canoes circled the big ship closer and closer, ignoring the plunging wheel in the dark brown water and the cocoa waves of its wake. The rhythmic pounding of war drums rose above the engines. A blasting shriek of the steam siren deafened the passengers and crew gathered at the side of the vessel, but made no difference to the paddling Indians. No one on the ship had ever seen so many natives gathered together in one place.

"Get out of the way, ye blasted savages," the captain bellowed through the bullhorn.

The chief in the prow of the lead canoe raised his right hand holding the long clay pipe of peace.

"Get out of the way!" Van Buren shouted again.

A deep, bass voice boomed from the lead canoe. "It is you who are in the way, white man. These waters, this right of way was granted to the Great White Father in Washington many moons ago, but it remains sacred to us. We come in peace, but the way is ours."

"Who are you? What do you want?"

"We come in peace. In exchange for your safe passage through these sacred waters, we ask only that you take us to the Great White Father on the back of your engine canoe."

Van Buren and his officers exchanged puzzled looks. The savages were blackmailing them. Indians hadn't done that in thirty years. Lottie, from her position next to her chaperon on the deck, breathed heavily at the sight of the muscular, half-naked war party. She imitated the beat of the drums with tiny taps of her folded fan on the railing.

"Who are you?" the captain demanded.

"I Running Fox, Chief of Middle Nations," came back from the canoe. "Here my daughter, Princess Little Deer. Great White Father has sent for us. We want ride in big engine canoe."

Captain and officers looked among themselves again, baffled. After all that had happened on this voyage, the old man was relatively unsurprised. The drumbeat hastened its tempo, joined by barking war cries from the young braves.

"We don't go to Washington," Van Buren called back, stalling for time to think.

"We know. We travel only to Port Huron. Great White Father have council."

Chapter 23

Curious passengers crowded the quarterdeck when the gangplank was lowered to receive the Indians. Van Buren, after hastily comparing the cost of giving in to the Indians with their possible mischief, acceded to their demand for passage. Ship masters might not be engineers; but as a diplomat, the captain was pragmatic. It was not so unusual after all, and a free ride to Port Huron was a pittance compared to the bribes he'd paid in the West Indies and Panama. Out on the water, canoe after canoe dipped in farewell to the chief and his daughter.

Van Buren watched with sympathy as Chief Running Fox and Princess Little Deer mounted the unsteady stair with great dignity. In them, the old sailing master saw much that was like himself, a dying breed. The Chief, a wizened old man, carried himself with unflinching pride and a look from his good right eye scorned the gawking whites. An old scar, perhaps from a tomahawk in an Indian war or a saber cut from a federal troop, slashed across the left side of his face. The feathers of his war bonnet and the deep reds and blues of his blanket, tokens of high rank, gleamed in the sun against the white ship. Short and stocky but strong, the Indian must have been a fine figure as a young man. Over his shoulder, he carried a gunny bag which probably contained everything he owned.

The chief offered the clay pipe of peace, a gift to the captain, and bowed, sweeping the air with his right hand to his daughter who walked a respectful three paces behind.

Princess Little Deer apparently wore all the finery of her tribe at once. From the beaded moccasins to the single feather worked with sparkling shells in her braids, she shone in the sun like an Aztec idol. The captain detected something extraordinary about her eyes, a consequence of mixed breed perhaps or a childhood disease. Her loose fitting doeskin jacket was completely covered with red and white and blue glass beads in fanciful tribal designs. The beaded outline of a deer's head, no doubt her personal totem, stared glassy-eyed from her back and a six inch plait of woven porcupine quills hung from neck to waist. Each of the quills had been sanded as smooth as ivory and each was tipped with a bead of pale lapis lazuli. Lady passengers blanched, aghast at her ritual doeskin leggings instead of a respectable skirt.

Van Buren noticed that Lottie seemed lost in fantasies, eyes half-closed, no doubt imagining the sensation she'd create in the Indian's costume at dress-up parties. Mrs. Hill touched her arm, cautioning.

Again, the captain found the ceremony full of sad prophecy: A *peace pipe, an Indian Chief, an Indian princess. The idea of calling the modern technology "engine canoes" was laughable. No wonder the government was disposing of the primitives. There was a hint of the future in the two natives, among the last of their kind, on the way to see the President of the United States.* Barker, the First Mate, and Smith, the Chief Engineer, blue cloth and brass button replicas of one another, bowed as the captain accepted the pipe of peace. The First mate kept his eyes fixed on the lovely princess. He elbowed the Chief Engineer.

"Chief Running Fox . . . " The captain cleared his throat solemnly. "Chief, please come to my cabin. Come in peace aboard this . . . ah . . ." He looked about, forced himself to look respectful. " . . . this engine canoe. Please follow me."

The captain sat behind the desk in his cabin to maintain a remote distance from the unusual passengers. The two junior officers perched on mate's chairs, flanking him like gryphons. Chief Running Fox took the leather wingchair indicated for him. The princess knelt, sitting on her heels, behind her father.

"Now, chief," the captain began. "Let me tell you about the ship. This canoe is different from the ones of your nation." He stretched out his hands. "Bigger than any of those of your people. Because of that we have laws here you must live by."

The old man nodded, his face the color of seasoned walnut, registered understanding. His daughter's head bobbed, too, but she kept her gaze respectfully in her lap.

"First, there must be no cookfires on the deck."

The First Mate stared, his eyes roaming from her thigh to knee stretching the leather leggings, the swelling bosom beneath the porcupine quill necklace. Lottie, the young lady from Cape Girardeau, had caught his attention, but she was no challenge. The squaw, on the other hand, was a tempting adventure of more complexity.

"And, there must be no noise, no singing or prayers after dark."

Again, the nod of comprehension.

To allay any possibility of misunderstanding, Van Buren delicately approached the matter of their segregation. Poor travelers and colored people slept with overflow cargo on A Deck in the open, regardless of weather. Indians and gypsies were also confined there. "You will be on A Deck," he said. "Under the great stars. You will remain there. No go below. We will bring you food."

"Chief know." The Indian spoke blandly, inscrutable behind the brown mask of his face. "Chief know white man's law. You are kind. I give good word of you to Great White Father."

The captain smiled, sighed with relief. *How docile the old Indian was. He knew his place. How childlike. It seemed a pity somehow, that such simple people must be eradicated.*

On A Deck, the chief and his daughter dropped to their haunches at the corner next to the wheelhouse. A knot of slaves, the property of passengers, squatted not far away, regarding them with interest, but didn't speak. Whites, too poor to afford reserved bunks, kept well back from both groups, disdainfully scorning them as if to hide their own self-pity at having sunk so low as to have to travel with such vermin.

When they were alone, the princess leaned close to her father's ear. "We did it, Hawk," she whispered. "We did it. We got those fools to take us out of the reach of the marshals."

"Quiet, young Miss," the whaling man grunted through clinched teeth. "We're not free yet."

"You were perfect! And, to pretend you knew nothing about ships. It was wonderful to watch with a straight face while you let the old fool rattle on about ships."

"It was not me, Miss Reyna." Hawk, too, quaked with silent glee at the foolishness of the American officer. "Our friends, the tribe from President's Island, did it with their warrior canoes."

"Warrior canoes!" Tears of smothered laughter bubbled to Reyna's eyes. "Snake hunter dugouts! Warrior canoes! I must admit, Chief Running Fox, you look quite handsome in Tim Johnson's horse blanket!"

"Be still, young Miss."

"Just leave it to me," she insisted before going silent. "Just leave it to me to get to Drummond Island. I saw something in the young officer's eyes that will take us there. These white men," she said in a tone bitterly reminiscent of Rene DuPuis. "These white men are incredibly stupid."

As if to reassure herself of their chances of winning the risky game they played, Reyna put her hand out to touch the gunny bag which contained the portable altar, her most treasured possession.

Chapter 24

That night, the masquerade Indians, sitting up, leaning against the bulkhead on A Deck, slept more soundly than they had in a week.

A large party of marshals had been deputized in Memphis to hunt them down. When scouring the city and countryside produced nothing, they headed for President's Island. As Tim Johnson had predicted, the slaves had been able to fade into the households of the many free black farmers on the island, but there was no place for a white man to hide from the marshals. Then, the friendly Indians of President's Island offered to help them escape in the only boats they owned, dugout canoes used for snake hunting in the swamps and bayous.

Now, the problem Reyna wrestled with was how to get to Drummond Island. The *Joy of Cincinnati* went to Boston, but that was too dangerous. She was known there. If she could get to Drummond, she figured, she could hide with Grandma while Hawk went on to see the Gardners or Ned. Perhaps, she thought, she could enlist the aid of the young officer with the hungry eyes. It was just a week to Port Huron; seven days to get his help.

Unfortunately, the Captain, the tow-headed twit of a school girl, and the hatchet-faced chaperon had also noticed the First Mate's stare. The captain had scowled in disapproval while Lottie hurled daggers of envy and Mrs. Hill huffed and puffed her outrage at a ship's officer looking so boldly at a woman, particularly a savage. Reyna would need to take care with all of them.

Each morning aboard ship began with a great clatter and clamor of metal against metal, the clank of bunks being lifted and stowed away in the Gentlemen's Cabin, the tinkle of china and glass in the makeshift Dining Room. The smell of frying bacon drifted up from the galley. Two coal black stewards rolled out carts of hardtack and ersatz, chicory coffee and set up temporary buffet tables on A Deck. The breakfast service was but a way to be certain open deck passengers would not wander down to the dining room and create an unpleasant scene before their betters. A line formed, winding down and around the ship's internal stairs to C Deck for the solitary toilet available to A Deck.

There were no tables or chairs. In order to eat, the ragged passengers of that level could only sit cross-legged on the deck itself, perch on capstans or on cargo boxes. Reyna and Hawk hunched against the wheelhouse, solemnly munching hardtack and sipping coffee from tin mugs. No pretext of even commonplace civility was possible under the circumstances.

While they were eating, the officious First Mate appeared, inspected the service and ordered the stewards about. She cringed when he glanced their way. Squatted ungracefully on the deck, Reyna fantasized making a fool of him at her Boston table of crystal and china and heavy-weight silver. He made no attempt to hide his lust.

She recognized the arrogant self-assurance. His immaculately pressed jacket and perfectly polished buttons insulted she who had access to water only after waiting in line for the single necessary.

Passing her, the young officer turned, presented his profile obviously for admiration, showed off his well-defined chest and narrow waist in his tailored jacket. To Reyna, it seemed he believed his best feature was his face — a strong chin and blue eyes beneath a square, masculine brow. He kept his head turned just so and a swath of honey-blond hair waved down across his forehead under the bill of the officer's cap. Apparently, it had never occurred to him that anyone might find him less than irresistible.

Reyna looked away, pretending shyness. She hated the man, loathed him the more for her own ignominy.

Before leaving the deck, he strode over to them, cast an ominous shadow against the bulkhead. "Good morning, Chief," he said. "Princess. How are you today?"

"We good, Captain," Hawk said, adding the rank to feed the man's ego. Reyna favored him with a smile.

She listened to the click of his heels, retreating to the stairs to B Deck. But she knew he would come again.

Seventy-five passengers sharing a single convenience meant a continuous file down the stairs. That night, seething from the humiliation, Reyna was standing in line waiting for the toilet when the First Mate passed with the flirtatious girl on his arm. Mrs. Hill trailed in their wake, a stern watchdog at the door to the temple of virtue. The Indian Princess was at that turn where the stair intersected the wide, central passageway of B Deck. In the distance, the brightly candled Dining Room was laid with crisp linen and crystal. White coated stewards hurried to and fro with porringers of viands and vegetables for the evening supper. The lower classes of the deck above had already collected their ration of stew on tin military plates. She dropped her eyes at the officer's approach.

As though he was uncommonly amusing, peals of giggles from Lottie answered his rumbled phrases. The First Mate halted. The girl ogled Reyna's Indian garb with open curiosity from behind a petite, aqua silk bonnet and clouds of teased, white-blond hair. Her wide, blue eyes twinkled, as if she saw something comical about the costume.

"Good evening, Princess," Barker said.

Reyna mumbled something indistinct, toyed with the quill necklace across her breast and, as if inadvertently, unveiled the tiniest bit of flesh at the base of her throat.

"I hope you're enjoying the voyage," he went on despite Lottie's tug at his arm.

"Yes, Captain," she said. The dark crescents of lowered eyelids shadowed her elegantly arched cheekbones. Her pale flesh was creamy-soft. Barker's stare was so blatant, she thought he was about to reach out and touch her.

"Princess, if there is anything I can do to make you more comfortable, don't hesitate to ask."

"We will, Captain," she breathed. "We will."

They were gone in an instant, the First Mate, the little fool, and the stalwart matron, gone in a swish of silk dresses and broadcloth uniform down the passageway toward the Dining Salon. Lingering behind the quick departure was Lottie's lilting words about "how like animals squaws are" and "the shame it was that such creatures could never learn to be decent Americans."

Reyna woke in the night. Propped up alongside Hawk against the wheelhouse, she sat quietly listening to the pulsing throb of the growling engines and the slapping paddle wheels. Narrowing her eyes to slits, she cautiously peered about. Nothing moved in the darkness, yet she sensed a presence there. The white ship's rail glowed with an eerie, almost luminescent blue-green light across the night. The inky blotches of fellow passengers huddled in their usual places on the deck. Then, she saw him.

A tall form leaned casually over the ship's rail, a shadowy outline in the dark. The figure calmly, unhurriedly puffed on a pipe and, from time to time, glanced back in her direction. No need to make out the features to know who it was.

Slowly stealing her hand to their bag, she felt for the padded leather of the altar. "Great Vodu," she prayed, "come to me now. Help me at this hour. Save me from these barbarians who believe in nothing. Watch over me in the days to come."

She didn't move. Not so much as a hair. Closing her eyes again, she drifted back and forth between waking and sleep for the rest of the night. She never knew when he left the railing. *Let him wait. A little while.*

Carefully timing her trips to the necessary, the Princess was on the stair each time he passed on the way to the dining room. After it became a part of her scheme, the debasement of the line to the toilet no longer mortified her. He never failed to stop, to invent something to say, to devour her with his eyes before moving on.

In the following nights, his nocturnal visits to A Deck to suck at his pipe and gaze off into the murky sky and water became a game. She might have learned her patient stalking from the Canadian hunter, Charles Pilar, but she couldn't remember when; it surely hadn't been a deliberate teaching. Still, it was very much like hunting an animal, watching, aware of every muscle without moving a one.

It was always the same. Crouched on the deck, her back against the bulkhead, one hand touching the sacred altar, she watched with nearly closed eyes. Only three bones of her spine touched the wooden wall before the lower back arched to where her tailbone met the deck. She could feel a wrinkle in her leather leggings and the grain of the rough, wooden deck through her moccasins. One forearm across her knees made a pillow and her knees and heels and butt made a triangle. Hours passed like that, attending to minutiae, in and out of light sleep, before she knew he was there.

She sensed his presence without a single motion. The sensing must be like Pilar's after days of blind waiting for game, like the slaves stockaded in the pens in Memphis, like oppressed people everywhere divining friend or foe from instinct. Whatever it was, she felt the presence of the figure at the rail through an inner telepathy. Without opening her eyes, she could sense the tension underlying his calm pose, feel the wanting in his body. At the same time, by some uncanny transmission between them, she also knew he recognized her knowledge of his need.

In her bunk in the Ladies' Cabin, Lottie closed her eyes without the slightest chance of sleep. The girl had never been so excited in her life. Mr. Barker, First Mate of the *Joy of Cincinnati*, had set up such a dither of emotion in her, she thought she'd lose her mind. All the others, the men and boys, transients and residents of Cape Girardeau, had been banished with the first flash of the First Mate's eyes. She realized now that this was what true love was really like. She'd only thought she'd known before. She'd never have done those things otherwise, never have allowed herself to get in her present condition. But this was different and she was different now. She'd been only a child then. Now she was a woman, a woman in love. This one was real. This could be forever.

How to advance the affair was another matter. How to bring about romance, real romance that is, whispered words and passionate embraces, baffled her. First, there was the Captain of the ship to contend with. The cranky old man seemed always to find something for the junior officer to do just when he showed the most interest in Lottie. Then, there was Mrs. Hill, her companion, more warden than friend, who never let her out of sight. Finally, Lottie couldn't understand why on earth the First Mate insisted on speaking to the dirty Indian squaw. In spite of all of them and their suspicious spying,

Lottie vowed to find a way.

At dinner the very next night, opportunity presented itself. At the captain's table, the first mate mentioned navigation and plotting the seas by the course of the stars. Lottie, a pastel vision in pale blue fichu, fixed her eyes on him, pretending to be enchanted with his knowledge of astronomy. The Captain looked likely to fall asleep. Next to the Captain, the Chief Engineer, named Leander something or other, a plain-faced, good-hearted boy no more interesting than Cape Girardeau lads, leaned across the table eager to join in. Mrs. Hill, carefully observing, nodded in time to some unheard rhythm in the discussion. No one could see the girl's blue satin-slippered toe stroke the back of the First Mate's calf. Nor could they see her eyes behind the fan peep at his lap to judge the effect of the dainty game under the table.

When they parted at the door to the Ladies' Cabin, the First Mate remarked, "The Constellation Orion is particularly notable at this time of year. I would very much enjoy showing it to you. On the deck."

The forward suggestion was instantly squelched by the ice that hardened on her guardian's face. But, when Barker bent to kiss her hand, Lottie bowed to receive the gallantry. "Two hours," she murmured.

At that muggy time after midnight when the Mississippi River cools itself and steams the creeks and inlets at the shoreline, Lottie sneaked from her bed and crept up the stairs. The Captain shifted about in his bunk with only a sheet over his knobby knees. Mrs. Hill, properly covered in full sleeping wear, including a lace cap to ward off the fevers born of night air, rested serenely, unaware of her ward's empty bunk on the other side of the curtain. Chief Engineer Smith didn't try to sleep while waiting for his cabinmate to return with tales of his escapade.

The First Mate met her at the door to steer her away from the port side of the wheelhouse where the Indians slept.

"That's Orion there. The one with the five-starred tail." He kept his voice low.

"Oh." Lottie pointed far to the left. "That one. The one with one, two, three stars in its body?"

"No, let me show you." He stepped behind to take her arm to point. "Now, sight down your little finger while I hold it directly toward the star."

His arm folded along hers; his body formed about her back. His lips were next to her ear, nibbled at her ear.

The girl was about to turn when they heard a footstep sound in back of them, something scurrying across the deck. They froze.

"Who is it?" a voice called out.

Startled, the First Mate pivoted about, freeing Lottie to pull back and stand alone.

"Who is it?" came again from the darkness.

It was the Indian woman, walking the deck, choosing this most awkward time to stroll. The First Mate blushed furiously in the dark.

"Oh, it's you, Princess. It's me, Mr. Barker, the First Mate," he said softly. "I was just showing Miss Bremerman the stars we use to steer engine canoe."

Lottie was silent, brushed at a nonexistent wrinkle in her skirt.

"What are you doing up?" Barker went on.

"It warm. I no sleep," Reyna replied, feigning the accent the whites expected.

"Perhaps you'd like to join us looking at the stars. We're looking at Orion. We use it as a compass at this time of year. But, then, your people have always known about the stars as guides." Talking, pretending legitimacy, seemed to calm the First Mate. He regained his composure. "Much of what we do is based upon ancient civilizations. The Egyptians knew, for instance . . ."

"Mr. Barker," Lottie interrupted. "The Indian lady," sarcasm dripped from the title. "The Indian lady couldn't possibly have an interest in science."

"My people know star well. Use many years."

Lottie fought back tears. The situation was becoming impossible. This might be their only chance alone together and the young man had actually invited the filthy heathen to stay. In two days they'd be in Port Huron where she was to leave the ship. She inched closer, touched his arm, "Perhaps we should go to the rear of the ship where our voices won't disturb the lady. Let her get her rest."

"You might be right, Miss Bremerman." The First Mate was no less distressed than the two women. The sudden shower of fortune, two ladies on the dark deck alone with him, was worse than none at all. "Will you excuse us, Miss Running Deer?"

Reyna bowed her head subserviently. "Of course, Captain. Running Deer sorry to disturb."

They had taken only two steps when Lottie shrieked and grabbed her side. A sharp needle of pain pierced just below the ribs. For a moment, unable to catch her breath with the stab of it, she could only moan, "Oh, Mr. Barker! Mr. Barker, oh!"

"What is it, Miss Bremerman? What is it?"

"I . . . aagh —" the sounds strangled in her throat. "I . . . ah, I'm having an attack. Vapors or heart. It burns like fire! Oh, it hurts! It hurts!"

The First Mate held her to him, not knowing how to help. Confused concern blanched his face. Princess Running Deer rushed over to support the other side.

"What happen, white lady?" she asked. "What happen, white miss?"

"I don't know. It was like a hornet sting, but a thousand times worse." She straightened stiffly, gripping the assisting arms hard in her tiny hands. "It's better now, but it burned like fire in my side."

"Are you all right? Shall we call the ship's surgeon?"

"No!" she gasped, terrified. She would die before being discovered on the deck after dark with the man. "No, I'm better now. Truly, much better now."

"You sure, white lady? We call doctor."

"I'm better now." She gulped at the night air, bravely forcing a wan smile. "I'm better now, but perhaps I should go below and rest. Please, help me to the Ladies' Cabin."

Neither the First Mate nor Lottie saw the Indian Princess restore the porcupine quill to its place among the others in her necklace.

Chapter 25

"You've agreed to stop the fuckin' ship?" he roared. He slapped his own face as if to wake himself from a dream. "Stop the whole fuckin' ship for a fuckin' piece of tail?" The Chief Engineer turned over in his bunk to face the oak bulkhead, unable even to look at his cabinmate.

Behind him, Barker seemed undaunted by Smith's dramatics. He knew the prank was bold; but, he also knew, when it came right down to it, he could count on the man's help. Smith would come around. He always did.

"C'mon, Leander," Barker bawled. "Get outa that bunk. This will take both of us and we've got to hurry."

"What's this *we* bullshit? Don't bother me, Jack," Smith muttered into the bulkhead. "This time you've gone too far. You're thinking with your balls instead of your brain. Remember, this is a packet ship. *We've* got a deadline to meet." Because they carried the mail, both law and contract held packet ships to scheduled arrival and departure times.

Barker said, "It'll only take two hours. I've got it all figured out. C'mon, you know I'd do the same for you. Besides the Old Man will never know the difference."

Smith stirred a little, relenting.

Finally, the engineer slowly turned and swung his long legs over the side of the bunk. In the one-piece underwear he wore summer and winter, he resembled a sleepy scarecrow propped up in the bunk. From their first days in school, the First Mate had been the leader of the two, overwhelming the engineer with his daring and bravado. Barker knew that Smith envied his devil-may-care lack of concern because when he participated in Barker's adventures, Smith thought some of the glory shone on him, too.

Barker held no such delusion. He didn't give it a thought. Smith was his friend, in the way best buddies often are, one a leader and one a follower. Men like the First Mate needed followers to help in their schemes, audiences for their genius. Barker liked and needed the engineer's admiration and rewarded his friend's loyalty by granting him the pleasure of his company.

"Now, tell me again," the engineer said. "Just what the fuck are WE going to do?"

"Well, you know the Indian girl. The one on A Deck, the little squaw traveling with her father, the chief."

"Yeah. I'd sure like to give her eight inches."

"What you mean is that you'd sure like to have eight inches to give her. "

The two spent hours each day discussing women, those they had bedded, would like to have bedded, and intended to bed. In that, too, Smith was apparently inferior. Neither ugly nor handsome, the engineer was simply undistinguished. His smile, open and broad, perhaps even charming, somehow lacked allure or the suggestion of masculine appeal.

"Anyway, after the other night, when Miss Bremerman took sick, the squaw gets kind of friendly like. Then, next day, I met her in the passageway without her father." Barker paused for effect. "I kind of figured, you know, that she'd been watching me all along; but with the chief there, I couldn't say anything. Anyway, to keep to the story, I met her alone in the passageway and she said, just as bold as you please, for me to come up to A Deck with her. Seems her old man was taking a leak and then . . ."

"Aw, come off it, she never did no such a thing."

"Man, that's exactly what happened, I tell you." The First Mate flipped his head to toss the handsome lock of hair away from his eyes. "But, the best part is that on the way to A Deck, the squaw bumps against me like it was the motion of the ship."

"Jaysus, man! Christ!" the engineer said, eyes wide.

"You're fuckin' right, she did. An' I got a good feel of her through that Pocahontas outfit, too."

"Mother of God, no?"

"Yeah," the First Mate rubbed his hand down the fly of his uniform. "An' I'll tell you it was somethin'!"

"God help you, if this gets out!"

"Yeah. Now, here's where you come in. I asked to see her later, but there's no way we can do it with A Deck full of passengers and crew and her father watchin' her like a hawk. Then, I asked if I could see her ashore, but she says her whole fuckin' tribe will be at dockside."

"Aw, fuck. So close and yet so far."

"Not so. Here's where it gets good. I came up with this brilliant idea. You're gonna love it."

"Oh, no, I'm not so sure. Somehow, I think this is where I come in to my everlasting regret."

"Naw, it ain't nothin' like that. Anyway, li'l Pocahontas says if we can get ashore for a minute that we can make time to become friends."

"Friends? That's a good one! Friends!"

"You're getting' the idea, Leander." Barker clicked his heels and saluted.

"If I ignore your smart talk, will you tell me where I come in?" the engineer grumbled.

"Well, you come in in a very big way, Mr. Smith. You're the one that's providin' the excuse for Pocahontas and me to go ashore for an hour or so.

That means stoppin' the ship. Now, out of the Great Lakes and in the canal on the way to the Ocean, we're only ten hours from Port Huron. So we need an emergency that can't wait. Somethin' we've got to do now."

"Such as?"

"Such as an oil leak. Even the captain knows that if we don't got oil, this tub'll blow higher than the big dipper. Now, if we've got oil trouble, either it's got to be repaired or we got to supply enough fresh oil to keep us going."

"But, we ain't got no oil leak."

"Oh, yes we do. When you go on watch, look at the pressure gauge on the 1700."

"Nothin' wrong with the 1700. I checked it myself two hours ago."

"Well, better look again. When I left the Engine Room, the needle was dancing around like St. Vitus."

The Chief Engineer straightened, expressive blue eyes almost pained in concentration. The greatest danger in steam engines was overheating the massive boilers that provided the power. Unstable valves, a shortage of oil or water, or the slightest additional pressure on the seamed copper plates could cause an explosion blowing them all to Kingdom Come. Hardly a month passed without word that it had happened somewhere in the fleet. Most often, the ship, the crew, and the passengers were gone in a few seconds, a giant firecracker of flame and steam and debris over the water.

Smith reached mechanically for his trousers. The chance of an explosion in the main boiler was not a joke.

"Don't look so scared, Leander," the First Mate said. "We easily got an hour or two before we shut down."

"What do you mean, we got an hour or two?" One long-johned leg had already found its way into the uniform.

"I mean we're only losing about three gallons an hour. Lost about six so far. . . . that gives us another couple of hours."

"How do you know?"

"Guess! Just guess how I'd know a thing like that." Barker smirked as though he'd discovered lost treasure.

"You!"

"Right you are, my friend."

"Oh, Jack I don't think we should take chances . . ." The Chief Engineer shook his head, turned pale at the seriousness of the trick. It was one thing to play practical jokes, another to risk five hundred lives.

"Too late, buddy. It's done. There's not really any danger because we know just what the problem is and how to fix it. The little redskin gets a hunk of this —" He grabbed a handful of his crotch. "And, you get a commendation from the Old Man for saving the day."

"What did you do?" Smith asked, the worried look still in his eyes.

"Ready to salute my genius? You know the valve at Number Three Aft, next to the bilge? Well, I simply completed a "Y" Cross to release oil, a little at a time, into the waste water system. When the level was down enough, I poured in all our extra oil to bring it back up to normal. Now, we're running on the last there is. Brilliant, is it not, my friend?"

"No. Brilliant it is not. You're taking a fuckin' big chance."

"Oh, don't worry."

"Seriously, Jack, if anything changes. The temperature, the pressure, a stress weakness in the inner boiler skin. You know, almost anything could make her blow."

"Don't be such a nancy, Leander. None of those things are gonna happen."

"But, they could!"

"But, they won't."

As if verifying the danger, the familiar noises of the ship magnified in the room. The continual thump of the logs thrown from bunker to boiler, the slap of the paddle wheel against the water, the smell of steam and hot oil, all of it suddenly was ominous. According to reports, there would be absolutely no warning of any kind before one of the gigantic boilers went.

"Right now, Mr. Smith, get the rest of your pants on and go check the 1700. The captain will let me take the gig for oil. We're about a half hour from Whitby Bay on Drummond Island. They'll have oil to sell there. And, while the supplies are being loaded, Minnehaha and me will take a quiet walk down the beach."

"All that's fine, Jack. You've got it planned down to the last minute."

"I told you it was a work of genius."

"But, you're forgetting something."

"What's that?"

"Me. What's in it for me? What do I get out of this caper? You've got the deal made with the Indian. O. K. She's probably got the crabs anyway. You've sabotaged the ship. Maybe kill us all. And, I get to go to the old man with a big cock and bull story so you can go ashore with the tribe tramp. But, what's in it for me?"

The First Mate stopped in mid-sentence. He had never considered any compensation for the engineer other than the bonus of being a part of his scheme.

Chapter 26

The captain alerted passengers and crew of a delay at Drummond Island to take on "supplies." It would save time, he said, to send a boat ashore rather than take the big ship into the harbor and tie up. When the time came, so the young officers wouldn't wonder why he didn't forbid his daughter's escapade, Hawk placed himself prominently in the line for the toilet. The First Mate and Chief Engineer made things ready for the supply trip. At last, the dangerously overheated engines were shut down and the big steamer bobbed from offshore moorings like a bottle in a washtub.

An hour after sundown, four oarsmen, two officers, and an Indian Princess lowered the captain's gig to go ashore. If the deck hands were curious about the woman, they didn't mention it aloud. A brisk, Atlantic breeze reminded Reyna how much she preferred saltwater air to the brackish climate of inland rivers.

Except for grunted exclamations from the seamen shoving the awkward gig away from the ship's side and handing in the officers and the woman, there was no talk. Seated aft, between the men on the U shaped bench at the rear of the longboat, Reyna kept her thoughts to herself. Nor did the junior officers speak. The Chief Engineer self-consciously examined the clasped fingers in his lap while the First Mate reared back to study the starry sky overhead. It would be a bright night. The constellation, Orion, winked down at the little craft.

The men couldn't know what this short journey meant to her. She couldn't escape the ugliness of the events of months that had passed, but returning to Drummond and Grandma's offered refuge for a while. It felt like going back in time. It was as though she'd never had a life in San Francisco. Now, there was none for her in New England. Perhaps, here, in the unhurried serenity of Drummmond, there would be time and place to think her way out of it. Or, into a real life for herself.

The First Mate jounced against her on the bench, interrupting her bittersweet reverie. She hated the greedy look in his eyes, grown impatient for that promised walk on the beach. His engineer partner peeked about, envious of his fellow officer's boldness. Reyna recognized the engineer's insecurity. *Unsure of what might be in store for him. Unsure of how he might respond.* She smiled to herself: she must bide her time with these two.

The old, familiar row of warehouse sheds of Whitby Bay seemed to ride out to meet the captain's gig. They had not changed. Closer and closer they came, scattering the gloomy mood simply by virtue of their unaltered faces. There was the Goodman Import House and the warehouse where fish was salted for shipment and rendered for liver oil. At first sight of the launch, the dark forms of two warehousemen, indistinct in the shadowed night, clambered about on the pier to identify the craft and to help with the lines.

On the dock, a little apart from them as they ordered the oil to be put in the boat, Reyna wanted desperately to run, but forced herself to appear calm, to stand there quietly. Although not cold, she shivered a bit and shrank her hands up into the sleeves of her decorated smock. Now and then, the warehousemen glanced at her with contempt. Stifling the desire to make a futile plea for help, she remained mute, turned away from their scorn. Her timing must be precise if she were to get away.

If she could elude them and make her way to Grandma's, there was still much to do. It was only a matter of time before the slave hunters of Memphis traced her north. Hawk would send for Ned and with his assistance and the Underground, there was a chance she could be smuggled to safety. It all hinged on breaking away from the ship's young officers.

At the end of the dock and warehouse row, the pilings fell away to a narrow beach of coarse sand and golf ball-sized pebbles. Three hundred yards from the ships, the beach ran headlong into an abrupt cliff of fallen rock, sheered away and dropped into the sea during some prehistoric time. An invisible goat path, barely the width of a human foot, made its way up the rugged, jutting promontory to reach the meadow opposite Grandma's store with its secret cellar.

"Let me take your arm, Princess," the First Mate said as they stepped onto the rough footing of the shore beyond the wharf. "Allow me to assist you."

The Chief Engineer fell back to follow ten yards behind them.

Barker's hand shook when he took her arm. A smug smile lighted his face. Unbeknownst to him, at that precise moment he had sealed his own fate. That single touch and condescending look removed Reyna's hesitation about manipulating the young men. While her plans had been forming, she had reserved an ounce of pity for their youth, but not now, not after the touch and look, the mirror into the First Mate's soul.

Now she knew him. Now, she felt only contempt. *The officer seems not to have the slightest qualm of morality, his trembling is derived from anticipation. His arrogant self-certainty glosses over any doubt that he should have less than superior intelligence, physique, and sexual prowess. He seems to believe women are fortunate to receive his favors. In this case, a mere Indian squaw is lucky indeed.*

When they had traversed a quarter of the beach, the fingers at her elbow squeezed. They stopped. The First Mate mashed his mouth on hers. Startled at first, she tried to yank herself free, then gave in to the rough embrace. She made herself yield, offered her mouth, formless beneath the hard kiss. In his roughness, his teeth bruised her lips.

Over his shoulder during the embrace, she could see the engineer halt, stare gape-mouthed, gawk in admiration..

Reyna, trapped in the First Mate's arms, let her body go soft, limply accepted the caresses, the hand at her rear, his tongue pushing its way into her mouth.

"You like me, don't you Princess? We be good friends, no?"

She said nothing.

"You like me, don't you, Princess? C'mon, admit it." His hand drew hers down the front of the uniform, forcing her to touch his stiffened sex. "You like me?"

Her head nodded twice.

"Say it, then," he insisted. "Say it."

"I like white man," she whispered.

Barker put both hands on her shoulders to push her down to the rocky beach. "Let's lay down here."

"No." She shook her head. "It better far from men on dock."

"Oh, I get it," he laughed. "You're shy."

He kissed her again, then his fingers groped for the breasts under the quill necklace.

"If that's what Princess want, we'll do it." He stood back. He took her arm again. "We'll do it, Princess. Let's us walk some more."

She allowed him to take her by the hand and guide her, his body jarring against hers. When they reached the end of the beach where the tides had hollowed out a nest alongside the cliff, she turned.

"This good," she said. "This good."

Behind them, Smith halted, too, and went back to his stupid gaping, shivering a little whether from cold or anxiety she could not tell.

Barker bent forward to cup her face with his hands. His mouth found her lips. All at once she was cooperative. Her tongue joined his in his mouth. Her delicate teeth nibbled at his lips and chin. She ground her body to his while she worked to unbutton his coat.

"Oh, Princess," he gasped. "I knew it, knew you wanted it."

Reyna stopped his talk with her lips. A good swift jerk and she had pulled his shirt tail free and sent her hands plunging inside to stroke his belly and chest, to scratch lightly at his nipples. He reached for her, fingers frustrated with not finding an opening in the leather top. Still, her mouth kept at him.

Nimble fingers undid his belt, ran down the buttons of his fly. The uniform trousers fell in a heap about his ankles. The fingers continued on to brush about his scrotum held up tight by the swollen penis. She fell against him, then, the porcupine quills sharp against his chest. Back the eager mouth went to his.

"Let's lay down," he begged. "I can't get your shirt off standing up like this."

Princess Running Deer bent down close to his rigid member. Behind them, she saw Smith lean forward.

"Not so fast. Slow down!" the Chief Mate cried out.

"Yes, Captain. Yes," she said. She made herself gasp, faking heated exertions. "You stay, please. How you say, 'lay down.' Running Deer go prepare for Captain. Lay down, please."

The Indian went behind the rock of the cliff to disrobe for him modestly, he supposed. Pulling the trousers off his ankles, the First Mate carefully folded and placed them where they would be handy as a pillow. The throbbing of his sex had not stopped and he hoped she'd hurry. The grainy sand scratched his naked ass when he sat, but a minor thing like skinned knees was nothing alongside what awaited. Forming thumb and forefinger in a circle, Barker signaled triumph to the engineer.

It was several minutes before Barker and Smith heard a scrambling sound, the disturbance of rock and gravel on the cliff above.

"Captain," a voice like the wind came from the sky. "Captain!"

"Who is it?" he called.

"It Princess Running Deer," came back. "I sorry, Captain. I cannot bed with you. You not yet man. I look. That thing between your legs is too small. My people have saying. 'It sin to take minnow before it grow up'."

Before the blush had reddened to the roots of his hairline, the officers heard her laughter fill the air about them.

Then, there was nothing.

Captain Van Buren was dragged from sleep by the banging of a heavy object on his cabin door.

"What is it?" he called out lamely, not fully awake but fearful about the nature of some new tragedy on this ill-begotten voyage. The beating on the door continued.

Hustling from his bed while tucking his nightshirt into his pants, he shoved his arms in the sleeves of his uniform jacket. As he hurried to the door, the captain muttered a vow to kill the steward who'd let someone find his way to his cabin without warning.

"Who is it?" he roared, yanking the door open to face Chief Running Fox who looked as mean as a cornered mountain lion.

Startled by the unexpected appearance of the Indian, Van Buren calmed himself a little, squeaked out, "What is it, Chief?

"You lose princess!"

Running Fox growled again, once more commencing to rap at the cabin door a staccato rhythm to accompany his demand. "Where is Little Deer? Where is my daughter?"

"Calm down, Chief. I don't know what you're talking about."

"Little Deer go on island with your young braves."

"She did what? Oh, my God!" Van Buren groaned, the color draining from his face. The old seafarer instantly understood what First Mate Barker had been up to. "How did this happen?"

The chief stopped pounding on the cabin door but was no less demanding. "Princess Little Deer and I argue about her marriage to tribe warrior she no like. But I make marriage deal with family of tribe warrior and in our tribe deal is honorable promise. She much mad and go ashore to take walk to settle her head. First Mate and boat now back from shore, but princess no come."

"I'm sorry, Chief. I will see that my First Mate is punished but what can we do? We can't stay here. We'are six hours behind schedule now and as a packet ship we have promised to be on schedule. What can I do?"

Running Fox held his head, seemed to shake the anger out of body and at last looked up. A sudden flood of tears poured from his blind eye.

"I think I know where Running Deer is," he said, thoughtfully. "She run to her mother's people who live two days' walk toward the rising sun from here. I think I can send hunting party to get her back."

Van Buren smiled and sighed with relief. That solved, he could take his time to find suitable punishment for a young officer who'd dallied with an Indian Princess whose father was a friend of the president of the United States.

"It will not be easy," the chief continued. "And it will cost many furs to bribe my wife's tribe, mink and raccoon and beaver. If you pay for skins, I can trade to return Princess to my village. This can be deal between us. You pay for skins, I no tell Great White Father about your young brave."

Although he nodded his head in vigorous agreement, pleased that the chief would settle for the bribe, Van Buren's stomach churned over the loss of the voyage profits, and his fingers itched to settle about his first mate's throat.

Chapter 27

Reyna scrambled and clawed her way up the narrow path on the cliff. Her breath came in raw gasps and she prayed the displaced rock falling into the abyss on her right would not give away her location. Her left elbow, which she'd struck against a rock outcropping, throbbed. Knees scraped, hands bruised and bleeding, she pulled herself along the steep precipice. She had no choice but to keep climbing. There was no going back.

She mourned, too, the temporary loss of her altar. She had known from the beginning of this plan to escape that she must travel lightly, leave her hands free for this climb, but she sorely missed the proximity of the spirit world of soothing herbs and seeds. The mere touch of the box had given her comfort aboard ship. Now, she must wait. Hawk was to transfer the cabinet to Ned who would bring it here when he joined her in a few months.

When at last she reached the rim of the cliff, she stood tall, squared her shoulders and gulped the air as she looked out over the bay. Despite a chill in the night, perspiration poured from her face and itched beneath her leather garment. Turning from the overlook, she headed toward the roadway that followed the crest of the hill. Grandma's house and store lay less than a mile away.

She limped along the country road, knees, hands, elbow stiff and sore. The moonlight filtering through a curtain of clouds cast a surreal pall on the clumps of sand dunes, low-lying shrubs and rock. An uneasy feeling settled upon her when the dark silhouette of the barn which had housed Grandma's store did not appear. She was certain the store lay near the sandy plain at the top of the goat path. Still, she plodded along, grateful for her escape.

All of a sudden, the silhouette of Grandma's house came into view, but she couldn't find the outline of the store. A moment later, she realized she was standing over it.

The charred remains of timbers and clapboard siding had caved into the foundation of Grandma's store. The store had burned to the ground and had fallen in upon itself. The acrid stench of burnt lumber still clung to the place.

Reyna cried aloud, "Oh, great Vodu! What has happened? Where is Grandma? Is she safe? Is this the foul play of marshals? Has Grandma been discovered and jailed?"

At that, she sped across the road, raced up the three steps, and beat upon the front door. When there was no answer, fearful of calling attention to herself, she paused a moment, thought back to her time on the island. Grandma had always kept a spare key in a crevice of the bottom step. *It was there.* Snatching it up, she cautiously turned the lock.

Closed up and unaired, the cottage reeked of mildew. A thick layer of dust had gathered on the surfaces. Otherwise, as she trailed from room to room, she saw that everything had been left tidy as though Grandma had simply gone away.

That night she reclaimed her old bedroom, superstitiously recoiling from the thought of sleeping in Grandma's room. The old slant-ceilinged room under the eaves, the primitive country made furniture, welcomed the fugitive like a warm heart.

Reyna rose before dawn to search in Grandma's closets for suitable clothing. Her luck was better than good for she found three dresses and a cloak, Quaker-styled in yesterday's fashionable color, Continental Brown. With only slight alterations, a bodice here, a waist there, she was able to make them presentable enough for the simple life of the island.

Her next task was to visit those members of the sect she had met on her visit with Mr. Shield when she first began working with the underground.

Reyna waited patiently for Zimmer's Hardware and Dry Goods to open. If anyone on the island knew what had happened — that is, what *really* happened to Grandma's store — Mary Ellen Zimmer would be the one. In the week since her return, Reyna had met a wall of silence as impenetrable as an iron mallet.

Like Grandma, Mary Ellen Zimmer was one of a kind. A thick-bodied midwestern farm woman, she could lift and haul, plow and harvest alongside the best men in the county. Knowing that, it was easy to guess that she'd take over her father's hardware store when he passed, and that farmers for miles around would accept her as an equal in what had always been a man's business. Reyna had suspected Mary Ellen worked with the railroad, but had no proof.

Hearing a shuffle of movement inside, she rapped lightly on the door.

"I'll be there in a minute," came from within.

When she opened the door, Mary Ellen stood back a moment, her aged eyes blinking in the morning light. Then she rushed forward to encircle Reyna in a full-bodied hug, crying out, "Oh, child, how good it is to see you — after all this time. I heard you were back and if you'd not come down today, I was going to come up there and see for myself."

She pushed Reyna away, held her at arm's length, "Land O'Goshen, you ain't changed a bit. Prettier than ever. How long are you here for?"

Caught up in the enthusiastic welcome, Reyna found herself laughing aloud. "I came all of a sudden — a business trip — and because I had a few days, I just thought I'd stop off and see old friends. And then ... and then, I found Grandma's place." She paused and caught her breath. A cloud of moisture floated across her eyes at the thought of Grandma and the loss of the store. Telling it to this woman who had been Grandma's best friend brought her grief to the surface.

"Come in, come in," Mary Ellen said. "You look like you could use a cup of tea."

When they had settled in the snug little kitchen behind the store, Reyna said, "I was shocked to learn of Grandma and the store."

Mary Ellen brought her cup to her lips, took a sip. "I'm sorry you had to find out that way, but we didn't know where to write — and, we'd heard about Edward so we didn't want to add to your troubles."

Watching her face, Reyna detected no sign of evasion in the woman's clear blue eyes. "What *did* happen? It just doesn't seem possible — after all these years."

Mary Ellen's hand flew over to cover Reyna's. She said, "Don't follow that direction, Reyna." She looked away for a moment as though studying a spot on the wall, looked back and continued, "You know all of us sometimes try to find something extraordinary about everyday events, especially when they bring grief. We don't know what hit the store, lightning or a lamp left on — could have been a lot of things that night, but in a way what did it don't matter. She's gone and nothing we can do will bring her back."

They spent the morning between customers in the store talking about old times, Grandma, people they both knew on the island, and new babies born to local families. No matter how subtly Reyna designed her questions, there was nothing more to be had from Mary Ellen Zimmer. Perhaps it was the woman's obstinacy about the matter that persuaded Reyna there was more to the story.

Mrs. Elizabeth Steele, a widow from Connecticut, had taken the old Pardee cottage down the lane. A soft, plump woman with pale blue eyes in a face as round as a sunflower except for her pointy chin, the woman was cheerful and bright albeit a little too talkative for Reyna's taste. But, that trait, she decided, might come in handy as a source of information. Close neighbors, it was natural for them to become friends, stopping to chat when they passed each other on the lane, in the fields and, from time to time, sharing tea in their kitchens.

It was on one of those occasions that Reyna learned the truth of the fire in the store and Grandma's death. Not wanting to appear too eager, Reyna had settled into her tea that afternoon, munching a bit of a gingerbread cookie, a specialty of which Mrs. Steele was quite proud. Looking deep into the older woman's milky blue eyes, Reyna asked calmly, "Can you tell me about my friend, Grandma, who died the night of the fire that burned her store?"

"Oh, my, yes," Mrs. Steele declared with her chirpy, bird-like voice. "We'd become quite good friends. We left each other space, don't you know, never intruded on our need for privacy. But, I found it a comfort to have her there and I think she felt the same about me."

"I'm certain she did."

"But Grandma was also very independent. She had her life and I had mine, don't you know."

Reyna closed her eyes, remembering the stubborn set of Grandma's chin. "Yes. I found her quite an inspiration," she said, "but, tell me what caused the fire in the store? What happened to Grandma?"

Mrs. Steele pursed her lips in a tight little circle and answered slowly, as though the telling was painful still, "Well, it was a Saturday night." She paused. "I'd not seen her for a couple of days . . . not that that was unusual . . . sometimes she'd just seem to disappear for days at a time. Oh, I always knew where she was with the store and all, people coming and going, of course. Sometimes she'd have night visitors, maybe a dozen people or more come to her house after dark. It wasn't that I was nosy or nothin', I just kept an eye out for the old lady, to make sure she was all right and not needing help, don't you know."

Yes, Reyna did know. She also knew that some of the comings were not so innocent. She reached her hand across the little table and patted the back of her hostess' hand in reassurance. "You're a wonderful neighbor."

"Anyways," Mrs. Steele went on, rolling her eyes for effect. "It was a terrible stormy night with wind howling off the harbor. I looked out my back door and couldn't see my hand in front of my face. It was pitch black, but I was scared enough to think I saw shadowy figures moving and running around Grandma's store. It gave me a fright, I can tell you. I set about locking my own shutters as tight as a drum. Anyways, sometime later, I peeped out again and I could see what looked like the sky lit up over there, brighter and brighter and dancing in the dark. I nearly fainted when I realized the store was on fire!"

"And I swear to God," Mrs. Steele continued, "I heard what sounded like human screams. Loud cries like people in pain. I've not told anyone else but you. Now you can see why I hate those storms!"

Mrs. Steele fell silent and gave her guest a look so piercing that Reyna realized that the widow feared she'd not be believed. Reyna knew the woman sought confirmation that she'd not dreamed it all in some ghastly nightmare.

"Oh!" Reyna said. "It must have been horrible! You've been very brave to go on living here alone."

Mrs. Steele nodded. "Well, I ran for my coat and hat and winter boots, even though I didn't have an iota of an idea in the world about how I could help but I *had* to do *something*. I couldn't just stay here as worried as I was about Grandma and all."

"No, surely not."

"Well, when I got up there it was really all over. They say the wind must have broken a window pane and blown over an oil lamp. The store being made of very old wood and all, the fire was mostly over by the time I first noticed it."

"How brave you were. What a good neighbor," Reyna exclaimed.

"Then, I run across the road to Grandma's and up the stairs. The door was half open, the wind opening it and banging it shut, over and over again, a banging like the sound of a cannon. And . . . and, there was Grandma sprawled out in the front hall, eyes wide open but gone to the Lord. Seems she'd had a heart attack on her way out to save the store. No more'n got the door open before it hit her. It was peaceful." Mrs. Steele's voice suddenly went soft. "And it's a blessing if you ask me."

"Yes, " Reyna murmured, "a blessing."

"She suffered no sufferin' and she was saved from having to see her store like that. That store was all she had."

Reyna bowed her head nodding. She knew then that she'd never know for certain what caused the fire or what had been in the cellar of the store.

Chapter 28

Life on Drummond Island crept along at its own pace, an unhurried snail's crawl. Nothing had changed. The island was as settled as the dust in Grandma's unoccupied house. Nothing marred what had been. Although no doubt legally Phoebe's cottage now it would always be Grandma's.

It was hard to believe she was gone. Sometimes Reyna had to remind herself that Grandma was not just in the other room. Now and then, she called to her in the world beyond. *Help me, Grandma. Use the wisdom of the spirit world and tell me what to do.*

In the early morning, she often went for walks to the settlement at Whitby Bay carrying bouquets to the sunken place that had once been a mound over the remains of Grandma. She went to the store and kicked about the rotted timbers roiling with ants. She often paused to dream there, swept away with remembering how exciting it had been when she first came here to learn about the railroad.

Every day she hiked up to the spear grass meadow overlooking the bay to watch for Ned on the daily packet ship. With no one around in the meadow, she loosened her hair from her bonnet and pins. Thanks to Vodu and Lucy and her unknown father from Virginia, she had good thick hair and it had grown long again. The wind took it like a sail.

On the island, temporarily safe from slave hunters and traders, her fears gradually dissipated and the days were long with waiting for Ned. While the solitude allowed her to collect the scattered fragments of her life; she still was not content. That part of her that gloried in the thrill of danger grew restless with inactivity. There, in the timeless quiet on Hammond Island, Reyna began to put together the intricate pieces of a new plot.

She knew without asking that she could rely on Ned. It had become their way. It didn't occur to her that it should be different. He was nothing more than a useful and sometimes sexually satisfying pawn to her. Besides, she had a new scheme to counter any reluctance he might have. Now, she wanted him and bitterly resented the distance that separated them. *Hurry. Hurry back to me.*

When at last she spied the packet ship, she ran, hair and skirts flying, all the way to the wharf. Arriving breathless, hair gone wild in the wind, it wasn't until she saw people glancing at her with the special look reserved for a mad woman that she realized what she must look like. She slapped the dust out of her skirts, straightened the waistband of her gown and hid her hair in the plain brown bonnet.

Her assessment of Ned was brutally accurate. He had paced the deck of the packet ship all the way from Boston.
　　He leaned hard against the rail, too anxious to sit, oblivious to the spray of wind and salt air stinging his face. He could think of nothing but how she would look, hope for nothing more than her favor. The way she used him had not changed that. If anything, he wanted her more than ever.
　　He supposed — no, he knew — he was in love with her, but it was a most confounded love. Love was supposed to be a joyous thing, a walk in the clouds. Their affair had never been likethat at all. When his heart and head and loins ached with craving, she either sent him away or left. He could never do enough to please her, didn't even dare confess what he felt because of the scorn such an admission would surely bring.
　　How to save her was another matter. He had troubling news to tell. Her escape would not be easy. He was prepared to lay down his life for her and the crisis was so dangerous that sacrificing himself was not entirely improbable.
　　Then he saw Reyna running like a school girl to meet the ship, throwing propriety aside, her skirts fluttering above her ankles, beaded mocassins on her feet, indecently bareheaded, swinging her bonnet by its strings. She sprinted from the high meadow, pitched recklessly down the goat path on the side of the cliff, and swept across the stony beach to the harbor. He could see her flaming cheeks and heaving chest as she joined the little crowd on the dock. Only then did she halt to plop the bonnet on her head, set it in place, and poke inside the loose strands of hair at her temples.
　　From his position at the rail, Ned looked down, waved and smiled. She never failed to amaze him.
　　"It's good to see you, Ned," she said, as calm as the wind after a storm. It vexed him to know she could play-act so well for he never knew when she was genuinely sincere or pretending to be.
　　But the sudden flush of moisture in her eyes was genuine as she eyed the outline of her altar in the carpet bag at his feet. "I'm glad you could come, Ned," she said.

On the dusty lane to Grandma's cottage neither of them spoke much. What conversation they began was just as quickly aborted, a sudden blurting out, then drawing back. After the tumultuous events of their time apart and the sharpness of the waiting, now that they were together, it seemed they couldn't bring themselves to speak their minds.

"I've missed you, Reyna." Stubbornly plodding on, she didn't even look his way. "We were worried. There was no word of you at all."

"Well, we were all right," she said. He looked foolish in Drummond with his Virginia farmer's clothes, the bulky carpetbag banging his leg. She was grateful for this island composed of a vast mixture of races, red and black and white, where Ned would not be thought different because of his color. She continued, "And when we weren't all right there was nothing to say. We got through it somehow."

They were silent again. The afternoon sun dampened his forehead. Her head hurt from squinting in the sun.

"I hated to see Fairfield go. It was good land," he said simply.

"Couldn't be helped. Maybe it was just time to move on."

Little puffs of dust rose and fell on the path and startled grasshoppers leaped across in front of them.

"I need to talk serious while you're here, Ned. The farm is gone. A thing of the past. What we need to talk about is the nexts . . . the nexts are all there is. The pasts are all behind us."

"I 'spect you're right," he sighed.

Mrs. Steele stood in the door of her place as they passed.

"Afternoon, Reyna," the widow called out. "I see the boat finally got here."

"Yes, ma'am!" She waved in greeting without slowing down. "This here's my friend, Ned."

"Howdy do," Ned called out politely, saluting the widow with his soft brimmed hat.

They walked on then, their strides lengthening and hastening, toward the cottage that would be theirs together. This would be the first place they could openly share. Here, with the nearest neighbor a hundred yards away, they could scream or laugh out loud if they chose. Still, she found it odd to show the cottage to him. In a way, she hated sharing it, resented surrendering her solitude and memories.

The cottage seemed so small, so crude and Spartan. Perhaps having always seen her in grandeur, he'd not like it.

"As you can see, it's not elegant, but this is a special place. It's where I began my work with the underground."

"I know that."

Just inside the door, she was about to tell him to drop his bag anywhere, had actually formed the words with her lips, when he grabbed her.

"Oh, Reyna, don't you know?" he muttered. "Don't you know that I know what this place . . . what Grandma was to you? Thank God you had this place to come to." His lips covered hers, smothered her talk while he kissed the mouth he had wanted for six months.

She reared back, stumbling against the carpetbag. "You must be weary," she said curtly. "Let me fix a cup of tea."

The big man, outsized in the cottage grown small with his presence followed her to the tiny kitchen where she readied the water and added kindling to the fire. All the while, he hungrily watched her every movement.

They sat at the table where she and Grandma had sat, Reyna in the chair of the old woman. The mug warmed her hand and the setting sun streaked the windows just as it had then.

"Ned," she said, gently caressing the rough knuckles holding the country mug. "Ned, I may be cold sounding, but I don't mean it. It's just my way."

"I know that," he said. His eyes glistened. "I've come to know a lot since I came to know you."

She continued stroking his hand, glancing up from time to time, smiling. "I don't mean anything by it."

His hand opened and caught hers like a bird on the wing. "But you could go a little softer, ma'am. And you could go a little slower."

As she freed her hand, her voice took on a sharpness. "It's beginning to get cold in here," she said, then looked away toward the hearth. "Please, Ned, build a fire. Not a big fire, just enough to take the chill off."

The farmer set about the chore quickly, seeming glad to turn from her unspoken irritation. "Now, that's cozier, isn't it?"

Again, she remembered how it had been in this place, just the two women then. *Help me, Grandma,* rang in her ears, actually moved her soundless lips. *Tell me what to do.* The image faded and was gone.

She studied Ned's silhouette, his golden complexion, duskier in the fading light, before she began the conversation she needed to have with him.

"It's about the work," she said. "I want us to reorganize. Regroup. We'll have to work out of Boston. Slavers are getting more and more angry with abolitionist states. For them, it's a battle they've already lost. The sad thing is that the more impossible their situation gets, the harder they fight. We must work faster . . ."

He put out his hand, fingers across her mouth to silence the talk. "Stop," he said. "There will be no more." His hands went to her shoulders leaning over the table to pull her closer. "No more."

"No, Ned. I can't stop so long as a single one of our people is in chains."

"Goddamnit, woman!" he exclaimed. "Do I have to say it? You're through! It's over for us."

They stood then, found each other and clung together. Head buried against the big chest, she could only mutter between clamped teeth. "I'll never be through, not so long as I still have a breath. Do you understand? Not so long as I live. We'll go to Boston and reorganize. They may know who I am, but I still have resources."

Again his hands found her shoulders, this time to hold her away. He shook his head sadly; his big, aquamarine eyes clouded with hurt.

"No, Reyna, there will be no more organization. The traders know who you are, but you have no friends on the other side either. They look for you, too."

"What are you talking about?"

His voice lowered to a rasping growl. "Just that. You have no friends in Boston anymore. They've arrested the Quaker women who helped you. The marshals are in Nequassett looking for Pilar."

"Arrested? Who?"

"The Quaker ladies who helped you. All of them. Marshals came the day after you left. Took the ladies away in your clothes. They were tried and imprisoned for over a month and now all the Quaker meetings are under surveillance."

"It can't be! Not in the north!"

"Oh, but it is."

"How awful!" Her hands flew to cover her face.

"Yes, it's bad and worse. The Quakers blame you for it."

"Me?"

"The word has gotten out that you talked."

"Me?" she cried out, unable to say more.

"Who else? It was your idea. You were the only one who knew."

"But, it could have been anyone . . . an accident . . . coincidence."

As the enormity of the charge sank in, her almond eyes widened with alarm.

"Sure it could." His head wagged slowly from side to side. "But, there's no proof of any of it. All that people know for sure is that you were the only one who knew. So you're to blame. They want nothing more to do with you."

Seconds lengthened to minutes as the magnitude of his news sank in. Goodwoman Stork and her daughter and friends jailed and publicly shamed, all because of her. Charles Pilar hunted. It seemed the end had finally come. But, still, she could not, would not, leave it alone. She could never lead a passive life. She could alter her plans, but would not leave the work.

It was after passionate lovemaking under the eaves that she told him. They studied each other in wonder at the ecstasy they shared when the rest of their lives were filled with despair.

"Are you sure, Reyna?" he asked, at last. "Are you sure it's safe for us?"

"Ned, leave it to me," she answered, a hint of irritation in her voice. "I'll take care of it."

The instant her new plan was born, Reyna pursued it as though there had never been any other. Perhaps this fresh idea had been there the whole while, buried in her, just waiting for adversity to flush it out. She had no intention of giving up, certainly not for a man as lacking in ambition as Ned.

Fall had passed and winter sent bitter Lake Huron breezes biting through the marrow of their bones. Reyna had forgotten the cut of the island winds, how one never seemed to get warm. In the old days, she had liked it, had been exhilarated by its icy fingers scratching at her face, bringing tears to her eyes. Now, the cold was just another annoyance. She itched to be away from here.

Maybe it was the waiting that finally broke through her pretense. After all, it had been five months since she had escaped from the First Mate on the island, but she saw no way to leave. Word had come that the Boston house, its furnishings, and the late Mr. Shield's brokerage business had been sold for twenty thousand dollars, a quarter of their value. Now she must delay till Ned carried an urgent message to Captain James and Phoebe Gardner in Boston.

When their fight began, it suddenly became obvious that what had been perfectly plain to her, hadn't been clear to him. The suggestion hadn't seemed unusual when she made it; after all, it was part of their plan, or at least part of *her* plan for them. Consequently, she was caught unawares when his face went gray with a sudden drain of blood. His look said he thought she'd gone mad.

"Go back to the underground?" he stuttered when he found his voice.

"Yes, Ned. You heard me right." She said it sharply as though scolding him.

"I believe you're actually serious, Reyna."

"I have never been more serious in my life."

He scratched his head. "If I wasn't hearing this with my own ears, I'd have said it was a bad dream."

"Stop it, Ned. We've already talked it all out."

"Then, let's not go."

She cut her eyes at him defiantly. "Don't . . . be . . . ridiculous."

"Ridiculous? I don't think it's ridiculous! Putting your head in a lion's mouth, *that's* ridiculous."

She stared at him incredulously. It had taken forethought to develop an alternative plan. His anger demonstrated his lack of appreciation for her cleverness. At the moment, any explanation seemed pale and she didn't want to appear defensive.

Ned kicked the packed carpetbag at his feet. "Well," he spit out. "I don't need this old grip. I'm not going any place."

"Don't be a fool," she snapped. "You are going to see the Gardners, then you're coming back and we're going to New York."

Ned turned away and went to the window to scowl at the desolate ruins where the store had been. His face was as sullen as the gray afternoon.

Reyna stood rigidly, debating whether to rail at him, storm out of the house, or command him to do as he was told. The pulse in her temple throbbed. After a moment, when she had calmed, she crossed over behind him, ran her arms around his waist, and lay her head against his back.

"It won't be so bad, sugar," she crooned.

The warm softness, the woman against him, melted him a little and his stiffness gradually subsided. He turned to take her in his arms and stare intently into her mysterious golden eyes.

"Don't you see, Reyna, that I'm just looking out for you?"

Her mind flashed back to Hawk's smoky quarters at Nequassett. This was the argument Hawk and Pilar had used then. Concern for her. Now it seemed even more like emotional blackmail. Wing clipping, she thought, to make her accept the supine position of women and Negroes.

"No," she said. "I'll not have it."

"You don't understand," he argued. "I'm afraid for you . . .for us. I could never forgive myself if something happened to you."

"No," she said before he put a forefinger across her lips to silence her while he went on.

He said, "I'm afraid of what the running and hiding will do to us. We've taken so many to Canada, why don't we go to Canada where we can be who we are? . . . and free. Not having to live by looking back over our shoulders any more."

"That can never be for me," she said. "Don't you see? Those of us who *can*, *must* help." She suddenly saw at the heart of this debate, the power of the blackmail the men in her life had used. She turned that logic on him. "Ned if you love me, you will support me in this."

He stared at her, a dumbfounded confusion clouding his eyes. Ned kissed her then, trembled a little rekindling the flame of his love in spite of his doubts. Working the same magic she always had, she returned the kiss, scratching his back with her nails. They walked arm in arm across the room to retrieve the carpetbag.

At the door, they exchanged a short kiss of farewell and she captured his right hand to bring it to her breast. Then, Reyna wrapped his fingers about the grisgris charm suspended in her cleavage.

"Ned," she purred sweetly. "Remember this. Remember the grisgris. If you ever doubt me again, I'll use it to fix you. Believe me, I can do it. You know I've got the power."

Part Four

The Rebel

Chapter 29

New York!

She was hardly aware of Ned in butler's livery at her side. She had traveled as Miss Reyna Shield, accompanied by her servant. They talked of momentary things like the weather and speculated about how changed things would be, but they kept their innermost thoughts to themselves. She was here to see to the business of freeing slaves and the charismatic abolitionist, John Brown. She had considered ordering new clothes, expensive new styles, flattering things to make her look prettier, or at least not so plain alongside Phoebe's radiance; but, then, at the last minute, changed her mind and settled for the Quaker garments that she had grown comfortable wearing on Hammond's Island. She was decidedly unenthusiastic about a reunion with the Gardners and, while it had been convenient in the days following Edward's death, she now resented the fact that the captain controlled her bank account.

At last they were on the East River within sight of the Empire City. The harbor lay cluttered with craft of all sorts, steamers and clippers, fishing boats and tugs. Reyna could see that here the merchant ships meant business and went about it with efficiency and speed. Railway lines and the Erie Canal linking Manhattan to the west and north and south had divested Boston of its title and proclaimed New York the foremost seaport in America, perhaps the world.

The sight of Broadway took her breath away. A double line of rails for horse drawn cars furrowed the roadway thick with carriages, wagons, and omnibuses. Traffic crept along a foot at a time. Pedestrians ran for their lives crossing from the east to the west and back. Streams of yellow and red omnibuses raced in wider parts and locked wheels in narrower sections of the road. Daring young businessmen, whipping the flanks of fast trotting horses, veered in and out of the crowd. Omnibus drivers never completely stopped, slowed only enough to allow passengers to jump off into six inches of garbage and mud and horse droppings. Above it all the constant thunder of policemen roared, "Move on! Move on!"

Her eyes ached with the strain of gawking at the magnificent buildings there. They passed Stewart's dry-good store, the greatest stock of merchandise under one roof on any continent. The immense solid marble building six stories high, occupied a full block. Broadway hosted Phineas Taylor Barnum's flag-bedecked museum, a gigantic opera house and three lavish theaters beside dozens of taverns and groggeries. Mansions of the rich, who were now being called "millionaires," presided over it all with granite and brown stone majesty.

Reyna was amazed to see, too, amidst the incredible display of wealth, that New York also cruelly ignored the poverty squatted in squalid alleys. Children in rags, mothers with the doomed eyes of starvation — whole families slept in doorways.

Finally, she was dismayed by sights and smells more odious than she'd known in the early days in San Francisco. Mire was ankle deep on Broadway, the narrow cross streets nearly impassable with refuse. Decaying garbage, cast off boxes and cartons, household wrecks, rusting utensils and piles of coal ashes lay where they had been thrown. By the time their carriage reached the St. Nicholas Hotel, Reyna had begun to rethink her image of the glamour of the Empire City.

Her dream of Eastern elegance was restored somewhat by the St. Nicholas Hotel which was so grand as to be intimidating. Green Venetian shutters screened all six hundred rooms of the white marble palace. A glassed in "sky parlor" on the roof permitted ladies to dawdle over tea and scones while laconically observing the panorama of fashionable nabobs promenading on Broadway six floors below.

On the way to the Gardner's suite, Reyna and Ned sank into rich carpets with half inch pile and were humbled like country cousins by the vast hallway of coffered mahogany doors. Neither spoke for fear of shaming themselves before the officious bellboy.

Phoebe and Captain James greeted them from the parlor of their suite, an elegant room in perfect mid-Victorian taste, but one that Reyna now found dark and depressing. The Georgian sofa and chairs, the Pembroke tables, and the Chinese import jardinieres seemed too pre-planned, too decorated. Undoubtedly carefully constructed, still the room was devoid of character. At that, for the first time, with painful clarity, Reyna realized the parlor of the Gardner's at the St. Nicholas was well-matched with them. They were like that.

Phoebe wore a gossamer, multi-tiered crinoline gown of as faint a color as her gray-blue eyes, a fashion that Reyna thought resembled a tea cozy. Alongside the confection of his wife, James, in a severe blue frock coat and beige trousers, seemed to be of a different species. His sandy hair, now lightened with the first streaks of gray, was flattened around the temples from his top hat which also left a red crease across his forehead.

The Gardners seemed strangely ambivalent in their welcoming Reyna whom they'd not seen since those final days at Louisburg Square when they'd quarreled about money and their damaged reputations by the guard outside the house. Suddenly appearing to remember his manners, the captain rushed forward, took both her hands in his great paws, and blustered, "My dear, Reyna. How good it is to see you. We feared every day for your safety."

Ned irritated Reyna by staring at his feet, looking the part of the obsequious servant.

Phoebe went to her husband's side and reached out to take Reyna's arm. "My dear," she said. When she bent toward Reyna the movement set the crinolines to bouncing like waves in a swimming pool. "You've not changed a bit. Come, let us sit down while you tell us all about yourself."

Reyna, suddenly aware that they had forgotten Ned, put in hastily, "Captain. . . . Phoebe . . . you remember our friend and foreman, Ned, from Virginia."

"Yes, yes, of course," Gardner said gruffly. "How are you?"

In her mind's ear, Reyna could almost hear the unspoken word "boy" in his tone.

The Boston couple took slat-sided Georgian chairs opposite a wood backed sofa for Reyna to begin a discussion that quickly became more cross-examination than conversation. Gardner drew himself up pompously in his chair, said, "Well, Reyna tell me. Why did you come back? Your letter was so mysterious about business and meeting someone, I'm curious."

Realizing that what she had to say would shock the Gardners, she carefully teased out a reply. "I'm on my way to meet a man from the West who's been very active in the cause."

She paused, glanced down at her nails diffidently. Gardner and Phoebe dared a quick peek at one another.

"You've probably heard of him. The man I've come to meet is Mr. John Brown."

"John Brown!" they both exclaimed, almost at once.

"Reyna!" Gardner added. "You don't know what you're saying. That man is poison."

"Tell me, Captain." She smiled faintly, leaned back against the support railing of the sofa. Although she had learned a great deal about Brown, she also valued information. "Tell me what you know of him."

"Well," he sputtered. "I'm surprised *you* know anything at all about him. But, if you knew as much about him as we do, you'd have nothing to do with him. I'm afraid you've wasted the trip if John Brown is what this is all about."

"Why?"

"He has the insane idea of establishing his own country. That's one reason. He believes he can set out a territory and that all the slaves will leave their masters and go flocking there. His nonsense is turning people against abolition and undoing all the work we've done. We've almost got the votes we need to abolish slavery. If not during this session of congress, then the next. Now, this idiot comes along and wants to start a rebellion. It looks bad for all of us. If he keeps up, we'll lose those senators who're sitting on the fence and we'll have to start all over."

Reyna thought a moment, then said, "But the man may be correct. Maybe the slaves *would* leave the plantations if they had a place to go."

"Don't be foolish!" James ridiculed. "John Brown plans to claim land inside the United States as a new territory. If the government would allow such a thing, which it won't, how could he feed and clothe the slaves till they learned to make the land pay? Surely you of all people can imagine what *that* would cost?"

His words brought a rush of San Francisco memories swarming back to her. Yes, she knew what that work cost and she knew how to go about it. She had done that work a long time ago. San Francisco. She said simply, "I could help with that."

"You?" James questioned. His skepticism was duplicated no less plainly on Phoebe's face. "You can't be serious."

"Oh, but I am. I want you to prepare a treasury draft for thirty thousand dollars. I'm prepared to pay the entire amount to Mr. Brown if his cause is justified."

"Don't do it," the captain said, chewing agitatedly on the corner of his mustache. Phoebe picked at a loose end in the petitpoint upholstery of her cushion. "I tell you the man is mad. He says he wants the money to buy food and guns for defense, but the truth is, if he gets his way, he'll lead us straight to bloodshed."

"I've seen a war coming from the beginning," Reyna replied serenely, unperturbed by his conclusion. "Slavery cannot help but eventually lead to war."

"I can't believe I'm hearing this, Reyna." His voice was taut and incredulous. "If you don't believe me, check with others, people you do respect. Wendell Phillips. William Morris. William Garrison. No one you know would give the man enough shot and powder to blow himself to kingdom come."

The more he talked, the redder his face became, the more violently he gnawed on the piece of mustache. His own words seemed to inflame him further.

"Well, thank you, Captain," she said coolly, standing to halt his rhetoric. "You've been helpful. I appreciate that."

"I'm sorry," he said, apologetically. "It does seem a shame for you to waste the trip."

"Don't feel badly about that. It's not wasted. We'll visit you once more when we've finished our business in Chatham."

"Chatham?"

"Yes," she smiled sweetly. "I'm attending a convention called together by Mr. John Brown in Chatham, Canada."

Chapter 30

At exactly 6:00 a.m., Fred Crawford left his little house on Short Street near the wharf overlooking the Thames River in Chatham, Ontario. He carried a bucket of white paint in each hand. Crawford turned up Kings Street and spied his friend, Tiberius Montgomery, who had left his own warm bed and was now struggling under the ungainly heft of a ten foot wooden ladder. Up so early on a Saturday morning, the two men hurried to finish painting the Negro schoolhouse on Princess Street before ten o'clock.

Neither man was a painter by trade, but Crawford had volunteered and with a tongue as slick as Tom Sawyer's had persuaded his friend, Montgomery, to help. Their after hours occupation to make the schoolhouse look spanking new took longer than they had thought and, although they'd already worked past dark two nights this week, there was still some touching up to be done. Despite the early hour to be up on a Saturday and the fatigue of a full week at the foundry of Thos. Martin and Sons, Ltd., a certain exhilaration lightened Crawford's feet that morning. The voluntary job had made him privy to earthshaking events.

"Man! You is about the luckiest nigger . . ." he started to say half aloud, then amended it to, "Negro . . . You is the luckiest Negro in the whole world." The new word, "Negro," still felt strange in his mouth, like it didn't belong there, but it was preferable to the one it replaced.

The pretty little township of Chatham was still asleep and dew furred the white frame cottages and picket fences. The gray-violet dawn haze lent a luminescence to the clapboard sidings and gleamed in the mist rising from the peaked roofs. In a precipitous, unlikely gesture, Crawford sucked in a deep breath of the morning, an inhalation that was tinged with an almost religious or medicinal feeling as though the air itself had a healing quality. And for Crawford and two thousand others like him, perhaps it had.

Chatham, sixty-five miles east of Detroit on the Canadian side of Lake St. Clair, had just about everything a person could want: a public stable, a feed store, a general store, a boarding house, two hotels, and a saloon. Chatham merchants supplied the needs of the town, the farmers from the surrounding country, and the ships and sailors who buzzed about the wharf on the Thames. To round out the town's self-sufficiency, there were also five churches and three schools.

As he walked up Kings Street before the town awakened that morning, the unexpected surge of well being so overwhelmed Crawford that he was forced to put down one of the buckets in order to wipe his eyes on the back of his sleeve. The town had come to mean a knowing and loving familiarity, and he wished to God he'd never known any other.

The peacefulness of Chatham was, by itself, more than ample to tug at his heart. At that hour, nothing stirred; even Big Boy. The large yellow tomcat from Sandy Taylor's Stable, Horses: Riding and Working, lay sleeping off a feast of field mice in the straw of the barn. The oil was nearly burned out of the lamp at Jeffery's Bait Store because Jeffery closed at seven, figuring that a man who wasn't fishing by six o'clock wasn't serious enough to be worth waiting for. Nothing moved at Grime's Feed and Fertilizer, neither light nor noise. Old man Grimes never opened before nine on Saturday. The smell of frying bacon was just beginning to float out the back door of the Britannia Rules Hotel, Ten Clean Rooms for Guests. At the core of the vortex of smoke and spattering grease creating that odor, the Widow Jones was wielding a spatula like a dueling foil. As good as her breakfasts were, they were nothing compared to her peach cobbler. Crawford's mouth went all juicy just thinking about it.

Now, the empty middle part of him complained loudly as he walked by without even so much as putting his happy black face in the widow's back door. Today was too important to waste on his belly.

The Villa Tavern, owned by the Barbour family, was full to overflowing, anyone could tell that from the horse apples back by the barn where, for all the extra business, no one had had a chance to shovel up. Probably had the horses two to a stall, too. That morning, the Villa seemed bigger, somehow swelled with the significance of its guests. Fred craned his neck on the chance that he might spot one of them, but it was too early and he hurried on.

Fred was one of the few who knew that history was being made in Chatham that day. In spite of the town's large number of self-manumitted slaves, less than a hundred people in the whole town knew what was to happen. Widow Jones didn't know, for instance, nor did old man Grimes. Jeffery, down at the bait store, didn't know even though a man who ran a bait store generally knew everything. Crawford was one of the few who knew and he nearly burst his britches with the knowledge. Just thinking about that, his own importance, made him step a little livelier, close his mind to the thought of the widow's biscuits and his ears to his protesting stomach. After another few steps he had to set down the bucket again and use his sleeve once more.

At the school, Tiberius was just where he'd said he'd be, but his posture was hardly energetic. Crawford's long-limbed friend had rested his ladder at a thirty degree angle against the schoolhouse wall and was half-leaning, half-lying, on it, fast asleep standing up.

"Jumpin' Gee Hosephat!" Crawford declared. "I swear, this man's gonna be sleep through his own funeral."

Tiberius Montgomery was a lanky six footer, the color of wood ash. When open, his eyes were quick and bright in a droll, round face that was cut in two by a smile of flashing white teeth. Despite his unceasing sense of humor, Tiberius was also an earth-bound realist, determined to enjoy the day, the minute, that was now. He was not even a dreamer during the ten hours of every day he spent sleeping.

Crawford stood a moment, hands on his hips still clutching the buckets, contemplatively considering the thin, black frame sprawled up the ladder. Tiberius' thick lips blubbered with steady breathing. For a moment, Crawford was tempted to snatch the ladder away and bring the rest to a crashing conclusion. He settled for putting the paint buckets down, removing his cap, and briskly cuffing the sleeper about the chest and upper arms.

Tiberius snapped his eyes open, looked about startled.

His partner grumped, "What you doin' fool?"

"Jes gettin' my beauty res'," the other drawled, smacking his lips between sleepy yawns.

"'Beauty res'? You should better be born a bear, then you got all the winter to do it in. Look like you needs it, too, boy 'cause you sure is some kind of ugly. Now get your ugly self together. We got work to do."

The two backed off from the building, a long, straight-sided affair of four rooms, one for each two grades of the school. They needed only to trim the window frames and sashes to finish it off. The shiny gloss of fresh white paint caught the first rays of sunrise and the smell of turpentine wafted pungently about the yard.

"It look like a new building. Just the place for a convention," Crawford said, admiring their work.

Even Tiberius squared his shoulders a bit, proud to have been a part of it. He had never been to school, didn't know how to read or write.

"That sure is a pretty sight. You ever think you gone see a schoolhouse for colored chillern, Tiberius?" The comment was rhetorical for he knew the answer. More than their church, the schoolhouse was the brightest beacon of their freedom; its very existence signified how far they'd come and why.

"A schoolhouse for colored chillern," he added. "Now we gonna have us a constitution."

Tiberius grunted noncommittally, but looked about nervously as though afraid of being overheard. He was less sure of the value of a constitution than the worth of reading and writing.

"Just put your mind on that, Tiberius, we'll have a constitution. A constitution! We gonna be part of history, man. You be tellin' you gran'chillern about this."

"Oh, man," Tiberius moaned. "I'm don' be up to making no history. I gets enough history just gettin' up at this hour of the night."

Crawford ignored that. "Don't you got no pride? Right here in this very schoolhouse, Negroes are going to make history. A free country with a constitution of its ownself. Negroes makin' history. We on the move!"

Tiberius refused to appreciate it, looked caterwampus out the corner of his eyes, said, "I wisht I'd knowed what this was all about afore I started. I don't know about any history, but it look like you Negroes is fixin' to get us niggers killed."

"Don't talk like that, man! Where's your backbone? Now, get you a bucket there and start on this side. I'll take the other."

"But, it's true, man," Tiberius insisted, slowly opening the paint. "What I want to mess around with no constitution for a free country for? I got a country. I ain't never goin' back to no United States. I ain't never forget those days." He smiled puckishly. "I got a country. I'm a British subject."

Crawford met the look with scorn. "British subject? You is a British OBJECT, that's what you is. You is a object!"

By the time the little town of Chatham awakened and started its day, the paint on the window frames of the Negro schoolhouse on Princess Street had dried to a sticky tackiness, its fumes strong in the mild breeze off the river. Crawford and Tiberius sat in front row seats of the eighth grade classroom as an officious looking group of Negro men began to file into the building for the alleged purpose of forming a Masonic Lodge. In fact, the men were gathering to ratify a constitution for a new, revolutionary nation in the Kansas Territory.

Chapter 31

As the delegates to this secret, so-called constitutional convention arrived, dribbling into the room in twos and threes, the magnitude of their aspiration, the deadly seriousness of their determination, choked the air with a feeling as sober as that of impending war. Finally, thirty-four Negroes had collected. Most were Canadians, a few were Americans; all were black men seething with hatred of slavery. William Monroe, a Detroit minister, shook hands with the prominent Chatham physician, Dr. Martin Delaney, and muttered something about burning slaveowners at the stake. C. J. Reynolds, who claimed to represent a Negro military force, said candidly that his troops would torch the capitals of every slave holding state. Fred Crawford, the erstwhile painter, had never heard such public talk, and he found himself feeding on the language and unquenchable rage of the bold, antislavery leaders. Tiberius Montgomery looked more and more anxious and worried.

A note of expectancy also hovered about the gathering in the deserted schoolhouse. Brief, vitriolic statements, threats of recriminations for slave owners would spew out, then abruptly break off, interrupted by a delegate's glance over his shoulder, a concerted tap on the face of a pocket timepiece, or startled listening, as though the speeches had all been made before and hung inconclusively, awaiting a final word. When at last it seemed the men might disperse, unsatisfied, a loud knocking commenced on the schoolhouse door.

The delegates froze. Conversation stopped. Outside, in the school yard, a bobwhite whistled its name, then returned to its search for grubs. Dr. Delaney, himself, hastened to open the door.

Although he was not tall, perhaps even a trifle short for a man, an overpowering sense of command was so natural to John Brown that he seemed to crowd the schoolhouse doorway. That aura of great strength, whether from his absolute certainty of righteousness or his inability to conceive of failure, permeated his every movement. It was there in his military stride and bearing; it forced itself upon his audience with the implacable jut of his heavy, square jaw; and, it menaced from his intimidating, index finger with which he pointed out God's will and man's fallibility. His presence electrified the eighth grade classroom, now transformed to convention hall.

He had an obdurate meekness, a refusal to accede to worldly trappings, that was not humility at all, but rather an indifference to worldly approval. He dressed in a dark suit of serviceable broadcloth so worn as to be faded gray at the seams and the edges of its wide-flaring lapels. A black bombazine scarf was wound, cravat-like, around the collar of his white shirt and the loose folds of his weathered and wrinkled neck. A lapelled vest, studded with pearl buttons, beneath the severe cut of the frock coat, was his only nod to fashion.

Combed straight back from his high forehead, Brown's thick, dark hair was shot through with gray as were his thin eyebrows pinched over the circles etched about his eyes. A deep creased furrow beside each nostril of his long, straight nose, extended nearly to the down turned corners of his large, tight-lipped mouth. Most prepossessing of all his features, however, were his intense, steel gray eyes, which captured and held anything they fastened upon.

Accompanying Brown were a dozen white men, fellow riders in his campaign that had been called the Kansas Massacre. His companion whites, all of them youths including his own son, Owen, were dressed in frontiersman's costume, leather leggings and doublets or jacketless farmer's jeans. They entered the hall ceremoniously as became a military brigade, executing precise turns to lead their captain to the front of the room.

The old man, for in that company Brown appeared ancient at fifty-eight, halted, flanked by his retinue, and faced the free black men of the Chatham Convention. A ripple of nervous excitation spread among the assembled delegates. Crawford elbowed Tiberius.

"Friends," Brown began calmly, "we are here to declare war."

There, the word was said; a name given to an idea carved in their hearts with years of guiding blacks away from their masters. Still, just uttering it made them squeamish. Tiberius paled, then looked around for a possible hasty exit.

"Do not be so shocked, friends," the leader of the Kansas Massacre said flatly. "Has there ever been any doubt of it? Has there ever been the slightest clue that the Godless sinners who would keep our brothers in chains would listen to reason or the dictates of moral teachers, would listen even to the teachings of Christ Himself?"

While many of the assembled gazed at their feet, incapable of meeting the fire in the steel gray eyes, none could deny his sentiment. They knew it first-hand from their own escapes and knew it from others they had assisted.

He echoed their thoughts. "No! the sinful in the quicksand of their own wickedness do not look up to heaven."

The preacher-like voice became confidential as Brown implored, "Upon the advice of Mr. Frederick Douglass, whom many of you know, I have asked you here to this Convention which seeks to redress the wrongs committed against the Negro race. I have had the honor this day of conferring with a very courageous female, Harriet Tubman, and she concurs with this. This is not an easy step for me to take, gentlemen, but one the Lord God has divined in His scheme for me a very long time ago. Some years back, after great deliberation and much prayerful guidance from the Lord, I went to the Kansas Territory to gain a footing on this matter."

The big, square chin quivered with emotion until his jaws forcibly stifled a tremor and he said, "From that time forth I have devoted my whole being, mental, moral, and physical, to the extinction of slavery."

Osborn Anderson, a printer's devil and clandestine publisher of seditious literature, permitted a tear to roll, unchecked, down his cheek. Crawford dug at both eyes with his knuckles.

"My company, twelve of whom are beside me — a number approximating the number of our Lord's apostles — and many, many more like them are prepared to fight."

The delegates scanned the hardy lieutenants at each side of the renowned abolitionist. At that, the young men about Brown stirred uneasily, unused to public attention. William Leaman, a lad of twenty with clear blue eyes, grinned sheepishly. John Henry Kagi nodded in greeting to the curious stares of the delegates as the Captain continued.

"We plan a new western terminus of the underground railroad. Under our modernized scheme, the railroad will be the SPW, the Subterranean Pass Way, and will link Virginia with Kansas."

William Munroe, the minister from Detroit, scratched his nose skeptically. Prepared to applaud any effort to stop the persecution of black people, all of whom he considered his personal flock to shepherd, he questioned the potential of any place for freedom on American soil.

"What we plan to do, gentlemen, is to invade Virginia." The old man had a way of making highly outrageous statements in the mildest possible manner, but with such conviction it was impossible not to accept them as fact. "Once we have provided the hope and direction, slaves on all the known plantations will throw down their chains and join us in the march to Kansas." His sentences flowed more rapidly then, his pitch heightened with his enthusiasm. They could see the black minions marching, joined by others all along the way, following this man, this Pied Piper, to Kansas. "And, yes, there will be still more to join us. The free Negroes of the north will also band together in this cause once they know of it. Faced with such numbers, the oppressors can never again impress their evil demand for human bondage."

An expression like awe, the sort of look that follows a mystic visitation, came over Anderson's face. In a voice more breath than timbre, he asked, "Are you suggesting, Captain Brown, you would lead thousands of unarmed slaves through the armed camps from Virginia to Kansas?"

The other Negro delegates turned quickly to Brown for his answer. The question was theirs, too.

Brown twisted his wide, thin lips in a gentle smile, worked over the congregation with the probing, steel gray eyes.

"I did not say unarmed, sir." He coughed lightly against the back of his big-knuckled hand. "There is an organization of men whose names I am not prepared to reveal, let's call them the Secret Six. At any rate, these Secret Six, wealthy men all, have agreed to furnish guns and supplies for the SPW. Our problem, then, is manpower, not money. Money can be had plentifully enough to supply us our needs."

"So much?" gasped Dr. Delaney, incredulous at the concept of financing such a vast undertaking.

"So much," Brown nodded, dimming the fanatical light in his eyes, then veiling the look with eyelids gently closed as in prayer or a moment's meditation.

His white companions beamed, unable to mask their pride in the canny foresight of their leader. After little more than a few seconds, the black delegates joined them in that pleasure, openly smiling and nodding at one another.

The entire assemblage was so pleased, that they were annoyed to hear G. J. Reynolds, the self-proclaimed general of an army of Negroes no one had ever seen, quibble, "But what if troops are brought against you?"

Brown's response shot back instantaneously, "A small force trained in forest warfare can easily defend the wooded ravines and hills against Southern militia or even from the U. S. Army." He paused and added gravely, "I earnestly hope with all my heart that there will not be much bloodshed." Then, he exhaled deeply, and as if an afterthought, concluded, "It is our plan to take hostages to assure our own safe passage and to ransom for still more of the enslaved."

"Just where is this place?" Munroe questioned, not so much from disbelief as curiosity for he was by then persuaded the man could do anything he set his mind to. "Where is this place that can accommodate such a migration?"

Brown accepted the inquiry affably, pleased to share his ingenuity. "It is in Kansas. I have built a fort, a protective enclosure, that can be expanded with the needs, on land that I own. There is adequate land for a hundred thousand new settlers and that number, too, can be increased. Our Army will lead those who have cast off their shackles to what we are now calling the new State of Topeka, a nation free of oppression."

After a moment, Brown continued, declaring, "And, now, gentlemen, for the main piece of business, the Provisional Constitution of the State of Topeka."

Chapter 32

Reyna and her "butler" arrived in Chatham on Monday. A hired cab took them from the wharf to the Barbour's Villa Tavern where her suite had been prepared. She had a headache that felt like someone was drilling a hole in her skull. Ned carefully stayed out of her way. A sulky silence lay between them. He'd been resisting her plans lately; a natural expression of his own freedom and independence perhaps, but not a situation she accepted readily. Just as she'd begun to add a brittle edge to her demands, so had Ned begun to disagree with some of her decisions.

For Reyna, the long list of disappointments had led her to the edge of despair. First had been the disillusion with New York. Her exile in San Francisco and her work in Virginia had painted in her mind a fanciful but completely false picture of America's largest city. What she had seen was filth and squalor that reminded her of the hideous scrambling of too many rats in a nest. New York's dirty screen of smoking factories blotted out the sky, and its streets stank of rotting garbage, and were crowded with starving indigents. She had expected glamour and culture but had found only the greedy pushing and shoving of self-centered provincials who had convinced themselves, and now seemed determined to persuade others, there was no other place like New York and no other people like New Yorkers. They were correct, of course, she admitted sadly, as she said goodbye to her fantasy. There truly was no other place or people quite like New York and its citizens.

Her depression had been deepened by the meeting with the Gardners. Despite their reserve and timidity, they had become a bellwether for her. The Gardners were the first whites she had ever known to employ free black people and they had been first to engage in abolitionist activities. Their opinions had always been correct, if more conservative than hers.

When they met at the St. Nicholas, she saw their pretenTiousness, their timidity, their lack of spirit, their personalities — as colorless as the walls within which they lived. There, in that overdone, too precious room, she had watched them ratchet up their pursed-lipped correctness. She had had to control her own emotions, and the reunion had turned foul. These people who had been most dear to her now seemed dull and ordinary. She was ashamed of not seeing them for what they were when she had first met them.

She grieved the loss and didn't know whose fault it was and couldn't readily affix blame. It simply was. The Gardners had not changed, nor had she. Perhaps no one ever does. What had changed was her perception of them. It left a hole in her heart not to think warmly about them, to imagine them as she realized they never had been. The fears that she locked away with her childhood returned; she was isolated and still all alone in an increasingly hostile world.

The trip to Chatham had been like that, a final, obstinate slap at timorous old Captain James because she didn't know what else to do. She begrudgingly admitted to herself that the Gardners were probably correct once more, this time about John Brown, the old radical. But she couldn't let it go without seeing for herself. She couldn't return to California and face herself as a failure.

Eased back in a club chair at the Villa Tavern, Ned sucked furiously at his pipe to get it lighted, then let the puffs of smoke cloud the air between them. He was done with hurting for her.

He couldn't remember when the pain of losing her stopped. Where he had been or what he had been doing when it went away, but he knew it was over and she couldn't hurt him anymore. Like sawing off a leg, it had been terrifying for awhile then it was gone, taking the agony with it. The single minded patience and determination with which he had bought his freedom and managed the farm in Virginia had become something hard, tougher, somewhat less human.

He didn't deny that he still desired her and that they still sometimes enjoyed pleasuring themselves in her bed. Nor did he ever doubt that she was an extraordinary woman. That was, after all, to be expected of Mamaloi in their religion. What bothered him was more disturbing than her superiority or even the spine-tingling fear of her unnatural power. Ned had come to sense a madness about her, an obsession with intrigue so demanding that she ignored or was indifferent to its consequences. The feeling was strong enough to turn his blood to water. At the moment, he wanted only to be finished with the business of John Brown.

The sullen silence in the pipe-smoked air was broken by a sharp rap at the door.

Reyna rose. "That must be Mr. Brown. Ned, would you be good enough to go down to the kitchen and ask for tea?"

He left to do her bidding like an obedient servant and, mercifully, she didn't see the way he grimaced. They had been together too long for him not to know when she wanted him out of the way.

Although she had never seen him before, not even a daguerreotype likeness,

Reyna recognized John Brown. His intensity, the searching eyes of a hawk, immediately distinguished him from his young Secretary of War, John Henry Kagi.

"Come in, come in," she called, touching the abolitionist's fingers. "Mr. Brown, Ned was just going for tea. Will you join us?"

Brown said, "I am glad to meet you, Miss Shield. Yes, tea would be delightful. Miss Shield, I would have you meet my colleague, Mr. Kagi."

Nothing about his inflexible, square jaw revealed it, but Reyna knew that Brown was roiling with high expectations for this meeting. She had implied in her letter that she was wealthy and intended to donate to his cause. She knew, too, that he desperately needed funds. The absence of influential Negro leaders, Harriet Tubman, Frederick Douglass, and the Secret Six, his financial backers from Boston, was a bad sign. Now, eager to begin the greatest crusade of his life, the old man lacked the visible support of famous Negroes and the money to carry out his plans.

Reyna went directly to the point. "How did your convention fare, Mr. Brown?"

Without hesitation, he exaggerated, "Very, very well. There is now a constitution to govern a new principality of free people."

Fortunately, the Gardners had prepared her for the man's daring scheme so she was not caught by surprise. Still, her heart leaped in her chest at the magnitude of his proposal. An idea so blatant as that would surely bring on a war between north and south.

By the time Ned had returned with tea, her mind had apparently accepted Brown's fantastic ideas and she had come to admire his almost mesmerizing charisma, yet something about him, the all too simplistic conviction of a fanatic, perhaps, or an obvious disregard for bloodshed, caused her to hesitate before playing her final card, the certified check for thirty thousand dollars.

"Just how, Mr. Brown," she asked thoughtfully, "do you plan to establish this free state?"

"I believe," he said, "the time is right for insurrection among the enslaved and that God has chosen me to lead a march on Virginia, the queen of the slave states."

Reyna's eyes rounded with the old man's amazing declarations. Somehow even casual conversation with him took on a quality of Convention Hall rhetoric.

Jabbing at the air with his forefinger, Brown continued, "Madam, if God be for us, who can stand against us?"

Reyna's cup chattered against her saucer as she lifted it to her lips. Over the rim of her cup, she gazed placidly into the steel gray eyes of the man who believed he had been personally chosen by the Lord. "Have you the troops to stand against the army and the militia?"

His companion, John Henry Kagi, a studious-faced man in his mid-twenties, sat quietly listening. He never once took his light brown eyes off the old man's face. Reyna had heard that the former school teacher had once claimed that he would gladly burn in hell if his death would end slavery.

Ned, behind Brown's chair, looked shocked by the talk.

"But I understand that we are winning seats in the Senate," she argued, "and, that soon we will see federal laws gradually extinguishing slavery."

He met the comment in an instant, insisting, "To believe that is folly. It is only through our Negro brethren rising up and throwing off their chains that this slave-cursed Republic can be restored to the principles of our forefathers and the Declaration of Independence."

"You may be right, Mr. Brown," she agreed in an effort to calm him as his voice shrieked with the ring of a pulpit declamation. "But what is to be done?"

The fire in his eyes turned to coals then, somehow more blistering than the blazing words. "I for one," he croaked in a voice so low that she had to lean forward to hear, "I am prepared to die for this cause."

He recovered himself, added tonelessly, "In fact, it is an honor. I have only had this one opportunity to be of service to mankind in a life of nearly sixty years."

Reyna's mind whirled through the facts about him she had gathered. *The man's words were more nearly true than his actual confession. In fifty-nine years, Brown had failed at every venture he had ever attempted. The death of one wife and half a dozen children from what was surely poverty, exposure to the elements and malnutrition, the bankruptcy of several businesses, and continual court harangues with creditors had so eaten away at him that when he found a ready ear for his God-inspired message of hatred for slavery, Brown had grabbed it as a drowning man to a life raft. This campaign, this single issue, offered him a chance to succeed at something.*

"I have heard," she said quietly. "Wendell Phillips, for instance — "

He interrupted. "Pardon me, Miss Shield, but I have noted that men who have the gift of eloquence such as our friend, Mr. Phillips, are seldom men of action. We need not talk of Wendell Phillips. It is men of action I wish to consult."

Although the rebuke was mild, it came so fast and heated that the room fell silent. Brown remained unrelenting, unapologetic.

Reyna broke the awkward pause. "I believe I can help you, Mr. Brown."

"Our mission can use all the help we can get."

For all the man's obstinacy and fanatical arrogance, his dedication and commitment were unquestioned and his ability to gather a following had been demonstrated many times. *It is just possible,* she thought, *that this eccentric old white man could accomplish what he says.* But his many failures disturbed her. She knew from her work with voodoo that in order to make a difference, a leader must be able to match the power of attraction with successful performance.

"You say you intend to lead a rebellion. Have you planned to prepare the slaves for it?"

"Not in any formal way," he said. "But, once they hear of it, they will rise up like Lazarus and throw down their chains."

"Forgive me, Mr. Brown, but I simply must disagree. Based on my experience, I honestly don't believe they know how. For one thing, they've been held in bondage so long they're afraid, and believe me, there's no unity among them. Had they realized the power in their numbers, they'd have overthrown their masters long before this. Someone will need to educate them."

While she talked, Brown studied her face, at first, curiously, then stroking his chin and nodding in agreement.

She continued, "Then, too, there's no system of communication among the plantations by which the message of rebellion could be relayed."

Brown nodded more vigorously, understanding, approving.

At last, Reyna summarized, "I think that education and the establishment of a relay system could be accomplished, but it would need to be done secretly so as not to alarm the owners . . . Someone would need to go to selected plantations and secretly meet with the slaves . . . it would take time to establish their trust in order to avoid confusion."

A flattering look of wonder at the cleverness of the plan lit up Brown's eyes as he evaluated her ideas. Ned began to regard her peculiarly.

"Once that's done," Reyna concluded, flushed with pride at a plan that had just bubbled out of her, but seemed to emerge fully formed, "then! Then, the slaves would be waiting for the announcement of your insurrection. Then, when the word comes to strike, they will join you."

"I think it's a wonderful idea, Miss Shield," Brown cried out wholeheartedly.

"I do, too," Kagi spoke up for the first time. "It's a truly good idea, Captain Brown."

"I think I can help you, Mr. Brown," she said, slowly reaching for her reticule. Drawing out a gray velvet purse, she handed it across. "Here's five hundred dollars. Will that help?"

The old man took it quickly, letting the ten dollar gold pieces clink against his long fingers. A sudden fog of moisture glistened his eyes.

"Thank you, Miss Shield," he mumbled gratefully. "You have no idea how much this will buy. This will arm a hundred men."

It distressed Reyna that he mentioned no supplies other than guns.

He said, "We will also steal your suggestion to send a spy to the major plantations. We'll begin right away. I must leave here in a day or so to go to Boston to order the weapons. We can work on your idea then."

"Do you have someone in mind to act as your undercover agent, Mr. Brown?"

Brown's cold, gray eyes met hers. "Are you volunteering, Miss Shield? Are you available?"

"Yes," she said. "I am."

"I was thinking while you were talking that you'd be perfect in that role." He stood and held out his hand. "You have just found yourself a heavenly errand, Miss Shield."

Ned had turned in such a way that Reyna could not see his face.

Although she knew that she could accomplish the secret mission, she also realized the fanatical leader had no way to know that. She also knew she could not count on him to wait till her work was done before he began an attack somewhere.

Reyna sat a long while and a touch of desperation lurked in the corners of her mind as she examined her options. Unused to failure, she couldn't imagine the shame of retreat. Brown's energy was like a comet, apt to incinerate itself with its own fiery tail. But, wait, she thought, grabbing a a single elusive thread. *I can work independently inside the old man's operation without becoming entangled in his personal character flaws. In that way, when he fails — and he surely will fail because of his brashness and overgrown ego — I can make sure that all is not lost.* She admitted, too, with a spark of indifference so cold that it startled her to recognize. *Let the white men waste themselves killing one another, thus sparing some of us from this brutality. The old man is pitiable but he can be cannon fodder for this cruel game we play.*

"Reyna!" Ned accused, actually raised his voice against her. "Are you mad? Can't you see that that white man is touched in the head?"

"What if he is?" she asked. "If that crazy old fool can help us then I'll use him. I'd work with the devil himself if it would free a single black soul from the hell of slavery."

"Oh, sugar!" he cried out. "Can't you see, I'm only saying this because I care about what happens to you and won't let you destroy yourself."

Her response came as dark as the expressionless eyes of a serpent. "You don't understand. I'm not asking your permission, Ned. I'm going to do this thing with or without you, I've made up my mind. I'm going to work with Captain John Brown." Then, her anger got the better of her and she added with a patronizing sniff, "You, of course, are free to do as you please."

"I think," he said slowly, "that you know I don't intend to kill myself for any white man. I can be a lot more useful to our people if I stay alive." His body bent toward her then as he said, "Ain't nobody else for me but you . . . and never will be; but when you're finished here, I'm going back to Charles Town. You know where I'll be. Let me know when you've come to your senses."

He turned his back on her then, and stared silently out the window where ight snow flurries turned cartwheels in the gusty breezes on the road.

Chapter 33

In June, Ashburyburg, Kentucky, fried in record-breaking heat. Without rain for 33 days, the parched topsoil dried up liked a tanned buffalo hide, then cracked, and disintegrated to fine dust to join puffs of late afternoon zephyrs and blow away. The town had come to a standstill. Nothing moved that didn't have to. Old men no longer sat on the benches in front of the courthouse. The shutters stayed closed at Owens' Mercantile and Drygoods Store until after sundown. Every twig and blade of grass turned brown, then yellow, then died. It looked like all of the crops, much of the livestock, and some elderly citizens would be lost if it didn't rain soon.

Ten miles out of town on the Post Road, Ironwood Plantation sweltered and suffered as much as the rest of Webster County. In the Big House, the white folks moved down to the first floor where it was cooler and lay about drinking prodigious quantities of flavored ades and nearly wore out the house servants, Jay Bee and Prissy, with their constant demands for a breeze from the broad-leafed palmetto fans.

The slaves deserted the cabins to camp along the bank of the pencil-thin stream of Dead Dog Creek, not because it was cool, which it wasn't, but because they imagined it was, a self-deception that allowed them to sleep a little.

In the mornings, they'd drag themselves to the quadrangle where Master John would bawl them out for being such useless niggers as couldn't take a little hot spell, then tramp them off with hoes to chop around in the dry dust and the remaining dead rows of worthless corn. There was nothing left to save of the crops; Master John just wanted to keep them busy and from making mischief.

It was a stupid maneuver. If Master John had the good sense to look out his own window, even he'd have spotted the richest soil of his land, loosened by the hoes that day, in league with the afternoon gusts, flying toward Wheatcroft Township twenty miles east. Unfortunately Master John was not very smart and would not learn that particular lesson until the next year.

Because of the uncommon weather, the master gave his people forty minutes for lunch. Rachel, Old Sally, and LuAnn, the plantation cooks, brought it out in buckets to the fields. That way, the field hands had time to gulp down a little fatback, take a couple of swigs of lukewarm water from the canteen, and fling themselves down on the ground for awhile. Mercifully, sometimes they drowsed in the suffocating heat while their guts worked away at the pork fat and water.

LuAnn's not inconsiderable derriere was scarcely out of sight before the field men and women began to fall to the ground to rest. James, Little Jim, Billy, and Donald dropped in a small circle of shade under the withering leaves of a runted cigar tree. Less than a foot around, there was room only for their heads in the stingy shadow of its branches. Bodies and legs stuck out around the tree like the spokes of a cart wheel.

The sun beat down relentlessly and bounced in undulating waves on the road. A crow lit on a fence post, mechanically opening and closing its beak, too hot even to croak. Hypnotized with the torpor, James watched with fascination as a soldier ant marched its way up his pant leg. The others lay motionless, breathing shallowly, so as not to waste their strength.

James was called James because he was the first man by that name on the place; not because he was bigger than little Jim which he wasn't. Little Jim got the name when he was an infant and by the time he was grown it had become permanently his. The naming of slaves had nothing to do with personality or identity, it was just a way of keeping them separate in the plantation ledger. Their names were considerably less useful than identifying marks, say the welts of severe whippings or the pale scars of a knife cut.

Billy. Dk. Male. 26 years. Notched r. ear. $900.

Notched right ear. That short entry was better than any name if someone was buying. Or selling. Or hunting. Alongside Billy, he of the notched ear, resting in the paltry shade of the cigar tree on Ironwood, were three other men: an eyebrow fretted with old adhesions; two missing front teeth; and a crippled left arm.

Nearly mesmerized with the lassitude of heat and digestion, it was several minutes before any of them attended to the spectacular sight on the road. The ear with the notch in it lay flat on the ground, flat enough to feel as well as hear the thud of horses' hooves. The crooked eyebrow lifted a little, but the head it was attached to didn't raise. The lips, slightly parted about his partially toothed gums, made the putt-putt-putt noises of slobbery sleep. At last, the crippled arm propped up its owner for a look.

"Well, lookee here," he sang out and whistled.

An eye opened beneath the scarred eyebrow. Otherwise, nothing stirred under the tree. The lazy-mouthed snoring continued; the notched ear lay just where it was.

"Get up here, you no 'count niggers!" he sang out again. "You be sorry if'n you miss this!"

Slowly and stiffly, the other three raised themselves.

Coming down the road at a gentle pace was one of the finest pieces of horse flesh those Kentucky slaves had ever seen. Its gleaming chestnut coat shimmered in the noonday sun. The animal pranced with the nervous, sideways step of a racer held back. From its tossing head and arching neck to its braided tail, the beast was such that inspired Kentucky dreams and sent men to digging out their last dollar for a wager. Best of all, the two year old had that crazy look, that particular madness about the eyes that shouted of its almost uncontrollable impatience to leap straight up and fly around a track.

"Laws, laws, laws! Lookee dat!"

As if the horse alone wasn't enough to set their hearts pounding, its rider sent the four field hands into a positive dither. A young, dark-complexioned jockey in pale blue silk pants, a blousing jacket tight about the waist, and with a matching cap of the same brilliant color and cloth, perched neatly atop the thin riding saddle. Spotless knee-length black leather boots and a broad black belt completed the enviable outfit. The lone rider held a short riding quirt in one hand and adroitly controlled the reins with the other, directing the stallion with a twist of an index finger. For a moment, the four, now standing slack-jawed alongside the little tree, were struck dumb by their proximity to such grandeur, imagining finery like that on them, a mount like that under them.

Still more miraculous, rather than riding on by without so much as a howdy-do, the horse and rider halted when they reached the tree and the awestruck group. Halted and spoke to them. Halted and spoke to them and dismounted.

"Howdy y'all." The drawl was rich and prissy, the high fallutin' tone of Central Kentucky, smack in the middle of horse country. The four slaves couldn't take their eyes off the elegant thoroughbred, the glorious suit of clothes on its rider.

"Howdy." James was first to break his enchantment enough to find his voice. "That sho' be some kinda animal. Fine, fine piece of horse flesh."

"Runs right smart, too," the jockey said. Then, "Any of you boys know a place called Ironwood and a boy called Little Jim?"

They looked back and forth among themselves as though they'd seen a ghost, the personal visitation of an angel. First, on a day hotter than the hinges of hell, a fabulous horse and rider appeared from nowhere, then stopped and spoke to them. Second, the vision called one of them by name.

"This be Ironwood and I be Little Jim."

"I seen your mama," the stranger said.

"My mama?" Little Jim said querulously. His mind wrapped around the idea, then refused to hold it. Little Jim's mother had been sold about five years back, sold off to no one knew where. "How could you see my mama?"

"She be up to the Jackson place this side of Lexington."

"How you know?"

"I been there, fool," the jockey said haughtily.

"Shoot! How I know that?" Little Jim asked. The doubt in his mind began to crumble with hope, the desire to believe.

"Your mama tell me to tell you she be a'right. And Maybelle be there, too. Yo' mama, she still think of you ever' day and that woman won't never stop talking about y'all all the time. She tol' me about the bob wire."

At that, a stinging rush of tears clouded Little Jim's memories. Maybelle had been his fiancee before she was taken away to be sold with the dozen that included his mother. The scar fretted through his eyebrow had come from a childhood accident with barbed wire fencing. James, Billy, and Donald had gathered around close, too, as if the story was theirs as well. It was a miracle come to earth.

"You want to see your mama?"

"'Course I does," Little Jim said. "What kind of a question be that? But, I'd like to have a horse like that'n, too. But, wish in one hand and shit in t'other and see which one fills up fastest."

"No, they ain't the same at all. Freedom's a'comin'."

Then, all four of them croaked with one voice, "Freedom! What y'all mean, freedom?"

"Just what I say. Freedom. It's happenin'. . . up north. When the word come, you gots to be ready. It's not goin' be long now, neither. Y'all knows old John up to the Toliver's place?"

"Yes?" they answered hesitantly.

"When freedom come, old John he'll come a runnin'. When he come, y'all light out. Follow the river north. 'Afore y'all go, you run on down to the Calden place and tell Isaac, then hightail it up the river. You be with yo' mama 'afore the month is out."

When they returned to the fields, James, Little Jim, Billy, and Donald worked as though there'd been a cooling breeze, as if they could smell rain on their faces. Freedom was not far away. They could feel the promise of it in every chop of their hoes.

The jockey in the brilliant clothing, long out of sight down the dusty road, was as much a dream as freedom had been. Reyna Shield, skin stained dark with the juice of walnut husks and dressed in blue silk pants, had made her eighty-ninth plantation contact in preparation for John Brown's rebellion.

Chapter 34

The surface of the old beaver dam at the bend in the Kaw River near Dry Switch, Missouri, topped 104 degrees this day. A foot below that, the stored heat in the dry twigs and the compost of mulch that bound them together added another ten degrees. Three feet further down, steaming moisture seeped up from the river. In the center of that sweltering blanket, between the steam from below and the intense heat of the blazing sun, lay a human form so lifeless it might have been dead.

Reyna lay there, four feet below the surface in the abandoned beaver dam, not knowing how long it would be before it was safe for her to sneak away. Although the threat of capture, tar and feathers, and finally jail were real enough, it was also true that she was not sure that she could tolerate this interment much longer. As best she could tell, she'd been there almost two days and her muscles had so stiffened she was uncertain she could move even if free of the debris that concealed her.

It had seemed so sudden somehow, the way things had changed. It had been slow, sometimes even boring once she'd mastered the rules of the road; and then things accelerated like a comet falling to earth. The night before she been at the top of her form, accomplished, efficient, like a sharp knife cutting clean for the cause of freedom. And then it all changed.

The moon should have warned her. As it was, its shadowed light peeked through the branches of a walnut tree and spread eerie phantoms across the meadow. The night and the place were special to Reyna for this was Missouri, a state whipped back and forth in its attitudes toward slavery. As such, the region mirrored much of the country, slave and free, as the nation lumbered toward murderous confrontation over the issue. Now, in 1858, an armed clash of north and south seemed inevitable.

Standing beneath the tree in the blue-white moonlight, Reyna was conflicted over the approaching war. She prayed for an end to slavery and she had wholeheartedly devoted herself to that cause, but she also feared a war could go against them and overwhelm the free states. In that regard, too, she knew that federal marshals hunted for her not five miles away. The thought of capture sent an icy chill the length of her spine. The sound of dry leaves rustling on the ground behind her interrupted the meandering thoughts.

She smiled at the whispered sounds of her community making its way through the woods. This trip had seasoned her, matured her skills and had justified Mr. Shield's trust in her. She'd perfected the ritual to demonstrate the power of the snake while traveling, leading new followers of the faith, adapting to constantly changing circumstances. She'd learned to live out of saddlebags swung over the rump of Camino, her chestnut stallion.

As this night's worshippers arrived, Reyna was amused by the look of disbelief on the faces of the farmers she'd met in her disguise as a jockey on the roadside, now seeing her in shimmering white silk, full bosom swelling her gown. The skirt, gored to the waist, revealed enough bare skin in the turn of her leg and the curve of her thigh to make the simple farming men hard with desire. Her hips swished slowly to an unheard melody as she patiently waited for them to assemble.

They filed in, men and women and children, naked to the waist, gathering about her in a semi-circle, leaning toward her, this gorgeous, barefoot goddess of their faith. Expectant, ready for the trance, the magic, and the laying on of hands. At the same time they were timid before the possibility of still another sham, tricks that life had played upon them many times. But they were here to try again for the magic of their childhood, the one life-sustaining force for them on the western edge of America.

Reyna closed her eyes, held her arms out at shoulder height, urged the assembly to link arms about one another to close the circle with a human chain. The voodoo queen began the familiar chant, inviting the Gods to come to them, to be with them in this enchanted circle deep in the forest outside their plantation quarters. Her voice had become a husky contralto, and now it was that mellow sound that called to them,

"Do se dan do go.
"Mande Heron. Heron Mande
"Tigui li papa, la bas papa."

Known to them, the familiar refrain began to work its magic, to call to them from a place they knew, another plane, one of liberation.

Because they dared not risk waking the master or the overseer, Reyna set a slow beginning pace for the dance which was basic to their ascent to higher planes. The customary drums would surely bring the white men and harsh punishment. Instead, their queen called upon Vodu to "set the table" to invite the spirits with finger snapping rhythms that they could imitate and maintain during the dance that led to the raw power of their religion. Left hand, *snap*, a full beat. Right hand *snap-snap*, a half beat for each. Then left hand *Snap*. *Snap*, a full beat for each finger snap.

Snap.
Snap-snap.
Snap

Snap.

They caught it up as she knew they would. Straight out of North Africa, a rhythm called the Ayoob, the Middle Eastern Two-Four, found its way to them, feet and hips, then worked its way into their bodies and they began swaying, then one by one pivoting, men shuffling, circling about the women like pigeons strutting in head-bobbing rites of mating.

Naked save for scant loin cloths, young males passed among them with gourds of fermented peach, as sweet as honey and with the kick of a mule.

As they loosened up with the movement and the echoing finger pops that drove them, Reyna gently quickened the pace of the dancing. The young men passed more of the peach nectar. Two elderly men, with hair the color of homespun cotton, moved forward and began the mournful fretting of the *aolus*, flute-like horns, blown against thin reeds and deepened an octave by slightly upward curves at the nether end.

Reyna quickened the tempo as the congregation relaxed, let their bodies become one with the music

Snap. Snap-snap. Snap. Snap.
Snap. Snap-snap. Snap. Snap.

As the peach nectar and the rhythm brought them to transcendental grace, Reyna raised her arms overhead. The music hushed.

She cried out, "Oh, my people. I am you and you are me. Believe! Let the magic be with us! Around you. Around me. All around this tree. In the universe, all things vegetable and mineral are related."

Again, she called, "I am you. And you are me. What happens to any one of us happens to us all." Then she turned around, revealing as she had at the funeral rite for Edward Shield the rutted scar tissue on her back. As it had been that long ago time, she heard afresh the involuntary gasp the wounds drew from a crowd. Then she could literally feel the atmosphere change as they bonded together. For her suffering, she was one of them. And they were a part of her.

Turning away, she thrust her hand into a large knothole in the trunk of the tree, the site of a rotted branch taken by the wind many years before. She pulled out of that cavity a young rattlesnake, as thin as a pencil and not more than two years old. Wrapping its body about her forearm and cupping its head in the tender flesh between her thumb and forefinger, she brought it to her face to enjoy the eyelash brush of its inquisitive tongue stroking her cheek. Her congregation stood transfixed by the sight of her transcendence as Vodu breathed his power into her. At that moment, she became Mamaloi, ruler of that domain, direct recipient of the power of the serpent, hence a conduit from her to them.

Carefully winding the snake around her neck so that its eyes looked out upon them from a point even with her own, Reyna gazed among them, intoned, "Brothers and sisters! Anything is possible if you put your faith in the snake. Believe! If you believe, you, too, will have the power of the serpent. A new day is a'comin'. Comin' from the president hisself."

The gathering shifted nervously, all too aware that merely hearing such rumors of insurrection was dealt with harshly by their masters. Only a fool would be blind to the increased number and severity of the beatings in recent years. There was hardly a young man among them who did not carry stripes of punishment on his body.

"Feel the power," she said. "Do not be afraid. Freedom's a' comin'." Reyna paused then, recognizing how strange and frightening such talk must be to these simple farmers.

"As you come forward for the healing touch," she said, "I want you to promise me you will march off down the road when you hear the word that freedom has come. We'll fill the roads and carriageways with the thousands of us walking north to glory."

Her disguise as a jockey had worked well for over a year. She had gone from plantation to plantation, showing up in the fields at rest times or at the slaves' quarters after dark to spread the word. Posing as a jockey had enabled her to travel freely and her power as a voodoo queen, as a farm owner, and as an underground railroad worker, had captured the imagination of rural slaves. Now, she was proud of her accomplishments. Her work had gone well. It had gone well; that is, until this night in June in the state of Missouri.

They had finished their ritual and the worshippers had gone home excited and motivated for the day of liberation. She'd been staying overnight with friendly slaves at the Cadwallader place when One-eyed Fred had come rushing in with the alarming news that marshals were on their way. Someone had informed the slaveholders about the itinerant jockey. A posse organized for her capture was headed toward the Cadwalladers. Although the slaves were terrified for her and for themselves for harboring her, Reyna herself was neither particularly alarmed nor frightened by the impending slave catchers. In fact, she received the news so calmly she amazed even herself. But, then, she had known all along that she was on borrowed time.

Some months before she'd seen the first of many notices tacked up on trees. A collection of slave owners had offered a reward of $10,000 to anyone who could give information leading to her apprehension. In the first rush of it, Reyna had actually been flattered by the size of the reward, to think that they would consider her so valuable, that stopping her work was worth so much. Unfortunately, it was also true that they posted a fairly accurate description of her as a woman, and a detailed account of her disguise as a jockey. They even mentioned her horse, Camino, by name. After that, she kept away from the main roads and ducked out of sight at the appearance of white people. But still, the borrowed time had been spent and now they were on their way to collect the dues.

After One-eyed Fred's news, Reyna hadn't waited for first light, but immediately saddled up the chestnut stallion and struck out on the back roads toward Thebes, Illinois. If she could make it to Dry Switch, Missouri, where the Kaw River meandered through swamps to join the Mississippi, she could make her way to a contact known to her only as "Auntie Maggie," a weird swamp witch, who could get her across the river to Cape Girardeau. She had a plan for Cape Girardeau. No one knew the exact location of Maggie's shack in the swamp. That wasn't necessary, they said. She always kept a candle in the window.

Despite a three hour head start, her flight was slow for she didn't dare give the stallion his head on the unknown road after dark. Her pursuers, good old boys of this county, knew that road well and rapidly gained on her while still more joined the chase from every house along the way. By ten the next morning, she could hear the furious roar of horses' hooves pounding on the road and, when the wind was right, the bloodthirsty shouts of their riders. There was no mistaking the reason for a large party of riders galloping like the apocalypse in the suffocating heat. Reyna had no doubt about the pleasure they'd take in punishing her. She knew she'd never make it to a jail, let alone a courtroom.

There was danger on the road the next day. She smelled it in the charged atmosphere, as strong as a coming thunderstorm. She saw it when a white man looked up from a field, spotted her, and ran toward his house, no doubt hurrying for help. She read it in the demeanor of the slaves who would have grinned and waved the day before, but now quickly turned their backs on trouble.

Bent low over her mount's neck, she whispered into his ears as they sped along, "Come now, great Vodu, protect your priestess as one of your own. Those infidels behind me mean only evil to your beautiful people. Save us now. Let your power flow though my body so that I may avenge the insult to you and your congregation. Help me, Vodu."

Late in the afternoon, the hard riding marshals had begun to gobble up the distance between them and she had spotted the swirl of dust they made behind her in the sleepy little valley east of Thebes. The excited baying of hunting dogs rang like an echo of doom over the gently rolling hills and dales. Her desperate flight had left her winded and perspiring; covered with Camino's slobber, too, as the racing horse reached out and ate the miles with his stride.

At last, even though it was still five miles from Dry Switch, she figured she needed to get off the road and travel where horse and rider couldn't go. Arriving at a gigantic blackberry thicket, she calculated it would be even more difficult for grown men to traverse its thorns. She slipped from Camino's back and loosened his bridle, but the affectionate beast, who'd been her most constant companion for more than a year, shook his mane and studied her with questioning eyes, not understanding that she meant for him to leave without her. Then, she slapped her riding crop across his rump, causing him to rear up in the air and canter on down the trail, all the while looking back over his shoulder with an expression of dismay and accusation. At that moment, her separation was no less confusing and lonely to her than it had seemed to him.

Was there anyone who truly cared about her or valued her work? Surely John Brown, the old fanatic, cared only for himself — he, as most men, used the plight of black people and the struggle for their freedom as mere tools for self-advancement. Who would there be to defend her if she were caught? Sadly, she could think of no one.

In the few seconds she paused there, a dozen images of the failures of her own past, rushed forward to fill her mind with dread. She saw her mother, the radiant Voodoo Queen Lucy, lashed to the malevolent cross in the slaves' quarters at Riverview Plantation, saw and heard the salted leather strap creating bloody furrows on her mother's back. Then Mistress Suzanne, her sadistic mistress, returned to her mind's eye, riding crop in hand, to beat her. A violent tremor shook her still when she recalled Master Joseph Hamber savagely raping her at *La Casa de Maria* in New Orleans.

The corners of her mouth turned down in an ugly rictus. Master Hamber might just be the one to free her. *What a twist that was*, she thought. *The pervert who'd bought her only to spoil her virginity was from Cape Girardeau.* She had received word that his father was a judge in Cape Girardeau. *Now the judge*, she thought vindictively, *had a reputation valuable enough to hide his son's ugly secret.*

Reyna shook her head to clear away the awful visions, then dropped to her hands and knees and began torturously wriggling through the blackberry brambles, trying not to disturb the brush, not to leave a clue for them to follow.

At first the sharp thorns seemed merely bothersome pinpricks against her hands and bared forearms. She was aware of their pulling her hair, scratching against her skull, and raking at her back. Sometimes a particularly vicious barb stuck to a finger of the right hand she used to clear away the brush in her path. Dragging herself forward, she could feel the rips where a branch of thorns tore open her silk shirt. Though the heat of the day was stifling, Reyna drew upon the powerful force of her Voodoo training for single-minded focus in order to put distance between her and the riders. She was only vaguely aware of the salt of her own perspiration stinging in her prickling wounds.

Then, too, the effort and the stinging scratches brought her wide awake after her long, sleepless night's ride. That energy doubled when the sound of the hounds revealed they'd reached the place in the road where she'd left it. Cuts and abrasions were minor compared to what that group back there had in mind.

Reyna's heart thumped against her rib cage. She'd taken a couple of bad thorns in her knees, forced clear to the bone by the weight of her own body slithering across a branch lying on the ground. Yet another thorn opened a painful gash across her cheek. Moments later, a two inch barb jammed into her forehead just above the eyebrow and lodged between the outer skin and the frontal lobe of her skull.

Forcing herself to take deep breaths lest she faint with the misery, Reyna lay down on her side and cautiously ran her thumb and index finger across her eyebrow searching for the sharp needle's point of entry. There, in the eyebrow just over her right eye, she found a short knob about the size and shape of a head of clove. Still, the throbbing was intense. Gripping that tiny head between the nails of her finger and thumb, she closed her eyes, took a deep breath, and yanked it clear. Pulling it out stirred pain so ferocious it matched the throbbing sensations, an agony so sharp she dared not even touch the spot to see whether or not all the spine had come free. She had only strength enough to lie panting like a dog in the dirt, trying to recover enough to go on.

The hunters had gone quiet for awhile but all at once a loud shout split the air, then died down, too. They were so quiet back there that she had hoped against hope that they had not found her trail and had left. But they'd begun again, this time accompanied by a metallic whacking she could not readily identify. Reyna lay quiet, praying silently for the pain to subside. *What were those men up to?*

Suddenly, she knew.

They'd found her trail, probably a bit of fabric torn from her garment, hanging like a flag from the brambles. Apparently, the marshals had gone to a nearby plantation to borrow scythes to cut a swathe through the blackberry thicket. Now they were back and hacking a path through the thorny briars.

Tortoise-like, one hand and leg dragging after another with excruciating pain, Reyna began her crawl once more.

At the point when she thought she'd no more body or spirit left, the blackberries thinned a little, then some more, then opened onto a creek of sluggish water and cat tail rushes. Without knowing where she was, the name of the creek or where it went, she eased herself directly into the water, soundlessly following the direction of its sluggish current.

Slime inched up over her immaculate black leather boots and oozed inside to squish about her feet. It rose to her thighs, her belly, the chest of her brilliant blue silk riding outfit as she deliberately strode away from her scent on the bank. Cautiously feeling her way along the channel with her feet, reaching for hard clay, she avoided the soft spots of deeper water.

It was then that she came across the beaver dam not more than a dozen yards from where she'd left the blackberries. The cries of the white men who'd also come upon the little stream sent Reyna underwater in search of the beaver's entrance to the dam. There she could lie above water, uncomfortable and cramped, but with less fear of discovery.

Unsure of what she could do, physically as well as mentally, Reyna studied her surroundings from the bowels of the Beaver Dam. She prayed to Vodu to help her get across the river, away from the slave hunters. Her life depended upon it.

Not until it was so dark she couldn't make out her hand at the end of her arm did she chance moving. Her heart fluttered in her chest like a frightened bird. From time to time, she heard barking dogs, crashing underbrush, and bellowed curses. As the night grew darker, sometimes she saw the flare of their torches as they searched the creek with dogs and rafts. Reyna estimated that at least a dozen men and twice that many dogs were out there, crisscrossing, foot by foot, through the maze of channels in the sloughs. *They wanted more than the ten thousand dollars reward. They wanted revenge. Deputized marshals, they did not intend to let her get away again. This time, they meant to bring her to quick and brutal justice, most likely from a limb of the nearest tree as a warning to other slaves tempted to run away.*

As cautious as a cat watching a bird, she lowered herself, head ducking under the water so as not to leave a ripple. Lungs burning for oxygen, she dared not ascend to the surface until she cleared the brambles of the beaver dam. At last, she felt the creek bed rise. She had reached the other side. She came to the surface gasping, eyes, nose, lungs stinging, but too terrified even to gulp for air.

About thirty yards up the creek, a stand of scrub oaks guarded the entrance to what seemed to be the swamps she sought. The oaks thinned out there and gave way to moss covered thickets and gray, diseased trees whose roots hung like string mops choking in the perpetual bog. High yellow grasses, head-tall reeds with razor-sharp leaves, and cattails flourished on the soggy banks of a winding maze of canals formed by water and muck from the annual Mississippi floods. Here and there, iridescent circles of oil slick rode on the surface and occasional bubbles boiled from the stagnant-water graves of decaying forms.

The rancid smell of dead plants and animals hung thickly about the place. Everything was dead, save the creatures who lived on the substances of death, water rats, spiders, flies, mosquitoes, and the snakes and lizards who fed on them all.

Reyna hesitated at the brink of the disgusting morass. Somewhere in there lived Auntie Maggie, a witch who knew her way about the bogs. *But where? A thousand deaths could claim her in the miles of twisting and turning mire.* The shrill yelp of a coon dog, very close at hand, forced her to decide.

At a bend in the swamp, forty yards from the place she'd entered, the bulking trunk of a cypress tree clung precariously, half-on, half-off the marshy bank. A clump of tangled roots as big as a bushel basket strung over the water's edge. Reyna struggled toward it, taking, long slow steps so as not to leave a wake of eddying muck to guide the marshals.

Breathing through her mouth to avoid the acrid stench and to calm a tickling gorge of nausea, she lowered herself to the chin in the mire, dodged under the roots, then rose till her head bumped up against the base of the tree. The rotten gray roots hung like a veil in front of her face, matted gray strands of hair on a cadaver. There, concealed in the fetid swamp, head behind and within the roots of the dead tree, she waited for nightfall.

After awhile the silent swamp came alive with the shouts and howls of men and dogs as they found the place where the scent of their intended victim had disappeared. Reyna froze in place till her muscles ached. A lot of excited talking and barking followed the discovery, then trailed off. Maybe an hour or more after that as the marshals went to obtain rafts. Reyna was tempted to leave her hiding place, but there was no place to go.

From her half-submerged vantage, Reyna counted three rafts loaded with grim-faced white men straining over the sides and animated dogs running fore and aft and back again, sniffing and barking, staring into the gloom of the slough. The raft poles stirred up the ooze and unsettled nested creatures. Bullfrogs leaped ahead of the boats and serpents slithered away on the bank. Giant gray-green lizards, ugly descendants of prehistoric monsters, clambered among the dense vegetation and watched with unblinking, half-lidded eyes.

As the hours trudged by, a hundred real and imagined aches attacked her muscles. The prickling premonition of a cramp threatened behind her right knee and her back ached from maintaining the stooped crouch necessary to clear the stump overhead. Her skin had become excruciatingly tender with the sustained exposure to the wet. As it wrinkled, it crept and crawled with a life of its own. Hot spots that she suspected were leeches broke out on her back but there was nothing she could do about them then, so she resolved to let them take their meal unmolested. A cottonmouth snake wriggled by, creating a tidal wave with its thrashing tail. It yawned open its deadly pink-white jaws not six inches from her face. Luckily, the myopic creature did not investigate the horrified new animal lurking in the old tree's roots. Worst of all was the high pitched whine of mosquitoes, buzzing about, lighting, biting, and sucking, then streaming away, abdomens crimson-full from her face, ears, and eyelids

Each of the dozen times she thought she could bear it no longer, prepared herself to move out into the light and risk capture, some new, menacing clamor from the hunters sent her scurrying back into her position. The longer the marshals searched without success, the more they seemed determined to find their feckless quarry. The night closed in on them and her.

Reyna lowered her head below the roots and noiselessly slipped away from the bank. Stabs of pain shot through her legs, stiffened with the constant crouching. She nearly cried aloud with the joy of being able to rub her mosquito-pimpled cheeks against the muddied shoulder of her jacket. Away from the tree, she hesitated, considering which way to begin her own search. Surely Auntie Maggie could not have remained undetected near the site of her entrance to the swamp, the center of the maelstrom of men and dogs. Groping with her toes for purchase, Reyna headed in the opposite direction from the one by which she had come.

She stopped again, two steps later. Her aching, paralyzed legs refused to budge.

Off to the right, a channel away, the rumble of male voices caromed through the night.

Trembling violently, Reyna begged the shooting spasm in her limbs to go away, her legs to move. She reached out with her toe, found the clay shelf of the bank and took a step. Then another. And another.

Voices shattered the stillness again. This time to the left. The diffused blaze of a torch flared up, lighting the rotting tree trunks on the bank above. It made her feel better to hear the voices, see the light. At least those signs told where her stalkers lay.

She took another step.

The slough she followed twisted and turned left and right so many times that soon she felt half mad with despair that she was going in circles. At odd times, the voices of the hunters came from totally different places. Still, she kept on wading, scanning the marshy hillocks for a light, a tiny light, a candle in a window to end her waking nightmare.

Turning a corner, she clung to the limb of a fallen tree jutting out into the slough so that she could peer around for her enemies before moving into possible view. She had no sooner leaned forward to peer out into this new channel than something hard and bony fell on her shoulder and slithered down her arm. Talons clasped her wrist.

Her heart jumped in her chest, then stopped with an almost audible thud. A violent screeching rang in her ears. It required all her self-control to force her head and straining neck muscles to turn.

The fingers on the creature's hand released her wrist, went to the lips of its grinning face and signaled silence. The bony arms beckoned for her to follow it.

Reyna carefully picked her way up the bank.

The cadaverous wraith led her along a path following the contours of the soggy ground, blending in with the ghostly vegetation. Ahead in the distance, a flickering candle shone in an unscreened window.

The shack was an assemblage of bark stripped from dying trees and bound together by hemp rope to sapling poles. There was an opening for a single window and a door on one side, but nothing covered the openings. The ghostly figure motioned for her to enter. Inside a simple, potbellied stove occupied one wall next to a rough hewn shelf of cooking utensils and crude wooden bowls. A pallet of faded quilts served as a bed against the other wall.

Winded, Reyna rasped, "You're Auntie Maggie?"

A thin and reedy voice, like one unused to talk, broke the stillness in the fetid space. "There's them what calls me that."

Auntie Maggie was a six foot tall scarecrow. She wore loose fitting garments, pants and jacket made of old tarpaulin roughly stitched together with rough twine. Her sallow skin was the texture and hue of a ripe mango. Jutting out of the flapping sleeves of a canvas coat, the strange one's arms and legs were more like bird legs and talons than human appendages. The dark, bony circles of her eyes seemed to be a skull in the half-light of the shed. In form and figure there was not the slightest indication of her, or possibly *his* gender.

"But how did you know?"

"Mr. Bird tol' me chile. Mr Bird tol' me."

"Mr. Bird?"

"Ayup, Mr. Sparrow. Mr. Coot. Even old Mr. Owl knows you out there. They all tell Auntie." The weird creature chuckled soundlessly at some unspoken humor. "And, white man know, too. They been tearin' up the swamp lookin' for you. Laws! I never heard such a racket as that beatin' aroun' the bushes dey doin'."

Auntie Maggie walked over to the hole in the wall that was a window. Her step in the rude little shelter seemed strangely stiff-legged and awkward alongside to the liquid way she had moved among the stunted grasses and weeds of the swampland.

"Come here, chile. Come on up to the light."

Reyna turned. There was no need in the tiny chamber to actually move to get closer.

"Chile," the witch said with a startled whisper in her voice. "You is a gal chile! Mr. Bird, he don' tell me you is a gal."

Reyna stared at her feet, shuddering at the thought that she might have become another Aunt Maggie.

At dawn, a pale sun stretched itself out in a long, thin line across the horizon, and danced in the shining ripples of the current of the Mississippi River. Midstream, a black woman in a polka dot calico dress with a polka dot scarf knotted about her head sat in the prow of a dugout canoe moving toward the Missouri side of the river. At the oars of the canoe was an old fisherman wearing non-descript clothes made of cast off rags from the waterfront. As the sun rose from first light, predicting another scorching day, it flashed on the old fisherman and brightened his complexion to the golden yellow of polished brass.

Chapter 35

Residents of Cape Girardeau, Missouri, feared only one thing more than tornadoes and cholera: Judge Cannon Hamber. The old man in Room 201 of the Court of Common Pleas terrified them. He produced in them the clammy terror of a coward facing the archangel of death. His court room was a Roman circus pitting Judge Hamber, the lion, against all the Christians of "The Cape." Young lawyers skipped lunch rather than pass his office on the way to the sandwich vendor. Secretaries, Deeds Recorders, County Clerks and all the other functionaries tiptoed in and out of his chambers praying not to be noticed. It was rumored that he regularly locked district attorneys in the tower of the courthouse building, yet most candidates for that position admitted the prospect was preferable to an encounter with the ogre in Room 201.

    He might have inherited his ferocity from his father who had been a man so obese he kept his coffin under his bed and regularly lowered himself in to it and swore to diet when he no longer fit the box. But his physical size was not commensurate with his massive anger. Never more than 5'4" tall and 130 pounds, he had shriveled and shrunk him over the years to a spare 110 pounds of tiger meat on a 5'2" frame. While rheumatism and palsy had laid their claims upon him and left his hands a trembling bundle of brownish sailor's knots gripping the silver head of an ebony cane, not the slightest sign of weakness accompanied the disorders. Rather, one feared that his shaking arm might flail out at any moment to deliver a crippling blow with the stick.

    If any one were so bold as to express pity to him for the pain that went with the crippling the judge put an end to it. "I'm fine, " he'd say, fixing the asker with a wintry glare. "The rheumatiz' simply reminds me that I'm alive."

    At eighty-five, he combed his hair straight back in oily, gray-brown threads over his collar. His liver spotted skin had stretched so tight across his face there was hardly enough left for his eyelids to blink and it pulled his mouth into a permanent, lip-spreading grimace that exposed his small yellow teeth. When angered, his chin thrust up in a sharp point that nearly met the tip of his aquiline nose.

    As mean as they were, his appearance and manner painted an unfair portrait of him. Hamber was not fundamentally a wicked man, a dissembler, or a conniver. It was the erosion of his pride in himself and his community that made him seem so hateful, a kind of futile grasping for the last vestiges of what he thought proper and just. At the heart of it all was something he could never confess: he felt betrayed.

Cannon Hamber had been born at the time when all of Missouri and much more belonged to Upper Louisiana. He had been a man of twenty when Americans bought it from the Spanish. Cape Girardeau had been proclaimed the capital and the young Hamber based his dreams on its future. In 1815, all that was snatched away when the country seat was moved to Jackson and the Cape fell into decline. The Hamber family fortunes and aspirations died with the town.

Further, the Hamber clan proved singularly inept at producing sons and heirs. His only daughter married a vagabond profligate and his worthless brother's daughter ran away with a common tradesman. The burden of maintaining "family," and the respect that naturally goes with such a thing fell heavily on Cannon's shoulders. At last, in despair, he had adopted a young man, a distant cousin, as his son and heir.

In 1836, the town and the Hambers experienced a rebirth. Cannon was sixty-two years old, but even at that advanced age he recaptured the dream. Because of its strategic location on the river the Cape boomed once more. Mississippi water power made it important as a milling town for grain from nearby farms and the logs floated down from "up north". Pork packing plants were established along the levee. Culture sprouted, too. Vincentian priests brought St. Vincent's College in '43 and in '49 Presbyterians opened a seminary for ladies.

Unfortunately, to Hamber's eternal chagrin, once again the promise proved to be false. The brief flame of Cape Girardeau's candle was doused by the political clout of St. Louis. The slavery compromise of '52 bitterly divided the state and everything fell apart again. The nickname for the region, "Swamp East Missouri," was coined, bandied about, and finally stuck, to the hilarity of the rest of the state and the ultimate humiliation of the Cape. Faced with such disappointment, it was not surprising that the old man fought for his pride which what he had left: his uncompromising personality.

On one of the muggiest days of the summer of 1859, Hamber sat fuming behind his desk. This day, his rage was unquenchable because it was the second time he'd badly underestimated his principal political rival, Senator Benton. Benton, or more accurately, his bitch of a daughter, was with the senator's help seeking the presidential nomination for her husband, the hopelessly incompetent John C. Fremont. They'd damned near captured the new Republican Party, too. Again, Cape Girardeau had been ignored as if it didn't exist. The judge was as furious as he'd ever been in his life.

Clements, his secretary, a freckle-faced lad of twenty-two, had been coming and going all day with his eyes lowered, holding his breath, almost sliding along the wall to stay out of the firing line of the judge's tongue. He entered more boldly at three o'clock and advanced to stand meekly before

Hamber's desk. The judge noticed a smugness in the young man that had not been there since the ill-temper began that morning.

The judge glanced up, eyed the young man as if searching for a soft spot. "Well, what is it, you nincompoop? Don't just stand there. Can't you see I'm busy?"

"I'm sorry, your honor," Clements stammered. "You have a visitor."

"You're sorry! I'm sorry!" The gnarled knuckles waved over the paper-cluttered desk. "I can't see anyone. Show them away. Are you some kind of fool?"

The secretary screwed up his mouth as if in pain. "I know, but she won't leave, sir. I've told her all I can."

"She? What's it all about?" the old man roared. "What's so important? Send her away! Send her away!"

"She says it's personal. A matter of importance to you."

The judges blue eyes lidded to half mast. It was so unusual to have female visitors that it was possible that this one brought news of the campaign against Benton. His pointed tongue brushed hungrily across his row of yellowed teeth.

"Show her in, then, Clements," he said, then added, punctuating the pronouncement with a crooked forefinger. "But if this is some sort of tomfoolery to waste my time, I'll have your head when I've got rid of her."

No one in all of Swamp East Missouri could have been more astounded that day than Judge Hamber when he saw a woman, *a colored woman,* in polka dot plantation garb, step into his office as though she had a right to be there. The sight so unnerved him that for a long moment he was too dumb struck to bellow out. The judge swore a solemn oath to strangle Clements with his own hands as soon as the interview was done.

In addition to the mere fact of her presence in his chambers, an uppity quality about this particular colored woman took his breath away. A seedy-looking thing in the cheapest possible calico, her face and hands seemed streaked with grease or dirt. Some sort of unhealthy bumps marked her face and swelled her eyes half shut. Despite her pathetic appearance, the creature strode boldly up to his desk.

"Well, gal! What's on your mind!" Hamber raged when he could find his voice.

"I'm looking for work," the woman answered. The northern dialect in the woman's mouth stunned the judge even more. A northern accent from a plantation woman, an escaped slave by the look of her, strained his credulity. "I'm a cook and came to ask about a place in your household."

"What's the matter with you, gal?" He was so livid he had not enough breath for more than a squeak in his voice. "You dare to gain admission to my office to ask about a thing like that? Are you mad?"

The woman seemed unimpressed by the obvious anger boiling over in his eyes, the thin, vicious line on his lips. "I'm sorry, judge, but you're the only one

I know."

"You don't know me, you sassy wench. Where'd you hear my name?" Veins stood out like twisted rope in his neck.

The visitor stared back at him impassively. "Does the name Joseph Hamber mean anything to you?"

The judge turned pale, so pale the dark spots on his hands and face looked maroon against his blue-white skin.

"Joseph Hamber," she repeated. "My master a long time ago."

In the second's time it took to utter the short phrase, the judge's heart dropped like a rock in a well. All the misfortunes of the Cape and the Hamber family name were wrapped in those few words.

"Now, Judge," the strange intruder said again. "Do you have need of a cook?"

"Where is this Joseph Hamber?" he asked, still clinging to the hope of discovering that the woman was a clever fraud. If so, he'd see her in jail within the hour.

"Pardon me, Judge, but you know very well that your adopted son is dead. He died when I was only thirteen. He had sold me to a house of prostitution by that time. Raped me and sold me into prostitution when I was still a child."

"Can you prove any of this?" Hamber asked only half-heartedly for he knew the answer.

"I'm not here begging or stealing, Judge Hamber," she said. "I work for what I get. I'm a good cook and I need work. Your daughter's name is Katherine. What must I tell you to prove that I am what I say I am, your adopted son's former slave?"

Staring blankly at the papers, suddenly unimportant on his desk, Hamber said without looking up. "I don't need a cook."

"Do you know anyone who does?"

A long pause followed the request. Still, his eyes didn't leave the surface of his desk.

"I can give you a letter of introduction to the Sloans at the plantation next to my place. They're new. There's no guarantee, but the Hiram Sloan may need help."

"That's better," she said. He felt an irritating quality of self-satisfaction in her voice.

Later, quill in hand, Hamber asked, "What is the name that I should put on this introduction?"

"Reyna Royale," she said, "will be good enough."

Chapter 36

The Sloan plantation was as peaceful and serene as any place Reyna had ever lived. Five miles due west of Cape Girardeau, its fifty acres supported a crop of yams, several dozen apple trees, and a hundred hogs for market each year. Although the Sloans used slave labor, they owned no slaves themselves; rather they rented small gangs of them at planting and harvest time. Four families of Sloans in Cape Girardeau County pitched in to help one another do the rest of it, the hoeing and weeding. The farm was sufficient to supply their simple needs.

Trudging along the road in her dismal clothes, the once-elegant, now ruined jockey boots hidden by the rag of a dress, Reyna fought against admitting for the first time in her life that she had no plan, no options. The end of this dusty road ahead was indeed the end. The plain wooden sign, "Sloan's Rest," pointing off the main road offered no cheer.

The narrow carriage way led past the house to stop at the barn some twenty yards behind it. A two-story farmhouse with a porch wrapped around it was all there was. She saw none of the grandeur she'd known on slaveholding plantations, no lofty pillars and second story galleries, no high French doors or elaborate cut glass entry ways. Instead, the Sloan house was sturdy and solid, painted a dull gray color and totally without pretense. Had she been asked, Reyna would have pronounced it "adequate" but no more.

Reyna made her way around to the rear, an approach more appropriate to a servant.

In response to her rap, a short, plump woman opened the door. A tall, thin man came from another room to stand behind her. Both were dressed as befitted farming people, denim pants topped with white jersey long johns, a calico dress only a cut above Reyna's own.

"Yes?" the lady inquired.

Reyna straightened up to her full height, met their stares calmly but not downcast. "I'm looking for work as a cook. I have experience in that line of work. Judge Cannon Hamber at the Courthouse is an . . .old family friend . . . and he suggested you might be in need." She held out the letter of introduction.

The Sloans, Hiram and Esther, complemented one another perfectly. He was a tall, bean-pole of a man with white blond hair. His face, neck, and arms were baked dark brown from work in the fields. Esther, a roly-poly dumpling, was not quite five feet tall. Alert and quick blue eyes darting about, her face was ever alight as if always ready to break itself in two with smiles. Both a talker and a listener, Esther was one of those people who made folks think she paid attention only to them in a crowd. Hiram was more reserved but never judgmental and he spoke quietly, usually offering profound observations on the nature of people and things. At first glance, the way a puppy can detect a friend, Reyna understood these people. She knew they would be friends because they cared about others.

Crowded around a tiny table in their small kitchen, the three of them waited to speak until Esther had poured tea, hot from the wood stove. There was a sad look about the eyes of the couple as they regarded their guest's obvious poverty, the bleeding sores on her arms and face. Once up close, able to see the desolation of the strange woman, they never again looked directly into her eyes that day. But, out of the corner of her eye, Reyna saw the sympathetic glances that passed between them when they thought she wasn't looking.

Esther said, "We hadn't really thought about having help in the kitchen."

"But, maybe, Esther, we could use the extra help. You know, we got the nieces' and the nephews' visits coming up. Kids always mean extra work . . .especially in the kitchen."

"Well, I guess . . ." Esther hesitated. Hiram nodded meaningfully, as though he'd made up his mind. Esther's hand flew over to pat the back of his. She said, "I guess you're right. We could use the help." Then, to Reyna, "We'd like to have you here, Mrs. Royale, but let's have a temporary period before we make up our minds. You can take the spare bedroom in the back and we'll try it for a couple of weeks."

When she had first come to Sloan's Rest and went to work in the kitchen, her relief was so sudden and so vast that she could almost feel the tension flow out of her as clear as the freshet bubbling over the water-polished stones of Loblolly Creek outside her window. Then, there followed a period of healing, the settling down and wound-licking, a time of repairing her mind and body. The familiar kitchen work soothed like a medicinal balm and occupied her hands while the rest of her knit back together.

After awhile, her anxiety dissipated. By the time a chill came to add its bite to the autumn air, she had come to hate the uneventful nature of the work she did.

When her reverie was done and she was healed again, she thought about her lack of future. She found herself in the intolerable situation of waiting until John Brown made his move. That dependence upon someone else made her anxious with uncertainty.

She had written carefully coded letters to the fictitious "I. Smith" at Portsmouth, Ohio where Captain Brown received his mail. Her letters urged him to use caution, advised him of her work throughout the south, and assured him that when he was ready, an informal network of slaves stood prepared to sound the alarm, to rise up, and to leave their masters. She'd walk down to the vegetable market near the docks at Cape Girardeau and dawdle near the sailors' haunts to eavesdrop in order to learn the news of the nation and the clouds of war. Overheard scraps of conversations, and fragments of rumor and conjecture were all she had.

When she learned that John Brown meant to attack the federal arsenal at Harper's Ferry, Reyna despaired. She had doubted the old radical could successfully plan and execute such a raid. The "Secret Six" had been reluctant to provide the necessary funds and Brown's "army" was reduced to antique blunderbusses, pickaxes, and staves, but Brown and his men prepared to lash out against hopeless odds.

Neither the cooking nor the Sloan family was enough to intrigue her. Without using a tenth of her ability, Reyna could whip up a better menu than they could appreciate, dispatching the job in less than three hours a day. The rest of the time was hers and it hung about her neck like a lodestone that grew heavier every day. Only one thing relieved the monotony.

A tremendous black walnut tree with lower limbs as big around as a grown man's thigh grew in the side yard. There a pretty, green-painted swing hung where a person could sit in the shade, swing a little, study the stream of Loblolly Creek, or watch the occasional country family pass by on the road. Reyna spent a great many of her interminable extra hours floating idly back and forth in that swing.

One day, Reyna got the unmistakable feeling that she was being watched. Someone from some hidden place was spying upon her. She could feel it like an itch on the back of her neck. The soft fuzz on her arms rose as she looked about to locate the stealthy observer without moving her head.

The hedge next to the trees parted and out stepped a lovely little girl of six of seven years. A cascade of red gold ringlets fell to her waist and the child's brilliant blue eyes flashed with the sparkle of polished jewels behind long, curling eyelashes. She wore a maroon satin smock over a yellow dress that gave her skin the opalescent look of fine bone china. A fluffy white kitten lay draped over the crook of her arm. At first, the child seemed so beautiful that Reyna thought her loneliness prompted her eyes to see more than was there, or that she was a witch sent by Satan to ensnare her.

The child stood a moment, staring solemnly. H'lo," she said at last.

Reyna said, "My! Aren't you a pretty little girl!"

"Yes, I suppose I am," the youngster said without hesitation, a remark of such audacity that it sent Reyna to chuckling, then laughing out loud.

The child stared back, smiling as the cause of the humor but not knowing why.

"What's your name, little girl?"

Again, without a pause the girl answered, "Sarah Althea Hill, the granddaughter of Mr. Jonathan Sloan of Cape Girardeau, Missouri." She stopped then, seeming pleased with herself for the long recitation.

When Reyna said nothing for awhile, the girl asked, 'I've told you my name. Now, what's yours?"

"Reyna."

The child thought about it only an instant before she said, "Reyna. We shall be friends."

Looking down at herself, the polka dot calico dress, the garb of a plantation mammy, it struck Reyna as humorous and she began to laugh again.

"Yes, I think so. I think we'll be friends."

In the days that followed, Sarah Althea Hill was a frequent visitor to Reyna's kitchen at the Sloan's house. The vivaciousness of the child, her rare beauty and winning smile, fascinated her and helped to while away the tedium of the long days of waiting for word from John Brown.

Chapter 37

Reyna's impatient waiting ended on December 2, 1859. John Brown was hanged that day. The raid she had predicted as suicidal had become just that. His followers were all caught or killed in the skirmish.

When the news came of the attack on the arsenal at Harper's Ferry, Reyna fled to her room in the plantation house and shut the door. Biting her lips to hold back shrieks of protest, she paced endlessly around the room cursing the old man as a bungler, a hard-headed fanatic whose stupid arrogance, whose need for personal attention, had destroyed her work of a year and a half.

With the capture of John Brown and the last of his men, she began to worry. *Would they talk? Name names of others involved in the conspiracy? The senseless killings would surely not go unpunished. Would they reveal me as the author of my letters?*

Inventing a dying relative, she resigned as cook, saying she would need to be away several months. She took up the Quaker dress again, to encourage the Sloans to believe it was respectful mourning. Finally, under the name of Miss Reyna Shield to retain access to her New York bank account, she booked first class passage on the *SS River Queen* bound for Panama.

On the morning she left, the damp wind off the river was so bitter cold that it slashed like ice against her face. The wooden docks shone blue with frozen slicks and snow mounded about the bollards. A knot of passengers, loath to step into the wind before they could board, huddled for warmth against a metal shed on the dock. An old woman, so ancient that not an unwrinkled inch of flesh showed in her face, turned to the metal wall for protection. Her shawl was worn through in places and her threadbare bonnet offered meager shelter.

"Laws, laws, laws," the old woman kept muttering. "I don't think these old bones ever gon' to warm up."

Reyna smiled sympathetically.

"Where are you going, dear?" the old one asked between chattering teeth.

"California."

The woman seemed amazed. "I'm going to Panama to be with my son. He's in business there. I hope this will be my last cold winter."

Reyna smiled kindly and nodded.

Two men in dark overcoats stepped around the corner from Main Street as the gangplank jerked and bounced against the chains that lowered it. They stopped and stood stiffly in a kind of parade rest position on the deck where the plank would land. Reyna's heart thudded in her chest when she realized that the men in dark coats were marshals.

There was something unmistakable about civil servants. Government employees seemed to buy their drab garments from the same shops. Nothing was ever quite right about their clothes; something always slightly askew. Security officials in particular were especially dedicated to dowdiness. Thus, seeing two slightly overweight, slightly ill-dressed men preparing to inspect boarding passengers terrified Reyna.

"Why don't we go inside and have a cup of coffee?" she said to the old women. "We still have at least a half an hour to board and we could get out of this wind."

Detective Lieutenant Robert Johnson and Sergeant Jack Garnett stomped their feet to revive their circulation as the gangplank thumped to the dock. The weather was miserable, the biting wind brought tears to their eyes, and they resented being assigned to the hick town. Johnson, from Memphis, and Garnett, from St. Louis, were unprepared to believe that anything important ever happened in a little burg a hundred and fifty miles in either direction from civilization, namely from Memphis and St. Louis. But, the chief had said go and they had gone and here they were at the docks watching the passengers board because a certain Miss Reyna Shield had booked first class passage on the *River Queen*. The Miss Shield they sought, a startlingly beautiful woman, was wanted for questioning in connection with the subversion of slaves. The purser, opposite them at the gangplank had promised to read the names of boarding passengers so they could make the arrest.

Sergeant Garnett said, "This Miss Reyna Shield is supposed to be a real looker and smart as a whip, besides. They say she rode all over the south rilin' up the darkies, trying to get slaves to run off. Rides like a champion and built like a Greek statue."

"If she's so danged smart, why you think she'd come here? If she's smart she'd go over land."

"Can't. Can't go that way. You know nothing moves out of Independence before April."

The Captain appeared on the quarterdeck to greet the passengers and the purser unrolled his manifest. Baggage handlers began wheeling carts of trunks and suitcases to the cargo nets for stowage. The travelers left the side of the building and moved toward the gangplank.

"Mr. and Mrs. Horace Brown," called the purser loud enough to identify passengers within earshot of the federal agents.

"Mr. Joseph Himmel."

"Miss Suzan Bausch and Miss Nellie Gage."

And, then, "Miss Reyna Shield."

The officers leaned forward. Reyna Shield was an old woman, wrinkled and hobbled with age, clutching a shawl as worn as she was. Detective Johnson smiled broadly. The elderly lady smiled, too, pleased with the kindness of the young stranger who had charitably exchanged a first class berth for hers in the hold so that a mother could travel in comfort to meet her son.

Chapter 38

It was mid-morning when the *SS Oregon,* Reyna's ship from Panama, docked at Long Wharf in San Francisco. A hand to her hat so as not to lose it in the breeze, Reyna gawked like the rawest tourist at the sight of the city now grown up all topsy-turvy on the hills of the city. More mature and outwardly reserved after her perilous adventures, to say nothing of the dangers of her criminal activities, Reyna restrained herself from any expression but the look of boredom on her face. She hoped that her stockbroker, William Sharon, had gotten her note and would be at the dockside to greet her.

An involuntary smile curled her lips at the thought of Sharon who had managed the fortune she'd amassed in San Francisco. Now that she was reentering white society as a white woman, Reyna was pleased that she had picked Sharon to replace MacGill to handle her accounts. He'd been but a realtor but she recognized the hunger in his eyes. She knew he fancied she wanted his investment advice when, in fact, it was that hunger and that he'd do precisely as he was told that she'd sought. Physically unattractive, a short bald headed man with a fringe of hair around his ears, Sharon dressed well and was willing to let rumors that they were more than just business partners add further cover to Reyna's ancestry.

She sighed deeply as a most confounded emotion overcame her. For all she'd seen and done, the triumphs and failures, at the moment she realized San Francisco was truly her home. It was where she belonged, this mining town, magnet to flotsam and jetsam from all the world. Here she could succeed. The sharp wind, the damp, the tumble down tents and houses marching up the side of those hills ahead and Fremont's Golden Gate at her back. This was where she belonged.

She spotted Sharon then, in formal dress, swallow-tailed coat and top hat, waving frantically to catch her attention. Gliding toward the gangplank, not yet accustomed to the awkward bustle on her gown after her months astride a horse, dressed as a male jockey. She forced herself to smile as a sign of her pleasure at seeing the little man.

At the front of the plank, he rushed forward, surrounded her with his arms for an enthusiastic bear hug.

"You look marvelous," he said.

"And you look very well, sir."

"No, seriously, you're even more beautiful than you were when you left."

"And you sir," she replied, tapping his arm with her fan. "You've not aged a minute. How are you?"

"Oh, he said. "We're fine. I know you'll be pleased to hear how well your money has done with us. Very well, indeed."

She smiled broadly, reminded that it had been a long time since she'd received any good news. The confirmation of her wise choice of him was good to know. Obviously, he was in a position to see opportunities for her investments and aggressive enough to buy her stock when the time was right. In addition, she liked his seriousness. Ralston had told her once that 'Bill Sharon would chase a dollar clear to hell.' In spite of herself, however, she caught herself thinking that his only flaw was his pale white skin: *What a shame that he's not black.*

"I'll go over your account tomorrow, Sunday, if you don't mind working on the sabbath." He touched her elbow, nodded toward an elegant black phaeton parked at the edged of the dock. "I've taken the liberty of bringing my own carriage for you, if you'll permit me to show you home."

"Why, thank you. You've very kind, William."

When they reached the carriage, Sharon called up to a shiny scarecrow of a black man seated on the box. "Please see to Mrs. Royale's luggage, Peter."

"That won't be necessary," Reyna stammered. "I've only the small satchel you see. The rest is coming overland."

Sharon handed her up into the thick-piled hunter green velvet upholstery, then ran around the coach to join her from the other side. They sat silently during the twenty minute ride to her little house on Stevenson Street; he, lost in thoughts of his lovely client; she, overwhelmed with the new buildings, the permanent structures of a city growing all about her.

At her door, he said, "I'll leave you here. I know you'll want to get used to your home after nearly two years away." He paused a moment, stared at his feet as though bashful. "I hope you won't mind, but I've arranged for a reception for you tomorrow afternoon at the Montgomery Block."

"You shouldn't have — " Reyna began.

He interrupted, "I wanted to. After all you're one of the Mining Exchange's most successful clients. Some people are calling you, the 'Queen of San Francisco's Mining Exchange'."

She smiled happily, delighted to be reintroduced to her former business associates and friends here, and she grinned at the new title, 'Queen of the Mining Exchange'. *If they only knew.*

Reyna's open cabriolet made its way up Washington Street toward the Montgomery Block in a sea of carriages, men on horseback, and pedestrians struggling with the tide of humanity hurrying toward San Francisco's most important office building. There, 150 bankers, stockbrokers, and merchants controlled the ebb and flow of west coast money, in particular that that came from gold and silver mines. Musicians, artists, and writers also rented space there. Mark Twain from Virginia City and Jack London from the Oakland docks kept working space in the Montgomery Block. Four stories high, tall windows watched the street from cast iron shutters.

Although she met many of her voodoo followers and employees in the first 18 hours after her arrival, Reyna couldn't contain her curiosity about a reception in her honor. Like leaping off the end of Long Wharf into the icy water of the San Francisco Bay, her abrupt dive into the management of boarding and parlor houses, a civic center stable, and a large saloon catering to Negroes left not a second for looking back. The transition from her months of running just ahead of marshals and slavers had made her increasingly cynical. She knew she'd have to soften the brittle crust of such feelings with her friends and employees in the days ahead.

Her godson, Jimmy-June, now handled the team guiding her through the traffic. As a child he'd been her greatest comfort during difficult times; now it appeared he'd be ready to manage her community stable on Sansome street when his father, James Smith, Sr., retired. This return to the continuity she'd left when she joined the underground now eased her depression that came from failing her black brothers and sisters.

Sharon, in formal wear, stood in the portico beneath the gigantic Doric columns of the Montgomery Block Entrance way. Leaping out to open her door, he said, "You're looking splendid, Mrs. Royale. As beautiful as ever."

He led her proudly to the ballroom beyond the massive marble stairs leading to the second floor. The ballroom, decorated with faux marble columns festooned with acanthus branches painted with gold leaf, looked as fresh as she remembered it from two years before. An eye-popping crowd of the city's most illustrious residents froze in place to applaud her appearance at the entrance. She stopped, at first confused, then deeply touched by the welcome home gesture of people she'd known more as business colleagues than friends. But then her life had always been dominated by business. Now, after two years away, and met by apparent affection, she blinked back the tears forming in her eyes.

The owners of the guest houses she managed, the Woodruff brothers, Black and Footer, and the Mintern brothers hurried over to greet her. They had sorely missed her management skills and were delighted for her return. "Welcome home, Mrs. Royale." "We've missed you more than you'll ever know." "I hope your business back East was successful and you'll be staying home a long time."

William Ralston, Cashier of the Bank of California, carrying a few more pounds on his big frame, rushed forward to greet her and the runty William Sharon, effusive in his exclamations of pleasure at her return. Ralston invited her to come around to the Bank the next morning to discuss a new line of credit he wanted to offer her. Sharon, as sly looking as ever, the fox in the hen house with feathers in his mouth, whispered that he'd joined Ralston in the bank as head of a new Virginia City branch of the Bank of California. Reyna surprised herself with how quickly she could fill in the details of that transaction She remembered hearing that Ralston's wife's Lizzie and William Sharon had been in primary school together in Carollton, Illinois. No doubt a word to Ralston from Lizzie had added to Sharon's prestige when he came forward with the Royale account.

Across the room, David Terry, tall, handsome, and gallant, a member of the Chivalry southern wing of the Democratic Party, tipped his hat to her. Reyna had no illusions about which side Terry would support in the inevitable war between the states.

In the excitement of the reception, Reyna had focused her attention on familiar faces in the crowd. All of a sudden, without warning, a single thought came to her, crowding out all others. This was the first time since she'd left San Francisco that she found herself in a sea of white people with no one of color in sight. A twinge of anger shook her, anger at a world so divided and unequal that one must choose people based upon attributes like color and race. She knew it wasn't fair, and had never truly believed it would be otherwise, but at the moment, recollecting all that she had been through, her anger threatened her self-control.

The mood was interrupted by Sharon's eagerness to introduce a heavy-set dowager in a wine colored gown and a neck covered with diamonds and emeralds. The broker said, "Mrs. Royale, I'd like you to meet Mrs. Hall Mcallister."

"How do you do?"

Mrs. Mcallister adjusted her lorgnette to scrutinize Reyna closely. "I am very well, thank you. It is so good to meet you. I've heard so many nice things about what a talented young woman you are."

A certain edginess in the lady's voice set off an alarm in Reyna's head. What Mrs. Mcallister said could not have been more polite, but there was also a hint, an inflection that seemed automatically to demand servility from the listener. Her lorgnette appeared to further the condescending look she bestowed upon those about her, as though there were something, a tiny speck perhaps, but no less low class about her audience.

Reyna said cautiously, "I'm afraid the gentlemen exaggerate my ability because I've been away from home such a long time."

"Nevertheless, I look forward to putting your name on our membership list."

"Membership list?"

"Yes, my dear, you'd be a perfect addition to our Ladies Welfare Society."

This she could do, and Reyna nodded. "I'd like to help with such things. Thank you, Mrs. Mcallister. I'd be pleased to do anything I can."

"Well, yes," Mrs. Mcallister said almost casually, "our current project is creating a primary grade school for colored children on Folsom Street."

Chapter 39

Before shed left San Francisco, Reyna had built a weekend hideaway for herself outside the city of San Francisco where the Mission Road ran alongside the San Jose Railway tracks. Although not a mansion, neither was Geneva Cottage small. It was a four bedroom, single story Spanish-styled rancho. A terra cotta-colored adobe with a curved Spanish tile roof, its windows were cross-hatched with fanciful iron work. Squat columns around the perimeter of the house held thick, stuccoed arches over a walkway of Mexican paver tiles. Once she had settled in and the healing progressed, the voodooienne's mind came alive again.

After such a long time away, this was the final salute to her return to the city, to reestablish her leadership in their religion. This night, St. John's Eve, June 23rd, she planned a Voodoo celebration that would outshine any other midsummer's night dream. It would rival the great Marie Laveau's Congo Square in New Orleans.

Reyna remained inside Geneva Cottage, spying through a crack in the shutters as her followers arrived. They stood, unspeaking, waiting to catch the first sight of her and for their religious celebration to begin. Like zombies, their arms around each other in the dark, they watched the front door of Geneva Cottage. Reyna could see Mama Doc with her brood of six skinny kids, right behind Sister Cecelia, the chocolate woman from Washerwoman's Cove. Agelica Sue sauntered in with her new lover, the one-armed opium dealer of Dupont Street. He gave her what she needed. More and more of them streamed in until the grounds were crowded with eager worshippers and secular hangers-on. From her hidden spot behind the shutter, Reyna's chest swelled at how many came. *Maybe five hundred. A thousand. They'd not forgotten her.*

Whites were there, too, some of them scrawny, middle-aged women, pale fleshed and pimple-scarred, to far gone in decadence to miss an event so sensual as St. John's Eve. White men avoided the sight of them. Old fat men, judges and politicians, clammy beads of perspiration pooling at the bases of their throats, waiting, restless with the passing minutes. Young white men, too, stood aloof, cool disdain plastered on their faces. Their excitement was betrayed by pinpoints of lust in eyes that darted from figure to figure among the half-naked women, and sometimes the men, in the collecting sea of black worshippers.

Conjure men and amateur witch doctors moved silently through the crowd, searching for clients. When a prospect was found, they reached in shoulder bags to offer their merchandise, grisgris of yellow ochre, cockscomb powder, the lenses of a rattlesnake's eyes, the ashes of a white stallion's tail. It was all there, all for sale.

Reyna felt the excitement flowing through the congregation when the musicians arrived with a tambourine, a snakeskin banjo, and orange gourds. The Sword of Samson, wires strung on the jawbone of an ass, lay alongside the bamboo drums. An enormous man-mountain drummer whom she'd not seen before straddled his hollowed out log. They spread themselves out in front of the entrance arch to form a narrow aisle for her, their Voodoo Queen.

Just ahead of the paved walkway, an altar had been prepared, a mammoth butcher block dazzling with thick Lifetime Devotion candles sputtering with rosemary incense. On wrought iron stands at either side of the altar stood six raven grosbecs, night herons who cried out like colicky babies.

Alongside the house, great logs burned beneath a huge vat. In the gigantic cauldron, half the boiler of a paddle wheel steamer, simmered thick, rich stew.

They were all there and still the crowd waited. They waited for their mistress of the ceremony, Queen of Voodoo. After awhile, a squadron of young blacks from the old What Cheer Hotel circulated among the congregation with buckets of sweet galli, a mixture of rum and fermented papaya juice which they offered from Cup of Life gourds. The liquor mellowed the night, made silhouetted trees in the distance seem to sway and teased a dancing mood from bare feet. The young men passed the Cup of Life gourds again.

Influenced by the rum, the night, and the tense horde, the giant drummer sprawled out, legs and arms spraddled across his log drum, looking like a sleeping alligator, to contemplate the images made by the moon shimmying through the clouds. At some unseen command, he slowly rose, upended the log, and began to palm the goatskin, a signal for dancers to take their places. A flute sang mournfully, repeating calls like a mourning dove. The grosbecs on the wrought iron stands, lulled for awhile by the still watch, stirred themselves, stretched their long necks and resumed their squawking.

Then, the door opened. The Presentation Sisters flowed onto the porch and formed an entry triangle for Reyna. Behind her shutter, Reyna felt her cheeks flush and her eyes mist at the sight of these lovely young women, her acolytes who tended her in the ceremonies. Flowers in their hair, garlands similarly strung about their necks, they moved to the banisters at either side of the paved walkway to take their places to assist the Queen.

Maurice, the Queen's favorite consort, in top hat and cape, filled the doorway. When he reached the altar, he flashed open his cape like the wings of a giant bat. Beneath the cape, the seaman stood before them totally naked. A grinning human skull wobbled on the shelf of his belly. Tattoos gleamed gray green against his brown sugar skin.

The whispered "aaaah" of a single voice escaped the crowd as Reyna appeared. A scarlet silk sarong hugged her body, its skirt slit to the waist, revealed her sinewy thigh. Mojo Hand, her ritual cobra, rode, hood flared, about her neck. She floated over, placed MoJo Hand in his basket on the altar, then stopped beneath the entrance arch leading to the garden and clapped her hands.

A shaking tambourine clanked out a funeral march. The big man softly stroked the bass. The steel-fingered hands that had once choked a man to death touched the skin to make a sound as soft as the lightest pulsation in the night.

The men from Dupont Street came forward and ceremoniously passed among the Presentation Sisters with full Cup of Life gourds of sweet galli, then served Reyna. The movement, the studied grace of the ceremonial offering, hauntingly reminiscent of a Catholic mass, mesmerized the gaping congregation.

After the priestess and her entourage, the gourd was offered to Maurice. Pushing it away the big man grabbed the bucket and lifted it over his head to shower rum down his face. The liquid splashed in his hair and ran down his body as his jaws worked spastically to drink A hideous grin lit his face when he returned the empty bucket.

"Drink my people," Reyna cried out to the masses. "Drink of Life. The Cup of Life is ours tonight!"

The sound of the drum picked up, louder and quicker. The men from Dupont hastened to the crowd with fresh buckets.

Reyna clapped her hands again.

A man of normal torso but stunted legs, appeared from the side. The color of burnished copper, as he came into the light, they saw that blue black ovals like water spots on heated metal covered his body and arms. The man with the dwarfed legs was Injun Bill, the snake-catcher. The marks were living evidence of the mistakes of his profession. He carried, at arms' length two thrashing, four foot rattlesnakes.

The queen regally glided over to accept the offered serpents, first one, then the other. Clutching them behind their heads, she squeezed hard to force open their mouths to inspect their fangs. A broken-fanged serpent brought the worst imaginable luck. Satisfied that the vipers were of sufficient quality, she took them, nodded to Injun Bill, and returned to the central position in her entourage.

The drum increased its tempo. An alto bamboo joined in, following the rhythm. When they both stopped abruptly, the beat lingered on in the minds of the onlookers.

Arms outstretched with the thrashing snakes, Reyna tossed her head back. Her eyes, gashed with carnelian, closed in meditation. The ritual chant moved her lips. When she'd completed the prayer, she paced sedately to the side walkway, gazed into the cauldron, considered a moment, then flung the rattlers into the boiling stew.

The queen turned once more to the assemblage. "Eat my people. Eat of life. The Bowl of Life is ours tonight!"

Reyna drew herself up, glided to the center of the stairs and raised her arms. Reaching for Mojo Hand, she restored him to his place about her delicate throat. As her familiar, his role was vital. He would pass the spirit message to her. The worshippers quieted, leaned toward the sound of her voice.

"Believe!" she intoned with a gutteral rush of breath. The congregation bent close, cupped hands behind ears to hear. "Believe!" came again, louder, and "Believe!" a shriek in the night.

Reyna Royale, their Voodoo Queen, had returned.

And her power was stronger than ever.

FURTHER READING: FIVE STAR FAVES

DOCTOR DUGGINS' NEW LIST OF FAVORITE AMERICAN HISTORICAL NOVELS

A Million Nightingales, Susan Straight
A New Orleans Voudou Priestess (Non-fiction), Carolyn Morrow Long
A Voyage Long and Strange (Non-Fiction), Tony Horwitz
All Other Nights, Dara Horn
Becky: The Life and Times of Becky Thatcher, Lenore Hart
Blessed McGill, Edwin Shrake
Bound, Sally Gunning
Charity Girl, Michael Lowenthal
Devil's Dream, Madisson Smartt Bell
Fire Bell in the Night, Geoffrey Edward
Freeman Walker, David Allan Cates
Gold Digger, Vicki Delany
Harriett and Isabella, Patricia O'Brien
Jarrettsville, Cornelia Nixon
Kincade's Fear, Michael Chandler & Loahnna Chandler
Mary, Janis Cooke Newman
Mayflower, Nathaniel Philbricker
Midwife of the Blue Ridge, Christine Blevins
Riding Vengeance with the James Gang, Donald L. Gilmore
Sally Hemings, Barbara Chase-Riboud
Shaman, Noah Gordon
Soldier's Farewell, Johnny D. Boggs
Someone Knows My Name, Lawrence Hill
Sweetsmoke, David Fuller
The Anatomy of Deception, Lawrence Goldstone
The Branch and the Scaffold, Loren D. Estleman
The Devil in the White City, Erick Larson
The Last Mountain Man, William W. Johnstone
The Long Journey Home, Laurel Means
The Spiritualist, Megan Chance
The Whiskey Rebels, David Liss
Thunderstruck, Erick Larson
Trail of the Red Butterfly, Karl H. Schlesier
Voodoo Fire in Haiti, Richard Loederer
Washington's Lady, Nancy Moser
West of Washoe, Tim Champlin
Woodsburner, John Pipkin

BOOKS BY SMOKE TREE PRESS

THE POWER: A NOVEL OF VOODOO
By Jim Duggins

The Power follows Reyna Royale, a slave girl, from her voodoo initianition on a Georgia plantation to study with New Orleans' Marie Laveau and to Gold Rush San Francisco where she becomes a successful madam and civil rights activist.

SLAVE STEALER
By Jim Duggins

An African-American whose complexion is so light that she passes as white, one who is clever enough to amass a fortune, and one who uses the power of voodoo to unify San Francisco's black community in gold rush California, Reyna abandons it all to join the struggle for her people.

GLAD HAND SALOON
By Steve Scott

When a mutilated body is discovered in the alley behind a Palm Springs gay bar known for it genuine rodeo posters and imitation cowboys, the Glad Hand Saloon becomes the target of an investigation.

CAFE RESPECT
By Steve Scott

After a beautiful new waitress is hired, a mom-and-pop cafe in Palm Springs becomes the epicenter of a series of bizarre murders.

ECHO PARK
By Steve Scott

Story is bordered by the Los Angeles' Police Academy, Saint Finbar's almost Catholic Church, a suspect sanatorium. . . all backdrops by people we seldom see or know: Charo, the Little General, Father Rudy, Neurotica Jones, Fabulousa and an elderly gay men's club called the Pastime Jocks.